Aja and Momo Shade, 2015
SANTIAGO FELIPE

Aja, 2018
SANTIAGO FELIPE

Haus of Aja, 2018
SANTIAGO FELIPE

Thorgy Thor, 2019
SANTIAGO FELIPE

Thorgy Thor, 2010
SANTIAGO FELIPE

Horrorchata, Merrie Cherry, and Untitled Queen, 2013
SANTIAGO FELIPE

Merrie Cherry, 2017
SANTIAGO FELIPE

Horrorchata, 2018
SANTIAGO FELIPE

BACKSPACE, CLOCKWISE FROM LEFT: Mary Jo Cameltoe, DiBa, Charmin Ultra (Charmy), Krystal Something-Something, Whiskey Dixie, 2011
SANTIAGO FELIPE

Krystal Something-Something and Charmin Ultra, 2011
SANTIAGO FELIPE

SWITCH N' PLAY, CLOCKWISE FROM TOP LEFT: Miss Malice,
Divina GranSparkle, Nyx Nocturne, The Illustrious Pearl,
K.James, Zoe Ziegfeld, 2019
SANTIAGO FELIPE

Miss Malice (in pink) and K.James (front), 2019
SANTIAGO FELIPE

Johnny Velour and Sasha
Velour, 2018
SANTIAGO FELIPE

Sasha Velour, 2017
SANTIAGO FELIPE

West Dakota, 2019
SANTIAGO FELIPE

Chiquitita, 2019
SANTIAGO FELIPE

Madame Vivien V, 2021
SANTIAGO FELIPE

Veruca la'Piranha, 2011
SANTIAGO FELIPE

HOW YOU GET FAMOUS

TEN YEARS OF DRAG MADNESS IN BROOKLYN

NICOLE PASULKA

SIMON & SCHUSTER

NEW YORK   LONDON   TORONTO   SYDNEY   NEW DELHI

Simon & Schuster
1230 Avenue of the Americas
New York, NY 10020

First Simon & Schuster hardcover edition June 2022

SIMON & SCHUSTER and colophon are registered trademarks of Simon & Schuster, Inc.

For information about special discounts for bulk purchases, please contact Simon & Schuster Special Sales at 1-866-506-1949 or business@simonandschuster.com.

The Simon & Schuster Speakers Bureau can bring authors to your live event. For more information or to book an event, contact the Simon & Schuster Speakers Bureau at 1-866-248-3049 or visit our website at www.simonspeakers.com.

Interior design by Hope Herr-Cardillo

Manufactured in the United States of America

10 9 8 7 6 5 4 3 2 1

Library of Congress Cataloging-in-Publication Data

Names: Pasulka, Nicole, author.
Title: How you get famous : ten years of drag madness in Brooklyn / Nicole Pasulka.
Identifiers: LCCN 2021055175 (print) | LCCN 2021055176 (ebook) | ISBN 9781982115791 (hardcover) | ISBN 9781982115814 (ebook)
Subjects: LCSH: Drag shows—New York (State)—New York—History. | Female impersonators. | Male impersonators. | Brooklyn (New York, N.Y.)—History—21st century. | BISAC: SOCIAL SCIENCE / Popular Culture | PERFORMING ARTS / Theater / General
Classification: LCC PN1969.D73 P38 2022 (print) | LCC PN1969.D73 (ebook) | DDC 792.702/8—dc23/eng/20220103
LC record available at https://lccn.loc.gov/2021055175
LC ebook record available at https://lccn.loc.gov/2021055176

ISBN 978-1-9821-1579-1
ISBN 978-1-9821-1581-4 (ebook)

CONTENTS

AUTHOR'S NOTE

I moved to New York City in August 2001. My life as a young person there was defined by post-9/11 anxiety, accelerating gentrification, and the stubborn refusal of the weirdos and artists around me to accept that the effervescent, hedonistic, grimy good life in the big city was a thing of the past. Over the following twenty years, I came of age mostly in Brooklyn amid queers who'd been grade-school children at the peak of the AIDS crisis and, as adults, found themselves able to get married, serve in the military, and be the protagonists on prime-time TV shows. None of this held much sway for those in my crew, but as some people and institutions became a little kinder to lesbians and gay men, we benefited from this growing visibility and acceptance.

In the early aughts, Brooklyn's queer scene was robust and exciting, but I rarely, if ever, heard the words "drag queen." In 2009, I left the city for a few years and, when I came back, the borough was brimming with joyful performance that proudly called itself drag. *RuPaul's Drag Race* had been gaining popularity, but that didn't fully account for the explosion that happened between 2012 and 2016. While drag has had a presence across the country for as long as there have been gay bars, and is now commonplace even in small towns, the Brooklyn drag takeover came harder and faster than pretty much anywhere else. The local scene was decidedly more messy, freewheeling, and avant-garde than what we watched on TV.

Why did all these barflies, show-offs, artists, and entertainers flock to drag at this moment? At first, I could only speculate based on how I felt watching drag in the city I'd called home for more than a decade. The sight of a performer who has embraced all the extremes and excesses of gender in order to transcend it, and who has done so in a cloud of sweat, spit, and makeup, while the music throbs and the crowd screams at the top of their gay lungs, is a reminder that we can be anything—at least for a few minutes—and we can be celebrated for it. In these lip sync shows, there was an honesty that only the baldest, most exceptional acts of exaggeration could convey. It was entertaining, but it was also real, and it was thrilling to see people re-create themselves and then lose their minds in a performance. Increasingly, lots of other people around the world understood how fun and infectious it was to watch drag. That, too, was mystifying after decades of seeing stereotypically gay people mocked and dismissed by mainstream culture. What had changed, and what did this broader embrace of drag mean for gay life in general?

As a journalist, it's been exhilarating to watch LGBT issues come to the forefront of American culture and politics. Many of these gains were expected and seemed like the natural result of an arduous, decades-long struggle. However, I never could have predicted that, in the second decade of the twenty-first century, loud, proud, unapologetic queerness would be the apotheosis of cool and drag performers would become wealthy and influential far beyond queer culture. Plenty of pariahs become celebrities. When an entire subculture moves from the back room to the main stage, it's worth trying to figure out how and why.

Some readers who are already familiar with local drag scenes in the United States may react to a book about Brooklyn drag with an eye roll and a—correct—assertion that there are other, equally influential scenes in other, less obsessively chronicled cities. However, few places are home to both the most experimental corners of the drag world and the most professional. Brooklyn drag is at once amateurish and world-class, and in this way it serves as a microcosm of the art form.

Drag, of course, is not one thing, and so I chose to structure this book in a way that allows me to highlight the many perspectives and styles that thrive in Brooklyn. I believe that a narrative told through reporting—closely following the stories of some of the people who have been hustling and innovating over the past ten years—not only explains what drag can be and contextualizes the art form for our current moment but also helps readers understand why so many people have fallen in love with this strange, wonderful community. The best stories reveal general truths through detail and specificity, and that's what I've endeavored to do here.

In a way, I've been reporting this story ever since I watched my first drag show at Pieces Bar in Manhattan in 2006. But the bulk of my reporting happened from 2018 until the Covid-19 lockdown in March 2020. During that time, I did around a hundred interviews and watched at least five hundred drag performances. Descriptions of drag performances, conversations, and events I couldn't witness myself have been re-created from interviews with participants, videos, and my subjects' memories. Whenever possible, these stories have been corroborated with multiple sources.

It's incredible how much drag terminology has crept into contemporary slang. I have frequently quoted people directly and reproduced their word choices in my own narration. There are terms and statements in this book that might offend some readers. I included this language only after considering it with care. The intention was not to be disrespectful or gratuitous but to represent my subjects and their lives faithfully and accurately.

On the subject of language, in the queer community—and, increasingly, the wider world—recognizing someone's gender pronouns and name is a basic form of respect. Because gender play and experimentation are critical to the art of drag, many of the people in this book use different pronouns and names at different times and in different circumstances. A performer might prefer to be called "she" and "her" when onstage, but want to be known by their "boy name" when out of drag. Other performers want to be known by only their drag names and pronouns. Others don't care or change their minds. I believe that any and all gender identities and presentations are valid, and I have worked to respect the individual preferences of the people in this book. I am aware this can sometimes require more care and attention on the part of readers, but one of the joys of telling this story was the way it demanded I embrace ambiguity and look past gender binaries.

I am immensely grateful to the numerous performers who spoke with me and do not appear by name in the book. They are listed alphabetically by their drag names in the acknowledgments.

This could never hope to be a definitive history of Brooklyn drag or a comprehensive description of that vast and varied scene. Learning and recording those intricacies would take decades—and thousands of pages. This is just one story—a small slice—in which I attempt to answer my own questions about queerness, city life, performance, and the nature of celebrity in the early twenty-first century.

PART ONE

CHAPTER ONE

Welcome to New York City

"Don't you fall," Aja warned, rushing Esai Andino toward the J train, their high heels scraping along the pavement. Putting Esai in the shoes had been a risk. Even in sneakers, the fourteen-year-old boy tripped—over curbs, steps, nothing at all—pretty much every day. The fat cans of Four Loko they'd polished off while getting ready in Aja's room hadn't helped Esai's composure. As soon as their makeup was dry, seventeen-year-old Aja had rushed Esai out the door and into the cold night: two Brooklyn teenagers in search of attention, cash, and adventure in the big city.

Then the pair turned a corner and, sure enough, Esai's ankle rolled. He screeched and keeled over. Fall 2011 had been mild, but in the evening chill his breath was visible in small puffs. Esai leaned on Aja as they hobbled into the station and up the stairs.

It was their first night out in Manhattan as drag queens. Their first night trying the thing they'd been talking about for months. Earlier that day, Aja had earned fifteen dollars reading a woman's tarot cards and used the money to buy Esai a pair of gold sparkly heels. Esai paced on the train platform, shivering and limping slightly. He had on black tights and a star-print skirt over a polka-dot bathing suit. Aja, who had been raised as a boy but prefers the pronouns "she" or "they," was wearing a floral shirt she'd made for a class project at the High School of Fashion Industries.

They arrived at Bar-Tini on Tenth Avenue in Hell's Kitchen early, to avoid getting carded. A drag queen named Holly Dae, who'd recently changed her name from Holly Caust, was hosting a competition for newcomers called Beat That Face! In the drag world, "beat" could be a noun or a verb meaning a face of makeup or the act of applying makeup. Esai had chosen a drag name: Naya Kimora, because he loved Kimora Lee Simmons, the fashion designer and former wife of hip-hop mogul Russell Simmons. Aja's name came from the chorus of a catchy Bollywood song. The other queens there had on long dresses and shiny, blond, expensive-looking wigs. Aja and Esai should have felt out of place—conspicuously underage and unpolished—but alcohol had steadied their nerves.

The bar filled up. When it was Esai's turn to perform, he collected himself at the center of the stage and waited for the DJ to cue his music. The drums began, and Esai started swinging his hips, turning slowly in a circle.

Esai lip-synched as JLo sang, "Let all the heat pour dooooown."

The shoes chewed into Esai's feet. The beat hit. He ignored the throbbing in his ankle, kicked his leg in front of him, pivoted, and began to twerk. People in the room tittered and politely cheered.

"Dance for your man," JLo commanded. "Put your hands up in the air-air-air—whoa oh-oh-oh," she sang. It was a good thing the words were simple, because he had not practiced. Esai left the stage panting and joined Aja, who had performed "Judas" by Lady Gaga, a song about toxic love, with dark synths and a wailing chorus.

Brave and foolish, these two New York City children had done something many older, wiser, and more experienced queers would never dare attempt. They'd gotten into drag, walked into a bar, and jumped onstage, without hesitation and with very little concern for the consequences. They were new, and they were rough around the edges, but even in this utterly amateur moment they had the priceless combination of guts and hunger that helped seemingly small people do big, scary things. Kicking and twirling while lip-synching in front of an audience felt like flying.

·····

Aja lived with her mom on Hopkins and Throop in Brooklyn, where hipster Williamsburg met working-class Bushwick. She was adopted and her father had moved out when she was young. "I was wild," she would later say about her childhood. At seven, she ran away from the babysitter, and when the police found her on the playground, Aja lied and told the cops her mother had left her there. Later, when Aja locked the door to her bedroom, her mom kicked it in. As a teenager, she dyed the family pug, Gizmo, blue with a spray bottle full of Kool-Aid and once threw an ice cube into a deep fryer in a manic desire to see what would happen. What happened was third-degree burns on her face that healed into bumpy pink scars.

People were always coming for Aja over her scars, her asthmatic wheezing, her swishy walk. Even old ladies on the street would offer unsolicited recommendations for clearer skin. "It's not acne," Aja would try to explain, and then sigh, "Oh, never mind." But Aja could give as good as she got. Bigger boys threw punches and skateboards, Aja threw them back.

Aja was a pariah but talented. By twelve she was hanging out on the East River piers, where queer kids from across the borough gathered to listen to music, trade insults, and dance. Aja was a natural, quickly learning to vogue, kick, and duck-walk as the other kids cheered her on. When Aja wasn't running the streets, she'd stay up all night perfecting sketches of Pokémon and Mortal Kombat characters. She could read a bitch to tears.

Aja met Esai, whose family occupied a crowded one-bedroom apartment a few blocks away, about a year before that first night out in drag. All the gay boys from the neighborhood crossed paths eventually. At the time, Esai was dating Timothy, a kid Aja knew from Fashion Industries. It wasn't really Aja's business, but she liked Esai and she couldn't stand the thought of him going out with someone with a boxy face, bad skin, and terrible breath. When Timothy heard Aja had been talking shit and threatened to fight her, Aja's response was a cool "Bitch, you're nothing more than gum on the street to me." Aja was not faking. Anyone who'd spent sixteen years disobeying a no-bullshit, always-yelling Puerto Rican mother wouldn't be scared of much either.

After a few months, Aja's dogged campaign against Timothy paid off. Esai showed up at Aja's house to talk about his "boy troubles" (some kid had sent Esai a Facebook message saying he'd been sleeping with Timothy, too) and they bonded over their disgust for Esai's—now ex—boyfriend. Aja felt protective of Esai. No one seemed to be looking out for him. Some of his close family members were moody and unpredictable—raging one day and sulking the next. Others were like ghosts in the house; the only signs of life were the liquor bottles they hid in the couches and cabinets. Esai's grandmother, who was from the Dominican Republic, tried to look out for him as best she could, but Esai, feminine and quiet, was basically on his own. Before he was old enough to grow facial hair, he was taking the train to gay house parties in the Bronx where he'd lie about his age and guzzle alcohol. Esai and Aja started hooking up. They'd both been with guys before, but this felt different. Aja wasn't used to being with someone so young. She thought she could help Esai avoid some of the struggle and drama she'd gone through.

For a while, they were a good match. While Aja sometimes tried to butch up, Esai never hid his girlishness. "I did not give a shit what anyone had to say," Esai later said about those early years. Ever since he was a little boy, he loved lip gloss and short shorts. His mother would buy him oversized pants and, by the time he was twelve, he was having friends with sewing machines tailor them to show off his ass and thighs. He wondered if he liked rainbows and sparkly clothes because he was actually a woman. In seventh grade, he asked a gynecologist about a prescription for female hormones. The doctor referred him to a therapist. Esai later said this was how he figured out that, no, he wasn't a woman, he just "wanted to look so soft and cunt" and, to him, that meant manicured nails, crop tops, and a big rhinestone Victoria's Secret bag.

As a kid, Aja would sometimes steal her cousin's skirt and line her lips in dark red to do a furious impression of the crass, no-nonsense former supermodel and *America's Next Top Model* judge Janice Dickinson falling down the stairs. Aja loved people like Janice Dickinson and Tiffany Pollard, who were fun to watch on TV. "I was always very thoroughly entertained by people who just didn't really give a fuck," she later said. The impression had her family howling with laughter and Aja basked in the attention. But it wasn't until 2011, after Aja and Esai had been hanging out for about six months, that she began to consider calling herself a drag queen. One of the trans girls at the piers told Aja that drag queens made money giving lip sync shows at gay bars in Manhattan. Aja and Esai had both heard of drag queens—men who dressed up as women and performed songs onstage—but they had never really paid them much attention. Now, Aja was intrigued. Money was always tight at home, but it had gotten especially so lately. A few years before, bullies had broken Aja's arm, and her mom had stayed with her in the hospital, missing so much work she lost her job. They lived close to the poverty line, but what set them apart from many other families in the neighborhood was the fact that Aja's mom owned her house. It was the foundation of their security and their relationship, the thing that protected them when Aja's dad left. After her mom lost her job she couldn't afford her storage space, and so she moved what felt like fifty Tupperware containers full of holiday decorations and old clothes into the house. These hoarding tendencies, her mom's refusal to throw away something she'd paid money for, had caught up with them and, just as they were at their poorest, they were surrounded by stuff. At one point, Aja came home to find that the lights had been shut off. On another occasion, she and her mom had to make an order of pork fried rice and chicken wings last for several days. Her mother made it clear that once Aja was eighteen she was going to have to support herself. Feeling overwhelmed and powerless, Aja messaged strangers on the internet, chased bullies in city parks, danced with friends at the piers, while, thanks to what Aja thought of as "the grace of higher energies," her mom managed to hold on to her house. Esai had started crashing with them more regularly, and Aja was desperate to bring in some cash, but hated the idea of a normal job. While voguing had originated in the queer ballroom scene, where kids of color found community and solace competing in categories like "face," "realness," and "body," being a drag queen meant entertaining other gays in bars and nightclubs. Those ballroom queens who ventured into the drag world found they could make real money with their fierce attitude and dance skills, but they were expected to dress accordingly—wigs, makeup, and stylish looks that sold the fantasy of a diva, tough girl, or pop princess. Drag required an outsized alter ego that had the power to make an audience laugh, cry, or get excited—that made them *feel* something. Drag in bars, as Aja and Esai would learn, existed at the intersection of commerce and art and consisted of doing things Aja loved—lip-synching, dancing, looking cute—but for money. It sounded too good to be true.

Esai was already used to wearing girls' clothes, so it made sense to dress him up, too. Though Esai was more naturally feminine on the streets, Aja was the one who knew how to paint to look really *female*. Posing for photos outside the house, Esai looked like a girl on her way to church: button-down floral shirt, pleated skirt, white tights. Esai didn't have any money for makeup, and no way was he going to ask his father to buy him some, so he mopped it from a local Rite Aid. Aja showed him how to use the stolen foundation and concealer, then they snuck into Aja's brother's house to *borrow* her sister-in-law's tiny skirts and dresses.

In the regular world, full of tired, yelling, frustrated people, Aja was treated like a nuisance, a person to be controlled or ignored. But dressed up in drag, Aja felt like someone else entirely. She felt special, not because of scars, or a lisp, or asthma, but because she was fabulous, glamorous, or shocking. In drag, Aja was strong and beautiful in ways she hadn't thought a boy could be. For the first time ever, Aja didn't want to hide. She wanted to be out in the world. This was a superhero cape complete with mystical powers. The teens hosted a drag show in Aja's living room. Fifty kids whooped, hollered, and jumped on the furniture as they lip-synched with abandon. Eager to test the moneymaking potential of this fabulous new persona, Aja scoured Facebook looking for drag shows and parties at Manhattan gay bars. For Esai, drag had become his escape from the gloomy atmosphere of his grandmother's house. He was happiest, in his words, "all pumped and perused," dressed up like a stylish woman. He wasn't going to be left behind. He asked Aja—the only other person he knew who did drag—to be his drag mother and take him out. Aja took to the role; it felt natural to be in charge.

In the fall of 2011, hours before their first Manhattan performances, they'd sat in Aja's bedroom, chugging their Four Lokos while Aja painted Esai's face and noticed that the gap between the younger boy's two front teeth made him look even more girlish.

After their performances, Holly, the host at Bar-Tini, called all the contestants up for the judging. Aja and Esai bounded onto the stage and stood next to the other competitors. All the others were aiming for what they called "fishiness," an arguably disparaging term that describes passable femininity—looking, moving, and talking like a woman. It reminded Esai of what he'd heard about drag pageants, where queens competed in categories like "evening gown," "swimsuit," and "talent," and the crown went to the most poised and put-together queen.

Despite Aja's efforts, Esai's makeup was thick and cracked. Their chins were square and reddish, like the shape and texture of a brick. "Grawlick chinnula" was how Esai and Aja sometimes insulted each other when their faces looked particularly busted. They were dressed in polyester skirts that covered too much of their legs and looked much more like schoolgirls than superstars.

None of this was lost on the judges.

"I loved your energy," said one judge. "But your outfit. Oooh, girl."

"Your performance was good," said another. "But you look . . ." She trailed off.

"You look just horrible," said a third.

Aja understood that they were long shots—it was their first time out, after all—but she hadn't been prepared to fail so spectacularly. She'd tried to create the illusion of a flat crotch with duct tape, what's known as "tucking." During the judging, the other queens made sure to point out that the silver of the tape was visible. Embarrassed by the reception and annoyed with themselves for giving a fuck, Esai and Aja left the club and jumped the turnstile for a silent ride back to Brooklyn.

Aja would later describe that night as both the beginning of her drag career and a continuation of all her troubles. Yet another sign that, no matter how hard she tried, no matter what she did, people would never accept her and would always stand in her way.

Aja and Esai, like so many Brooklyn drag performers who got

their start during the second decade of the twenty-first century, were striving to make money as artists during an unprecedented moment in gay culture. A cadre of drag performers that included Thorgy Thor, Merrie Cherry, Horrorchata, Switch n' Play, and Sasha Velour—would be the engine of this influential and innovative scene. Drag had long brought queer people moments of acceptance and rejection, but now it would also confer respect and visibility in the wider world. What Aja sensed back in 2011, before she was old enough to vote or even drive a car in New York State, was the growing power and influence of gay people—especially gay people in New York City—to make a performer's dreams come true.

Not that these opportunities would be equally—or fairly—distributed. Any truly ambitious performer had a rough road to stardom. . . . Years later, recounting her defeat at the Manhattan show, Aja was still bitter. As her emotions got hotter, her voice grew raspier and her Brooklyn accent thicker. "These bitches never made it easy for me," she would gripe, and Esai would laugh.

"Girl, your face *was* a brick," he said. "We looked horrible."

·····

A stage is a stage, no matter how small. For as long as there have been gay bars, there have been people who elbowed their way to the front of the room to find self-esteem, confidence, and opportunity by dancing, singing a song, or telling some jokes. If they were good, they became figureheads of the scene. From Alabama to Alaska, these performers brought glamour, excitement, and entertainment to the often maligned or ignored subcultures that formed in tiny rooms and dingy queer bars. On those nights when they were the flashiest creatures in the room, they found a certain type of fame among a crowd that hadn't yet been represented on Broadway stages, television, or in Hollywood. If they cultivated an alluring personality, gave good shows, and put the time in, they were recognized and respected by the network of friends, lovers, and acquaintances who made up the gay world in their particular city or town. Fame doesn't always mean your face on a Times Square billboard; it can just as easily be friends of friends you've never met, whose names you do not know, telling stories about your exploits and adventures. Unnoticed by the wider world, the gay community had quietly been forging stars like this for generations. Now, it was about to mint a few more.

On a chilly November evening in 2011, Jason Daniels was nursing a beer at Metropolitan in Brooklyn's Williamsburg neighborhood when one of the owners mentioned they needed someone to work coat check over the winter. Jason perked up. He had moved to New York City two years earlier from Berkeley, California, with two suitcases and three months of rent money, hoping to be somebody. He wasn't sure who, exactly, but somebody. Now, at twenty-eight years old, he found himself wasting his days in a windowless office, entering numbers into spreadsheets for a nonprofit alongside an overbearing boss and a bunch of uptight coworkers. He was living like a nobody in the most important place on earth, paying too much rent for too little space on Manhattan's Upper East Side. Even while people partied, screwed, and got rich all around him, Jason was friendless, bored, and broke. It sucked. Coat check seemed a step up, however small, plus he could use the money.

In Berkeley, he'd been raised mostly by his grandmother Ruth, who knew he liked boys but rarely talked about it. An only child, Jason spent a lot of time alone imagining a world where people wanted to get to know him. In these fantasies, he lived on Long Island—a place he'd heard about on TV—and belonged to the wealthiest Black family in the world. Everyone was fascinated by his rich, stylish parents, and all of Jason's friends were rich and stylish, too. Jason imagined that he had a twin sister, Jessica, who became a famous pop star after

Michael Jackson overheard her singing in the bathroom and cast her in his video for "Scream" instead of Janet. In reality, Jason's life was considerably lonelier.

Once, when Jason was around ten, he put on his grandmother's slip intending to "do a little show." His uncle walked in as Jason was mid-pirouette and made him change. As Jason got older, he got bigger—"two hundred and mumble mumble pounds"—and gayer, though he wasn't sure anyone could tell. Then, one day, Jason was hanging out with his cousin and their friends, when he noticed they were watching him closely. Studying him.

"Yes," his cousin said. "Yes. No. No. No. Yes. YES."

"What are you doing?" Jason asked.

"I'm saying when you're acting like a girl and when you're not," his cousin explained.

Jason hadn't realized he seemed feminine to other people. He'd never really thought about his gender as a performance—a *show*. To fit in, he let his cousin coach him on how to be more manly.

Overall, life wasn't bad—he got to go to summer camp and Disneyland, and his grandmother loved him—but there was lots of crying and slammed doors and frustration. In high school, he started going out with some cool kids, smoking weed, and downing beers. He went away to school in Boston but was kicked out for partying. He moved back in with Grandma Ruth and went out every night. Once, he was so confused and foggy from all the partying, he left the house for that night's adventure wearing two different shoes. He was suffocating in his grandmother's small, cluttered house. She knew it, too. One day, when he was twenty-six years old, he came home after yet another night spent dancing until five in the morning. "I love you for staying with me," Grandma Ruth said. "But you need to live your life."

But what was his life? Jason loved fashion, celebrities, and money. He had always dreamed about living in the biggest city, with the baddest, most important people. Soon after he arrived in New York, he reconnected with a rich girl he'd met studying graphic design in San Francisco. She and her friends were the kind of people Jason wanted to be around, the kind who regularly spent one thousand five hundred dollars on bottle service in a nightclub and vacationed in the Caribbean when the weather got cold. Jason soon fell into a routine. After work, he'd go to Metropolitan in Williamsburg for happy hour. He'd discovered it after fleeing some terrible bar full of straight people playing video games. He ran three blocks in the pouring rain and entered a dingy room full of sparkling, sexy gay men dancing to *NSYNC. At Metropolitan, he'd have a couple of beers most nights and then end up in Manhattan clubbing with his posh friends. It was a borrowed glamour, but it was glamorous none-theless. For his birthday, they had taken him for drinks at the Jane Hotel in the West Village. He wore a silk canary-yellow button-down shirt, a gauzy blue fascinator, and a swipe of eyeshadow. The music was good, and so he lost all six foot four inches of his gay self on the dance floor. As he danced, a crowd slowly collected around him. There was no one who looked like him in the club, and he could sense that people were taking pictures. It was the same feeling he'd had when he burst into spontaneous song-and-dance numbers at summer camp. He loved people's eyes on him, to see that he was making them laugh. But he didn't know how to hold their attention for longer than a song or a joke. He thought he was special, but he didn't know what to do about it. He sometimes danced or showed off while waiting for the bus, to try to get people to pay attention to him, and because he believed dancing made the bus come faster. But that was hardly a talent.

While Jason was scheming on how to rise up in the world, every-thing came crashing down. One night, he was so sloppy drunk he pissed off his friend's boyfriend. They stopped inviting him to the clubs. Suddenly, he had no crew, no bottle service, and very little money. What he did have, though, was Metropolitan.

Metro, as it's known to locals, was the biggest, busiest gay bar in Brooklyn. Windowless, on a residential street, it welcomed Jason with open arms. During the week, regulars gathered at the bar or pool table. In the summer, chatty groups of gay men and lesbians ate burgers and smoked cigarettes in the massive backyard. It was a dive, not a destination, and after a few months, the other regulars knew Jason's name, asked about his day and his grandmother's health, and bought him beers. As he plotted his return to the splendor of Manhattan nightlife, Jason took refuge among his fellow salty queers.

That winter, four evenings a week, Jason hung coats and handed out tickets. He didn't make a lot of money, but he met so many people—some of them celebrities, like clothing designer Alexander Wang. He was offered so many drugs. He loved it. He was still nobody, but the proximity to fame—and the pills and powders—made him feel one step closer to being somebody. In the Bay Area, Jason had sometimes dressed in drag for house parties and made people call him Jacquèline Baptiste. Just for fun, he started showing up to work coat check with a shimmery arch painted across his eyelids.

"Ooooh, you're wearing eyeshadow, I love it," people cooed as they handed him their coats—and left noticeably bigger tips.

You like this? Jason thought to himself. *How about if I come wearing lipstick, too?*

One night before he went to the bar, Jason had a friend do his makeup, and, an hour into his shift, a very drunk woman tipped him fifty dollars. Real money. *This is something I could get into,* Jason realized, and from then on he always worked coat check in makeup. Over the course of the winter, he added a wig, a tiny top hat, a bright red boa, and an obscene amount of glitter to his look. One night, Jason ran into a guy he'd slept with a few months earlier.

"Hello, Merry Cherry." The man came over to greet him with his coat.

"Merry Cherry?" Jason asked.

The man laughed, "I don't remember your name, but you were wearing red the last time I saw you and just seemed so happy. So I think of you as 'Merry Cherry.'" Jason waved his hand in front of the man and made a motion to snatch some imaginary object. "I'm taking that name," he announced.

Jason began introducing himself as Merrie Cherry whenever he was out. The handle was both sincere—he *was* merry—and satirical. "Mary" being a long-standing term of endearment and sometimes ridicule among gay men. He thought it was the perfect drag name.

Spring was approaching and, with it, the end of coat check, but Jason wasn't ready to go back to being a bored regular trapped in a day job, and he certainly didn't want to give up the extra cash. Jason thought of how much more excited people were when he wore makeup and a wig. In his final week, he cornered one of the bar's owners and pitched him an idea. He wanted to host a drag competition. The owner looked doubtful. Sometimes drag queens came in to meet up with friends after a gig in Manhattan, but there were no drag shows at Metropolitan. The New York City drag scene had waxed and waned in size and popularity over the past hundred years. In some eras, shows had been wild; in others, artfully restrained. Performances popped up in dive bars, nightclubs, dance halls, and theaters. But there had never been much drag in Brooklyn. In 2012, most shows took place at well-established Manhattan gay bars where a group of experienced performers and promoters determined who was good, who got booked, and who got paid. But Jason was adamant. His secret talent, he'd realized, was getting people to pay attention to him: on the dance floor, at the bar, even while hanging up their coats. If he could entertain that easily, then why couldn't he draw a crowd to Brooklyn for a drag show? Jason pushed and prodded, and the owner relented.

"You have one chance," he said. "But if it isn't successful, it's going to be a one-time thing." He agreed to give Jason one hundred dollars to host and organize, one hundred to pay a DJ, and fifty bucks for the winner. Jason left Metro and walked out into the cool spring night, a queer man, in the early years of a new millennium, in search of the holy trinity of show business: steady money, good times, and a stage.

·····

Drag was fun, no question. And the relative newness of drag in Brooklyn created an opportunity for creative expression that was rare in a city overflowing with competitive, talented show-offs. But could it pay the rent and provide a meaningful artistic outlet? Could it give performers the supportive community they'd need when times—inevitably—got tough? And could drag do this for everyone, or only a privileged—or lucky—few? Maybe, just maybe, it could make some people's dreams come true. . . .

Soon, these local performers would find the possibility of true celebrity beyond the grimy back rooms and raucous dive bars. *RuPaul's Drag Race*, at first just a small show with a niche following, would become a platform capable of launching drag queens to previously unfathomable heights of fame and fortune. After decades in the shadows, these performers would step onto a much bigger stage. It would be up to them to pack the house.

CHAPTER TWO
"Work Harder, Girl."

One Tuesday night in January 2012, a drag queen named Thorgy Thor was on a break between sets at Saliva!, her weekly show at the Ritz on Forty-Sixth Street in Manhattan, when the bar's security guard approached looking worried.

"There's five or six queens outside with no ID who say you'll vouch for them," he told Thorgy.

Thorgy sighed. "Aja?"

Though Aja and Esai's first night out in drag had been a disaster, Aja needed to help her mother stay afloat, and dressing in drag was easier than getting a minimum-wage job at the bodega and more reliable than bumming cash from her friends. The best way for a newcomer to get money was to win contests. Competitions like Beat That Face!, So You Think You Can Drag, and Miss Gay South Pacific came with a cash prize for the winner, plus a chance for a queen to show her skills in front of more established performers, many of whom had the power to book paying gigs at bars across the city.

On their nights out, Aja and Esai would jump the turnstile and take the subway to clubs in Hell's Kitchen, dodging bouncers by tagging along with older queens and telling anyone who asked that they were twenty-four and twenty-one years old respectively. Some of the other queer kids from school and the neighborhood heard about Aja and Esai's adventures in drag and begged to come along. Soon, a half dozen gay teenagers from Brooklyn could be found at the entrances of Manhattan gay bars, regaling bouncers with stories of lost IDs and friends inside waiting for them.

Once granted access to these clubs, they discovered that a current of rivalry and judgment buzzed through the scene. There were always more queens than opportunities. Job security and money were never guaranteed. And, like all divas, drag queens were loath to share the spotlight. When Aja and Esai performed, the other queens always had something to say. *Get your brows right. You're ghetto. You look gross.* Some of these performers had been doing drag for a decade and had strong opinions about how young queens should look, paint, and act. They enforced unspoken but well-established guidelines. In Manhattan, drag meant lip sync shows in gay bars, stand-up comedy in small theaters, and, occasionally, Broadway standards or Top 40 hits sung live in intimate cabaret settings. Lip-synching, an intense, theatrical pantomime that conveyed the emotion of a song and often queered or reinterpreted its meaning to suit the gay bar and the gay audience, was by far the most common form of drag performance. When it came to song choice, there were also tacit rules. Bigger, older queens, who could make the audience cry with a facial expression, performed soul classics and Broadway numbers (the musical *Dreamgirls* was a particular favorite); Beyoncé was for the more athletic girls who could dance and wore lots of hair; white girls in leotards performed to Britney Spears; older white girls in leotards did Madonna songs; and Adele was for those in gowns too heavy and cinched to allow for dancing. No runs in pantyhose, no tears in spandex, no tangled wigs. Absolutely no body odor. These nonthreatening drag performances appealed to tourists and buttoned-up locals looking for a wild night out. The wider an entertainer's appeal, the stronger her chance to make money and a name for herself. In gay and straight theater, cabaret, and nightlife, Manhattan audiences expected glamour. A flawless presentation was paramount.

Teenagers with no money and no experience, Aja and Esai were not particularly glamorous, and they certainly had flaws. Many of the established queens they met in Hell's Kitchen bars expected deference from Aja and got attitude instead. Esai was younger and less likely to lash out at strangers when he felt disrespected, but Aja was a fighter by nature—she just wouldn't show the older queens the respect they thought they deserved. The teenage crew quickly earned a reputation for chaos and drama.

"I was being me," Aja later said of these early struggles in the scene. "I was being hood. People were like, 'Oh my God, she's so angry, she's out of control.'" Aja insulted their hair and clothes and talked during their numbers.

Clapping back came naturally, but it took a toll. Aja would go off on someone and spend the next day under the covers at home anxiously replaying the conflict in her head. Despite all the swagger, she was just a kid. Gay—yes. Loud—of course. But also in need of love and support. Drag had seemed like an escape from the ugly, judgmental world but, after a few months, it had started to feel like more of the same. When the stress of rejection got really bad, Aja would sometimes have to rush off the subway, overtaken by panic, afraid that the train car was running out of air. For years, she'd been a full-blown hypochondriac, taking trips to the emergency room any time a rash appeared on her leg, or when she got itchy after eating a strawberry, or when she felt like she couldn't breathe. Her doctor eventually offered a bed in the psych ward. But her insurance wasn't going to pay for that, and plus, she couldn't imagine being away from her mother for that long.

·····

Thorgy Thor had heard rumors that Aja and her crew—who she suspected were underage—had been popping off and getting into arguments all over town. But Aja had been to Saliva! a few weeks earlier, and Thorgy had watched her give a fierce, if somewhat amateurish performance.

Oh, what the hell, Thorgy thought. "Let them in," she told the bouncer.

"It's on your reputation," the bouncer said.

Thorgy nodded. The young queens rushed inside and marched toward the DJ booth at the back of the club. A disco ball scattered blue and green light across the faces of the crowd, illuminating a coy smile on a bearded boy with a fade, making patterns on a tight white T-shirt, a set of pouty lips, a pair of long silver earrings. Thorgy stopped the teenagers in their tracks.

"Do *not* steal, and do *not* be a mess," she said, before instructing Aja and her friends to give the DJ their songs. If Thorgy's reputation was on the line, then she better get some damn good shows out of it. The kids took note of the warning. "I was trying to pretend I was twenty-four," Aja later recalled. "I could not afford to ruin that."

If any show in New York City was going to welcome a group of chaotic teenagers from Brooklyn who liked to dance and fight, it would be Saliva! with Thorgy Thor at the helm. In the überglamorous, hyperfeminine world of Manhattan drag, Saliva! was the refuge for weirdos, art school kids, and people whose personalities were too big and raucous for the more conventional scene. Typical Manhattan drag had deeply entrenched rules. At Saliva! there was no pressure to keep performances glamorous or accessible to straight people and tourists. The shows were full of inside jokes; homemade seven-minute song mixes that included dialogue; rude impersonations of bored housewives and butch lesbians; and costumes made from Halloween store castoffs, fabric scraps, and reimagined household goods. Polish was of little concern. Performances could be conceptual and sometimes downright stupid. People did eight-minute interpretive-dance numbers and wrote raps dissing other queens. They pulled things out of their asses and put them back in. They yelled. A lot.

At the center were the three hosts: Veruca la'Piranha, a queen from Pittsburgh who claimed to be the first drag queen to ever perform a Lady Gaga song and hailed from a spooky, punk rock drag family called Haus of Haunt; Azraea, a bearded queen who ardently rejected the notion that drag had to be feminine; and Thorgy Thor herself, a self-described "drag clown" who poured a steady stream of manic, sometimes vicious, always campy energy into her performances across the city. Thorgy and her cohosts' anything-goes attitudes had made Saliva! the late-night destination for nightlife denizens looking for truly crazy times on a Tuesday. At first, the hosts made fifty dollars apiece. By the time the party ended, they were taking home a hundred each from the bar—plus whatever tips they could cajole or coax out of the audience. It was a drag performer's drag show. To the monsters who populated Saliva!, bad drag was anything typical or expected: boring performers, in uninteresting clothing, with bland personalities. Good drag was surprising: fantasy, absurdity, risk.

"All drag is art, and all art is beautiful," Azraea liked to say.

Never mind perfect makeup, tights without runs, and shoes without scuffs. If a performance or a look transported the audience, made them feel like they were somewhere else and gave them *life*, then it was good drag.

A workhorse with a lot to say, it had taken Thorgy six years of constant striving to finally claw her way to a top spot at the Ritz. She'd developed her drag persona as a student at the State University of New York in Purchase, just outside New York City, which had a lively drag scene. For the school's annual Fall Ball, Thorgy debuted "Thorgy the Swan," a number later perfected at Saliva!, in which she emerged in a white leotard and tutu, her hair in a giant turban done up to look like a bird's neck, as music from Tchaikovsky's *Swan Lake* played. While she camped it up, trotting back and forth on tiptoe, a voice-over told the story of "a swan named Thorgy, on her way to the market to buy *Swan Weekly* magazine, granola bars, and a Tide bleach pen." The details changed over the years, but in every iteration of the number, Thorgy took a wrong turn, was threatened by hunters, and shot them with a handgun she pulled from her purse. Good drag.

This was a pure expression of Thorgy's deepest, weirdest energy. As a kid in the suburban Long Island town of Ronkonkoma, New York, the only time Thorgy—whose given name is Shane Thor Galligan—was quiet or focused was when playing violin or viola. Other than classical music, she liked dressing up, being crazy, having sex with boys, and getting attention. Thorgy's grandfather and namesake, Thor, had been a Norwegian Olympic ski jumper. She'd grown up doing whatever she wanted and trying not to care what other people thought. Being in the bars gave Thorgy a way to merge the discipline that made it possible to play Prokofiev on the violin, Tchaikovsky on the viola, and teach herself the cello, with her zest for the absurd. In college, Thorgy once cut class and traveled an hour and a half by bus and train to try to get a job at Lucky Cheng's, the legendary East Village restaurant staffed by statuesque drag queens. It was the only drag bar Thorgy knew about.

"I went in with a professional résumé, and they were like, 'We're transsexuals who give blow jobs to men from the suburbs while their wives are drinking martinis.' I was getting a bachelor's degree in fine arts, and they were like, 'Great! Can you suck penis?' I was that Long Island kid that didn't get it," Thorgy said of the audition.

After graduating in 2006, Thorgy rented a cheap apartment in Brooklyn and started going out in drag every night of the week. Thrifting at the Salvation Army or Goodwill she'd get inspired by props and one-of-a-kind vintage garments. She found some silhouettes that made her body look more feminine but cartoonish: a jacket or blazer over a bikini top; a cinched waist; French-cut bodysuits; XXL T-shirts over pantyhose; and belted jumpsuits with plunging necklines. She collected an arsenal of colorful looks, twisted and piled her long dreadlocks on her head, and covered them with an extra-high wig. For Thorgy, the idea behind a drag performance was just as important as the presentation, and she was overflowing with ideas. The elements of a typical Thorgy show were established early on: a strong narrative, a camp concept set to pop music, and prop comedy. One of her early numbers told the epic story of a woman who goes to a fertility clinic, becomes pregnant, then delivers octuplets. In the early 2000s, drag was still all but nonexistent in Brooklyn. With the exception of a few predominantly straight dive bars where she cajoled the managers into letting her host an occasional drag show, all of Thorgy's gigs were in staid Manhattan, where her sense of humor and strangeness weren't entirely welcome. She dressed as a penguin one night, a bumblebee the next; she'd pantomime to a violin concerto, then lip-synch to the song "Fuck Me," a parody R & B ballad by comedian Wendy Ho, with the lyrics, "You can fuck me in Pakistan / Blow my coochie up like the Taliban." When lip-synching to Beyoncé's "Listen," Thorgy pushed her fluffy wig aside at the first chorus to reveal a giant ear. It was funny and absurd, but Thorgy approached the jokes with the intensity of a prima ballerina on opening night.

All this conceptualism began to draw crowds, and the gigs piled up. She got some weekly bookings paying her the enviable sum of a hundred dollars, plus tips. She cracked jokes and passed the tip bucket relentlessly. *I'm one of the girls*, Thorgy thought, blissfully unaware of her relative weirdness, as other queens in leotards who performed megamixes of all the same pop songs rolled their eyes and gossiped behind her back.

"That was Manhattan drag," Thorgy would come to realize, but at the time, "I had no idea that I was different. I thought, *These are my friends and I just do different mixes. Of course we're all sisters.*"

Despite this gung ho obliviousness, she had her own set of standards. She would groan when drag queens showed up to a gig in a T-shirt and panties to do a tired Beyoncé number. "Work harder, girl," she'd implore.

Instead of putting a lot of effort into a look for a stale number, she'd advise younger queens to figure out what made them special, what made them *them*. "Some girls are very good with the mic in their hand—only. Some girls are good as a guest performer 'cause they fucking turn it. Some girls are terrible on the mic, even worse performers on a stage, but if you find out they're going to be working a party walking around and hanging out, you want to go there and see what they're wearing and who they're sitting with," she said during an interview with the local drag podcast *Grizzly Kiki*. Her knack for spotting talent and her bald ambition helped her convince the manager of the Ritz to let her, Azraea, and Veruca have free rein on Tuesday nights. Saliva! quickly became a destination for high-profile out-of-town queens looking to work out their most daring material.

"We brought the freak to Hell's Kitchen," Veruca later said. They were inspired by the club kids who'd dominated New York City nightlife during the 1980s and turned dressing into an art form. Aliens, horror, gore, feathers, latex, old Hollywood, and high fashion. But unlike the club kids, the Saliva! crew were performing drag queens. In addition to giving shows all night long, "We looked better than the other drag queens because we had these crazy fashions and we looked better than the club kids because we had our faces painted like we had plastic surgery," Veruca said.

At the Ritz, Aja and Esai had watched—baffled and delighted—as Saliva! upended everything they thought they knew about the rules of drag. On the night they visited, a queen with eyelashes made from scraps of paper and a purple ponytail glued onto her bald head knelt down and performed "I Will Follow Him" by the 1960s singer Peggy March, in an homage to the movie *Sister Act*.

"This is hideous," Esai whispered to Aja.

Aja nodded. But they also loved it. They friended Thorgy, Veruca, and the other artistic queens on Facebook and followed them to their gigs. Though several other bars had shut their doors to Aja and Esai, Thorgy had a ringmaster's instinct for spotting talent, and she believed that freewheeling fun was worth the risk of chaos.

"I'm not a queen who does, like, voguing and dropping to splits," Thorgy later said about her decision to let Aja and Esai into the club. "Put a mic in my hand, I tell jokes. I get butts in the seats. I give a good show." She was always trying to round out her crew of performers. When Aja danced, the crowd lost their minds. Thorgy didn't care that Aja and her friends were underage and messy. Good drag could be messy—some might argue good drag should be messy. Thorgy put Aja in the lineup for the final set. This was the late-night spot reserved for up-and-comers. Aja wouldn't get paid by the bar, but she'd be able to keep any tips collected during her number. At 3:30 a.m., the Ritz was still going strong, the audience assembled around the perimeter of the room with a stripe of floor left open for the performers. Aja mugged in a leotard and platform heels, and the DJ pressed play on the track.

During performances, Aja liked to start off slow, stomping up and down the floor, striking a pose, and tossing her wig. It built tension in the crowd. "I was fresh from the ballroom scene," Aja later said of these early shows. "Although I wasn't an expert at performing on a stage with people, I did know a thing or two about performing . . . period." Aja brought a kind of excitement and energy that was rare in the bars dominated by prop comedy and Broadway standards and, as she made eye contact and flirted with the people in the front row, an outstretched hand proffered the universal sign of approval: cash. While some queens stopped the show to eagerly grab a dollar, Aja knew enough to appear indifferent while taking tips during a hype number. Ballads provided time for a moment of connection, a little smile or wink, a squeeze of a hand even. But if the music was about to hit, you couldn't let the bills distract you and ruin the fantasy. They would always be there waiting for you on the floor when the number was over.

As Aja paraded and pranced, she kept her mind focused on the lip sync. Aja liked Britney fine, but she was more interested in female rappers—Lil' Kim, Nicki Minaj, Azealia Banks. Bad girls who didn't take shit from anyone. Oozing attitude, she'd toss off a line and strut, plant her feet, and then slowly bend her knees and swivel her hip to savor the raunchiest lyrics, like, "I'ma ruin your cunt" and "Lick my pussy and my crack." As the song grew louder and more intense, Aja would start to dance. First a few steps, voguing and making shapes with her arms, then she'd move more frantically. As Aja fell backward and slammed onto the floor, she'd kick a leg out toward the crowd. That's when the tips would really start to fly, tossed with whoops and cheers. The sight of a queen dancing like her legs were rubber bands and her back was on a hinge always brought the room to its knees. People gasped as she dipped onto the floor and bounced back up only to crash-land once more. The music had control of her, and she had control of the room. For Aja, all those months on the piers, dancing with her friends, were starting to pay off, literally, in small piles of crumpled dollar bills.

CHAPTER THREE

DragNet, Get Caught in It

Jason Daniels needed help. His inaugural drag competition at Metropolitan was rapidly approaching, and he had no money to hire performers, and no performers meant no audience. Even finding other novice competitors was proving difficult. There weren't that many young Brooklynites clamoring to get into drag. The DJ he'd hired had convinced his roommate to try drag for the first time and a barback at Metropolitan had enlisted his best friend to get dressed up and sing a song. But that left Jason three performers short. Enduring his office job in ill-fitting khakis and a white button-down shirt, Jason daydreamed about his debut performance as Merrie Cherry. He was planning to lip-synch to the "The Diva Dance" from the movie *The Fifth Element*, an operatic ballad with no words that turns into a dance track midway through the song. He'd listened to the track nonstop; he was even falling asleep to the music.

But he still needed a name for the party. Jason had wanted to call the event Miss Mister, because it would be open to all genders and types of drag, but his friends weren't convinced.

"Ugh, that's a horrible name," his friend Donovan said, shaking his head. Donovan and another regular named Gary exchanged a look. "Let's ask Grandma what you should call it."

The three men went outside, and Gary put the phone on speaker. "Hello," a hoarse, elderly voice answered.

"Grandma, how are you?" Gary asked sweetly, and Jason could hear the person on the other end of the line take a drag off a cigarette.

"I'm good, just watchin' TV."

Why is Gary calling his grandmother right now? Jason had no clue what was going on.

Gary spoke slowly into the phone. "Grandma, we have a new friend named Merrie Cherry who's starting a drag competition in Brooklyn called Miss Mister—"

"I hate it," the voice cut him off.

"What should she call it, then?"

The phone went quiet for ten seconds. Jason could hear the person audibly inhale again.

"DragNet," Gary's grandma announced.

"Yes. That's it. Thank you, Grandma," Gary said, and hung up.

"All right." He turned to Jason. "Mother Flawless Sabrina just blessed your party."

Though Jason didn't realize it at the time, he'd just received the imprimatur of one of the most influential and respected members of the New York City drag community, a performer who'd organized one of the first successful drag pageants in the 1960s, gone on to a have a career in Hollywood, and, now in her seventies, mentored a slew of young drag performers, trans activists, and artists—a legendary queen. The name was, indeed, perfect. As a kid, Jason had watched *Dragnet*, the classic police procedural, religiously.

Now that he had a name, it was time to announce the party online and test the strength of this network Jason had been building all winter. He began to post on Facebook every few days and then every day as the party approached. His tone was pithy and unhinged.

"One more day until the crowning of the first Miss DragNet. Expect pure creativity and magical cunt power. Bring your Depends because you may lose control of your bowels. . . . Thursdays are the beginning of the weekend, let's start acting like it." He sent the Facebook invitation to every single one of his friends, making it clear that DragNet would be open to all: "Fashion Queens ~ Beauty Queens ~ Lady Boy Queens ~ Hipster Queens ~ Butch Queens ~ Tranny Queens ~ Fairy Queens ~ House Queens ~ Rice Queens ~ Ghetto Queens ~ Old Queens ~ Twink Queens ~ Down Low Queens ~ Freak Queens ~ Daddy Queens ~ Leather Queens ~ Straight Queens ~ Vegan Queens ~ and every other type of Queen in between." All were invited to compete for a prize of fifty dollars.

•••••

On the night of the show, Jason, also known as Merrie Cherry, was panicking. She had to be at Metropolitan by 11:00 p.m. and, even though Donovan had promised to help clean up Merrie's look before the show, it was 9:30 and he wasn't answering his bell. At 10:20, Donovan came rushing around the corner. Merrie followed him up the narrow stairs, fuming. Earlier that week she had glued fat sequins to a black tank top. Merrie knew nothing about stoning clothes with crystals or how to make garments sparkle and had bought wood glue instead of E6000 adhesive. It was her first time wearing high heels, but thankfully they felt comfortable enough. Maybe walking in them wouldn't be as hard as everyone claimed.

The competitors were just as inexperienced. Merrie had managed to cajole a queen in town from San Francisco and another Metropolitan regular to fill the two remaining performance slots. Of the five people on that night's lineup, at least three were doing drag for the first time ever, including Sheza Lush, a cisgender girl who described herself as "cheeky, freaky, and downright creepy after years of binge-drinking, anonymous sex, and recreational drug use," and Hamm Samwich, the DJ's roommate, a rapper in pink tights who wrote lyrics like, "I got a pussy flown in from the fifth dimension" and "My vagina's sweeter than the best sparkling wine in all New York." It was extremely likely to be a messy night.

Donovan and Merrie arrived thirty minutes late and found the bar was packed. Everywhere Merrie turned, she recognized someone. They smiled and came over to swap air-kisses and wish her good luck. *This is my party*, she thought to herself as she walked over to the bar and asked for a shot of tequila. Then another. After forty minutes in the heels, her toes were aching. But, inwardly, she was thrilled. She was somebody. The other contestants were already there, anxiously downing drinks with their friends and waiting for the show to begin.

Merrie, now adamant that friends and bar goers refer to her with female pronouns in drag, picked up the mic and gripped it in her right hand. "Helloooo, people," she shouted, laughing, as she welcomed the crowd to the first ever DragNet competition. At her request, each contestant sent a short bio, which she forgot to read onstage, opting instead for ad hoc introductions that all amounted to the same thing: "This bitch? I know her. She's *fierce*."

The stage at Metro was right in front of the DJ booth and about six feet wide. Sheza Lush, who brought her own smoke machine, had sewn strips of fabric onto an old shirt to make it look like a gnarled tree, covered her face with gold leaf, and was wearing a white, faux-hawk wig full of twigs and leaves. She sang a Björk song and, at her performance's climax, doused herself with a packet of fake blood she'd hidden in her bra. Another cisgender woman, Ballerina Bizet, danced acrobatically in toe shoes and then stripped off her shirt and bra. Hamm Samwich broke a chair. The crowd went crazy.

Merrie had managed to find some thoroughly entertaining show-offs. She was serving a sloppy, deconstructed, gender-bending look and had on white eyeshadow and a red lip. "Diva Dance" from *The Fifth Element* starts slowly and sounds like a conventional aria, then, midway through, flips into a cartoonish banger. In the film, it's the calling card of a beautiful, preternaturally talented alien performed for the entertainment of a cosmopolitan and stylish audience. The alien in *The Fifth Element* is not a freak but an attraction: a beautiful anomaly whose difference is intrinsic to her appeal. Lip-synching at Metropolitan, Merrie tried to keep her performance classy. As the song's tone shifted, she could feel the people watching her and she began to sway back and forth on the tiny stage, waving her arms and pumping her chest with the beat. Her eyes stayed locked on the audience. Merrie moved her hands in circles in front of her face and twirled as the music swelled and trilled. Her feet had started cramping in the heels, so she kicked them off with a flourish and the audience cheered. *Oh, I don't have to wear these suckers*, she realized.

By the end of that first DragNet competition, most people were too drunk to notice when Merrie crowned the winner—the yellow-spandex-clad queen from San Francisco who lip-synched to "20 Dollar" by the Sri Lankan rapper M.I.A. (Hamm Samwich, the rapper, had been the crowd favorite but lost after she refused to lip-synch in the final round.) Someone stole Sheza Lush's smoke machine. For many in the audience, the attention-starved maniacs on the small Metro stage were a welcome reprieve from the bar's regular crowd of sweaty boys eye-fucking one another from across the patio. Blindly stumbling ahead, Merrie had busted open the doors of Brooklyn nightlife and invited the amateurs in.

Drag, Merrie realized, meant people knew your name when you went out. It meant they noticed you when you walked into the bar. Well, they didn't notice *you* exactly, but they noticed a persona you created, and that was good enough, maybe better even. Merrie knew that somewhere out there were girls who had been perfecting their crafts and personas for years, never missing a beat in their numbers, never an eyelash out of place. But she'd brought none of that polish or professionalism to the first annual DragNet, and it hadn't mattered. Merrie, who dreamed of becoming very, very rich, had not intentionally set out to democratize the medium of drag. And yet, instead of seeming like an unattainable version of a glamorous woman or a full-fantasy sex kitten, Merrie Cherry's haphazard aesthetic had signaled to the other performers that drag was, indeed, for everyone. Jason—who had very little money and only a couple of true friends—had gotten dressed up, stood in front of a room full of people in a dress and a wig, and the audience cheered and whooped and celebrated. The fantasy, for Jason as Merrie, was fulfilled, not by wearing the sparkliest gown or the tallest heels but by showing up and taking the stage.

·····

Ooof, who are these girls? Merrie thought. It was the third Thursday of June 2012, and a handful of teenage drag queens had just stomped through the door of Metropolitan for the third round of DragNet. The first competition had been such a success that Merrie had been able to spin it into a monthly event with a finale scheduled for the end of the summer.

"I am Aja Injektion Marie Von Teese," Aja said, reciting her full name—at least for that week—and cocking her head to size up Merrie Cherry. "This is Kaos Marie."

During that spring, Esai had changed his drag name from Naya Kimora to Kaos Marie because, as he'd explained matter-of-factly to Aja, "My life is chaos." Indeed, his home life had grown more turbulent, and his family members, on and off pain medication and drinking heavily, were increasingly volatile. They'd be manic one day, then dark and angry the next. Esai was considering becoming an emancipated minor. An older woman from the neighborhood, who lived near Metropolitan, would sometimes let him stay with her. He'd shown her pictures of him and Aja in drag, and the woman lit up.

"I walked past this bar and saw a flier for this thing called DragNet, with a guy called, like, Cherry Mary, or something," she told Esai. "You should compete."

The Ritz, where Thorgy hosted Saliva!, and Bar-Tini were Manhattan bars. Aja hadn't realized that people even did drag in Brooklyn. Brooklyn was where parents, bullies, and old ladies on the street tried to scare the gay out of you. A place that threatened to grind down anyone who couldn't break free and find their way across the river. Esai and Aja lived there because they had to. Why would any gay man, especially one who does drag, want to claim it? But as they would soon discover, Brooklyn had become a symbol of creativity, coolness, and rarefied consumerism. It was as much an idea—about the clothes people wore, the music they listened to, what they ate, and how they spent their time—as an actual place. The Williamsburg of Aja's and Esai's childhoods had been populated by Dominican, Puerto Rican, and Hasidic families. But, after more than a decade of development, a parallel Williamsburg had emerged, inhabited by young—often white—people with disposable income, artistic inclinations, and irregular schedules.

"Oh, bitch, you think I should do it?" Aja asked Esai after he told her about DragNet. If there were drag shows in their neighborhood, it seemed only natural to Aja and Esai that they would dominate them. In June, Aja messaged Merrie Cherry on Facebook, asking to sign up for the next round. Aja had been working hard on her looks and persona. On any given night, she could be found sitting at her desk, a rack of outfits behind her, wigs hanging from hooks on the wall, blue contacts in her eyes, pasting her eyebrows flat against her forehead with an Elmer's glue stick. Gluing down natural eyebrows made it possible for a queen to paint higher and longer eyebrows above them. Aja would spread the brows, now tacky and purple with the wet glue, up toward her hairline with a spoolie brush and fan her face to help them harden. Once the glue was dry, Aja pressed powder over her forehead to keep the brows from poking out when she inevitably started sweating. Next, a greenish primer went on the whole face to neutralize the skin tone, smooth the bumps in her skin, and fill in the creases. She'd lather it on and follow with foundation in a lighter tint for the areas she wanted to highlight. In order to beat the boy out of her face, Aja had to trick the eye and brighten up the center. This made her face seem smaller and her features more clearly defined. She roughly applied highlighter around her eyes, across her T-zone—the name for the area that spanned the forehead and the bridge of the nose—on her chin, and above her top lip.

With brown foundation and a skinny brush Aja would draw two sinister-looking hockey sticks above her glued-down eyebrows, and paint a thin line of white highlighter above the top and the bottom to give them definition.

"If the eyebrows are not on point, then you look ugly," Aja once said as two swoops that resembled a bird in flight took shape on her face. The real work, though, was in the eyes, which involved some configuration of liner, shadow, highlighter, contour, glitter, and lashes. Some queens approached their eye makeup with surgical attention to detail. Aja at seventeen was more of a butcher. Her eyeliner was a thick black chunk that extended diagonally from the tear duct across most of the eyelid and ended in a swoop at the far end of her brow bone.

"Do I go dramatic, or subtle?" Aja would wonder aloud. "I'm always dramatic, who am I kidding?" She'd painted a hazy ring around the otherwise dark and severely lined eye. This was the fiddly part, the point at which the face looked good enough to give her life and have her feeling herself, but when there was still lots of work to do. White liner applied at the eye's waterline, above or below the brows, and in the corner near the tear duct, widened, lifted and softened the eye. Then Aja would brush magenta blush across her cheekbones and hairline and line her lip bow, overdrawing the top into a heart and filling it with red lipstick. Slowly, stroke by stroke, Aja would begin to recognize the figure in the mirror as someone she wanted to be.

Properly applied, drag makeup both enhances one's natural features and creates a fantasy. For the eyeshadow and the lips, Aja took inspiration from manga and video games like *Zelda*. The look was, as she once put it, "alien warrior princess realness." The larger point, though, was to mix ugliness with beauty. How to successfully do ugly things while being beautiful was Aja's biggest challenge.

"I have a down-slanted face, my eyes go down, and I paint to snatch," she would later tell the *Grizzly Kiki* podcast hosts. "When you paint a downward face to snatch, it doesn't go up, it goes to the side. So I look like I'm grilling everyone. I look like I hate you."

In the bars, Esai would tell Aja to "fix your face" when she seemed to be scowling.

"This is my face; it's the only face I've got," she'd reply. Aja had always felt insecure in boy clothing, chasing down anyone who, noticing her awkwardness, called her a faggot or a sissy. Before drag, she had tried to butch it up, fronting that she was tough and masculine. And she was certainly tough, but performing masculinity was exhausting. Aja's godmother, who suspected that evil spirits were holding Aja back, had taken her to see a spiritual doctor and she'd been regularly attending Lucumí religious ceremonies, but the power of the spirits overwhelmed and scared her and it only made things worse. Then, one morning, Aja's mother woke her up. "I had such a weird dream about you last night," her mother said. "You were sleeping in my bed and there was a woman putting smushed brains under your pillow." In the dream, her mother had removed all the gore and beaten up the woman. Aja listened to the story and noticed that she felt good. The anxiety and fear were gone. From that point on, Aja said she had "the spirit of fuck you." Her drag began to elevate and she felt stronger and more confident on the streets as well. Now, when people made a point to tell Aja "I don't like you," she'd shoot back, "I don't give a fuck." And most of the time she meant it.

That night at DragNet, though Aja was just a drag baby, no one could resist her. She performed "This Joy" by Vernessa Mitchell in the same outfit she'd worn to Bar-Tini. She high-kicked, she dipped, she crashed onto the floor with every ounce of energy in her lanky, seventeen-year-old body. "I think they had never seen anything so Black at Metropolitan," she said. In the competition's second round, Aja executed a series of ruthless pirouettes, opening her arms and spinning until even the crowd was dizzy. She won and advanced to the DragNet finals.

Like Aja and Esai, now known as Kaos, Merrie's drag was rough, but she worked to seem like she had things under control. The teenagers caught this scent of responsibility and proceeded to hassle and harangue the older queen for exhibiting ambition and authority. They'd loudly read Merrie for her thrift-store looks, her flip-flops, her powdery beat, like two troublemaking teens at the back of the classroom. Which is who they were. But they kept coming back to Metro week after week, and audiences came with them. At Aja's urging, Kaos entered the next round of DragNet. When it was her turn to perform, Kaos walked onto the stage in a nightgown, her hair wrapped in a rag, back bent over and limping. "Wade in the Water" played. The music switched to an Aunt Jemima syrup commercial with a retro jingle describing pancakes without Aunt Jemima syrup "like the spring without the fall." While Kaos lip-synched to the jingle, she poured syrup onto the judges' open hands and they licked it off. The number ended with Britney Spears's "I'm a Slave 4 U." Kaos danced and shook as Britney cooed "Get it, get it, ooh." The whole thing was a mess. Merrie would later describe it as "so not PC, but fun." Though it was laughably offensive, confusing, and sloppy, Kaos was committed to the performance. The crowd giggled uncomfortably, and she slowly won them over with a mischievous, goofy smile and her natural charisma. By the end, they were cheering.

Also in the running that night was Untitled Queen, the drag persona of an artist named Matthew de Leon. Merrie Cherry had met him at a lesbian dance party in Manhattan where Matthew had been wearing a long pink wig and dancing wildly—his arms shooting up in all directions. From the moment he'd decided to get into drag, he brought a startlingly coherent and innovative aesthetic to the club. That night at DragNet, Untitled performed the opening number from the movie *Little Shop of Horrors*. The look was a cotton candy, man-eating-plant mash-up with a pink tulle skirt, a green leotard, and pink and green leafy accents. Untitled and Kaos tied that night, and Kaos was elated.

"We some badass bitches," she told Untitled. "Picasso come to life" was how she'd later describe Untitled's aesthetic. They would both compete against Aja and three other performers the following month.

The first DragNet finale took place on a steamy night in late August 2012. The stakes were high. The winner would not only get a cash prize of fifty dollars plus a fifty-dollar gift certificate to Bagel Smith, the all-night deli across the street from the bar, but would also cohost DragNet with Merrie for the next year—a steady gig was worth much more than a one-time cash prize. For the occasion, Merrie Cherry had upped her game—slightly. She'd used hairnets to style her white Afro wig into two poufs, one at the front of her head and one at the back. She'd glued pink jewels in a line from her forehead down the bridge of her nose and was wearing bottom lashes but not top ones, as she had only one pair. Esai and Aja, meanwhile, spent hours painting their faces and putting on homemade bodysuits, mohair jackets, and spandex shirts to transform themselves into Kaos and Aja Injektion. They spent pretty much all their time together; if either of them won, they'd be sharing the money, so instead of rivalry, they felt confident in their chances. A few weeks earlier, Aja had won another pageant, and her aim that night, was to look as fierce as possible and snatch the crown. They'd brought friends to cheer them on. Even Kaos's mother and older sister had come, in a rare moment of family support.

By the end of the night, Kaos, Aja, and Untitled Queen had all made it to the final round, where they were tasked with lip-synching together to "Let's Have a Kiki," a gay anthem about a drag queen house party. As the music blared, Merrie, watching from the DJ booth behind the stage, could tell Aja was killing it. Kaos and Untitled jerked and bobbed along with the beat, but Aja planted in the center of the tiny stage. Her energy was infectious; she was clearly the strongest dancer and knew every word perfectly. Yet, it seemed to Merrie that Aja wasn't sharing the stage. During the drum solo just before the song's bridge, Aja fell into a split, forcing Untitled to step over her. Untitled had on a tight, white long-sleeved dress artfully covered with dots of different sizes and colors and a wig that looked like a ball of cotton candy. No one was polished, but Untitled had a vision. To Merrie, she seemed like a star. Plus, Merrie had started to get to know Untitled. On nights when they weren't in drag, they'd go to a bar, order pizza and cocktails, then lose their minds on the dance floor.

After the song ended, the contestants stood panting on the stage, waiting anxiously for Merrie Cherry to announce the winner. Aja heard the crowd chanting her name. Untitled had been fierce. Aja was cunt. *But if she can't share the stage with Untitled, how is she going to share the stage with me?* Merrie wondered.

"Well, I think it's clear who won tonight," Merrie said. "The winner of the very first DragNet finale—and don't worry, there will be others—is my sister . . . Untitled Queen."

The audience gave a tepid cheer. Aja was gagged.

"Don't be rude, clap for my girl," Merrie exhorted.

Aja stormed past Merrie and off the stage, barely concealing her anger. The winner was going to cohost DragNet with Merrie for the next year, and Aja thought that had to be the reason she didn't win—Merrie knew that she would have overshadowed her.

Merrie found Aja after the show. "Babes, congratulations, you were great," she said, trying to smooth things over. "It's not shade, girl, you understand, right?" Merrie continued.

"You know what, Merrie? I can't talk to you right now. If I do, I will punch you in the face," Aja snapped. The sputtering, red-hot frustration that lived inside her began to pour out. The need to be seen, the anger at being taunted and misunderstood, the sense that no matter what she did, there was no satisfaction, no way out. Drag helped to channel this resentment into jokes or dancing, but it hadn't really changed anything, had it? Disrespect and disappointment were always lurking.

"Well, do you want to go outside?" Merrie stood up tall, wishing she'd kept her high heels on. She puffed up her chest to look as big as possible.

Aja paused and noticed that everyone was staring at her. It seemed to Merrie that Aja was surprised she'd stood her ground.

"I'm leaving," Aja announced. She felt like people always expected brown and Black girls to fight and she did not want to be a stereotype. Merrie wasn't worth her hands.

Merrie was gagged by the intensity of Aja's anger. It was crazy to be screamed at in a bar, but also shocking that anyone would be that upset about the contest. Merrie had no idea that Aja and Esai were teenagers. She had never seen them out of drag and had never actually wondered about the rest of their lives. Not because she didn't care, but because the point of getting dressed up, changing your name, and performing in front of a room of mostly strangers was to be something—or someone—other than your everyday self.

Everyone had aspirations, and everyone definitely had an ego. To Merrie, Aja and Esai just seemed to have something else that made them pop off so easily.

After Aja and Esai stormed out, shouting about "nepotism" and "favoritism," Merrie took a minute to collect herself, then walked back to her perch at the bar, where a throng of well-wishers gathered to congratulate her on a stunning finale.

CHAPTER FOUR
There's No Place Like Sugarland

Aja and Esai were always on the hunt for bars with inattentive or absent bouncers, where they could sneak into a drag show and perform during the third set, which was often open to newcomers or anyone looking to give a show. One night, as Aja was heading home, she passed a brick garage sandwiched between two brown five-story apartment buildings. From the street, a rainbow flag and the word "Sugarland" stenciled in red block letters were the only outward indications of life beyond the big black door. Aja, who was about a mile from her mother's house, peeked her head inside.

Oh, this is a gay bar, she realized. *Maybe they have drag shows.*

On any given night at Sugarland, shirtless bartenders poured drinks behind a massive, hand-carved wooden bar. (The previous owners were said to have salvaged it from one of Al Capone's favorite nightclubs.) The cratered floor was black, the brick walls were graffitied and crumbling, and a narrow balcony overlooked the dance floor. On Fridays and Saturdays, after midnight, it was as if a switch flipped and anything could happen. Pop music and go-go boys reigned, but there would also be guys in flip-flops and tank tops grinding with men in suits; straight couples furiously making out; and drag queens, lip-synching, climbing on the bar, and posing for photos in front of a massive salvaged stained-glass window. Even though the urinals regularly overflowed and it smelled like sewage, from 2008 to 2013, Sugarland was beloved among young queer people looking for dance parties, cheap drinks, and an escape from the long lines, guest lists, and VIP sections that dominated Manhattan nightlife just across the Williamsburg Bridge. Sugarland offered an elusive sense of belonging in a city that could feel indifferent even on its kindest days. Plus, as Aja suspected, it was also one of the only places in Brooklyn to see drag.

During the week, Sugarland offered its stage to a raggedy assortment of musical theater gays, aspiring stand-up comedians, and men in wigs who hosted parties celebrating nineties pop culture, trash-bag couture, and fetish wear. Thorgy Thor and her coterie of artsy, experimental queers didn't only gather at Saliva! in Manhattan on Tuesdays—they would go anywhere a bar manager was willing to toss them some cash for their raucous drag shows. This meant not just the Ritz in Hell's Kitchen but also bars in Brooklyn, where many of them lived because they could not afford Manhattan rents. Veruca la'Piranha, who lived in Bushwick in an apartment next to the elevated J train tracks, would finish a gig at the Ritz in Manhattan and end her nights at Sugarland, drinking cocktails with the bartenders until the sun came up. At Sugarland, Thorgy and Veruca cohosted Thunderwear Wednesdays with Misty Meaner and Mocha Lite—boyfriends who'd fled their respective sleepy Long Island towns for the big city. At Thunderwear Wednesdays anyone who surrendered their pants at the door got a free shot. The bar paid the queens fifty bucks apiece to ply partygoers with alcohol and berate them on the microphone, which, over the course of the night, became stained with lipstick. The tips were paltry compared to the Manhattan clubs, where wealthier clientele handed over bigger bills. On Sunday nights, however, Thorgy and the other Sugarland queens would show up even if they weren't performing in order to watch backSpace, a six-member experimental dance troupe from

Columbus, Ohio, led by a bald, darkly funny queen who was known as Krystal Something-Something.

By the time Merrie Cherry, Aja, and Esai started doing drag, backSpace was known to the Brooklyn queer nightlife devotees for their coordinated looks, elaborate dance routines, and deranged hours-long performances to mixes of TV dialogue, techno music, and their own twisted narration. On one typical Sunday evening, four backSpace members—out of drag but for a few leotards and some smeared makeup—stood on the Sugarland stage, dabbing at themselves and one another with white dish towels. As a remix of Benny Benassi's dance track "Who's Your Daddy?" began, the crew casually got into formation, each standing in front of a plastic folding chair. They stretched a bit, bending and lunging, rolling their wrists and ankles, nonchalantly checking out the surroundings. The song gained momentum. A robotic voice asked, "Who's your daddy?" and a shrill woman's voice replied, "You're my daddy!" The beat dropped and the dancers moved in perfect unison. They threw their hips and executed a series of flawless body rolls. They raised their arms above their heads and shimmied, running their hands down their bodies. They stomped, pivoted, and crouched on the floor. The dancers posed, then stood up tall in front of the chairs, as the song wailed, "You're my daddy / Come now I'll make you mine." Hips thrusting, they waved their ratty dish towels in perfect synchronicity. Their flawless execution and the complete sincerity while dancing to a corny techno song somehow made them seem impossibly cool. "I'll be your daddy," the robotic male voice chanted, and the dancers pointed at the ten or so gobsmacked, mostly drunk friends watching, and beckoned to them seductively before striking a final pose and grabbing their crotches.

"What the *fuuuuuuuck*?" that night's host shouted into the microphone. "*That's* what backSpace is!"

If Thorgy had the hustle and the strangeness and Merrie could pack a room, backSpace brought an uncompromising sense of artistic integrity and adventure to the scene. Their journey to the borough began at Ohio State University in 2005, where Krystal, an enigmatic, gay modern dance major originally from the small town of Circleville, Ohio, whose boy name was Aaron Kint, convinced a group of girls he'd met smoking on the steps of the dance department to create an eight-minute performance for that year's recital.

About a month before the scheduled performance, fliers with a close-up photo of cleavage or an image of a finger in a mouth that read, "TWEAK: Cum find out," appeared on campus. Professors began wondering aloud during class if the dance wasn't maybe too overtly sexual and if it possibly objectified women. Columbus was progressive, sure, but it was still the Midwest, where people apologize when someone bumps into them.

When the group finally did perform Tweak, the number was just as scandalous as advertised. The foundation of the choreography was a walk—hyperfeminine, up on the toes, shoulders bouncing, asses swinging—and a Good Charlotte song blaring the lyrics "Girls don't like boys / Girls like cars and money." The dancers wore white tank tops and plaid cheerleader skirts, punctuating their cutesy walks with perky high kicks and cartwheels. Halfway through, the dance turned dark and frenzied. Grinding feedback and techno music accompanied thrusting, pantomimed oral sex, and shooting up. Between artful falls and leaps, the dancers crossed themselves, sucked their thumbs, and, as the song reached its crescendo, peeled off their white tank tops and tossed them carelessly onto the floor.

The audience was divided. Some people walked out, while others cheered. This first taste of controversy inspired the crew, who were all eager to escape the stuffy constraints of modern dance. As teenagers in the nineties, they'd grown up in a world of music videos, porn, and hypersexual pop music, and they welcomed these dark, cheap, creepy influences into the hallowed art form.

·····

The next fall, Krystal recruited a freshman who had been raised as a typical Ohio boy, dressing in cargo shorts and polo shirts and always careful not to seem gay, but would eventually adopt the name Charmy full-time and use the pronouns "they" and "them." Charmy joined the group for Tweak 2. "You'll have to wear a skirt," Krystal, a senior in shredded clothes with a pointy black spike of hair on his otherwise bald head, told Charmy. Though plunging into something so strange made Charmy nervous, Krystal was exciting, if intimidating. "Yes . . . OK . . . thank you . . . when . . . ?" Charmy replied.

Despite the spooky and perverted themes, Krystal's choreography was always militant and precise. During rehearsals, he was blunt and exacting.

"That looks like shit," Krystal would say, shaking his head and making them start again.

"I'm so *bored*," he groaned when someone couldn't get their leg up or missed a cue.

Charmy tolerated it because it was exciting to be a part of Krystal's choreography. Plus, the dancers had spent their childhoods being yelled at by instructors. They were used to it.

Jessica Bennett, a petite ballerina from Canton, Ohio, who'd been partying at OSU since she was in high school, dreamed up the name backSpace for their group—it didn't have any larger meaning, but everyone thought it sounded cool, so the name stuck. Soon, they were getting hired to give shows at local gay clubs, where they'd spread out across the room, taking over platforms and balconies for performances that made people feel like they were at the Moulin Rouge or a sex party in Berlin. Krystal choreographed solos for each dancer.

For Jessica's favorite, "Backyard Betty," Krystal taught her how to twerk. Being trashy felt empowering; it was exciting to share a dark sexuality with the audience. Krystal insisted that Charmy dress up for their performances, and it was fun to show off while part of a group. Charmy started to loosen up and began to embrace looks that were familiar yet warped. A toddler beauty queen or a hoop skirt over leggings and combat boots. With makeup, the dancers drew shapes around their mouths and attached rainbow-colored ponytails to their heads. Charmy favored black-and-white-checkered prints and tight neon dresses. The girls would paint bright pink and yellow circles around their eyes and wear tutus with halter tops.

Even though the group had a name, no one knew how to describe what they were doing. Was it performance art? A cabaret act? Avant-garde stripping? At first everyone was confused, especially Charmy. They'd been a dancer performing in a recital, and now they were giving shows on go-go platforms in queer bars. One night, while wasted, Charmy admitted to being maybe bisexual. A backSpace dancer named Ashley Bono, who was high on Molly, gave Charmy a hug. "I love you," she said warmly. *I think you're actually gay*, she thought to herself.

About a month later, Charmy confirmed that yes, they were, in fact, actually gay. They weren't afraid anymore. Krystal threw Charmy a joyous coming-out party. Then, during one of backSpace's epic nightclub gigs, Charmy realized that of course this was drag. Though drag had been a mainstay of the queer world for a hundred years, some gay men looked down on the art form and avoided doing anything to seem feminine or campy. "We were the black sheep of the gay community—what we did was embarrassing," Veruca la'Piranha said of the time in the 2000s when she and Thorgy Thor started getting dressed up and performing. Even if some muscle gays or twinks would celebrate or tolerate pageant-style drag, they were freaked out by Goth or punk performers who didn't pad their bodies or shave. "You couldn't wear a colored wig without being called a clown," Veruca recalled, "and I couldn't get someone to go out with me for a decade because drag was seen as so uncool."

For Charmy, however, a love of dress-up and performance had made it easier to recognize that they were gay, and being gay made the drag that much more relevant to their life. Ever since childhood, Charmy had been fantasizing about being an artist in the big city. During Charmy's senior year, Charmy and Krystal visited a dancer friend who was living in Brooklyn, just a few subway stops away from the gay bars in Williamsburg. The first night in town, they both got into drag and walked out of the house and onto city streets already overflowing with cute queer people in wonderful outfits. What had felt remarkable in Columbus—two swishy kids in combat boots, dresses, and balaclava masks—was normal here. By then, everyone except Krystal wanted to move to New York. Krystal hated change; the idea of moving terrified him. In Columbus, backSpace was in demand. They had regular nightclub shows, sold-out theater performances, and a major following. But, really, how far could they go in Ohio? Turning out new choreography and looks at the city's three gay bars for, what? Another year, or five, or ten? There were so many more clubs and people in New York. Krystal was too driven, and Charmy was too curious, and the other dancers were too funny and talented. They had routines; they had energy; they were cute and confident. Ohio wasn't going anywhere. If they failed, or they hated New York, they could just leave.

In 2009, two weeks after Charmy graduated, backSpace found a few cramped apartments near Bushwick's Myrtle Avenue subway stop and began haunting Sugarland. At a poorly attended drag competition, Charmy and Jessica performed to the drum-and-bass song "Hide U" by the British group Kosheen. Jessica mugged in a teal jumpsuit and a white fake fur stole, while Charmy, with a thick black X painted over one eye, a curly ponytail, a pair of dangerously tall pink glitter platform heels, and an exact replica of the pink faux fur coat Reese Witherspoon wore in the movie *Legally Blonde*, improvised a delightfully unhinged interpretive dance. Charmy shimmied, cha-cha'ed, and grapevined, striking poses and ducking behind the flimsy gold curtain at the back of the stage. They didn't win, but they impressed the bar's manager with their willingness to act a fool in elaborately styled outfits, and he asked them to host a party the following week.

"OK!" Charmy replied before warning him, "There's six of us." backSpace approached the booking like the well-trained professionals they mostly were. Krystal choreographed new material, and the dancers spent hours rehearsing. Krystal didn't care if the moves hurt, if someone's knees were giving out, or if their hip was sore.

"It looks cool. Just shut up and do it," he'd insist.

Krystal, who'd chosen a drag name that felt white trash and evoked the tongue-in-cheek girlishness of his performances, gave everyone else a moniker. Ashley Bono was Mary Jo Cameltoe; Amy Campbell, a fellow OSU dancer who had come to New York to work as a stage manager, was dubbed Whiskey Dixie; and Jessica Bennett became DiBa. Ashley, now known to almost everyone as Mary Jo Cameltoe, got a job bartending at Sugarland during the week, and sometimes Charmy would bring a deli sandwich or takeout to the bar and eat dinner there. Their apartment was grimy and cramped, so Sugarland—also grimy, but slightly less cramped—became their living room.

That first party turned into more bookings, and within a few months they had a regular Sunday night gig at the bar. Theaters required intention and ticket sales, while bar performances had lower stakes. They could put on a mask every weekend to do whatever drunken random, high-concept or low-brow thing they wanted with no consequences. In addition to the Sunday night gigs, backSpace put on ninety-minute, multimedia, interactive shows titled Muffins in the Window, and 2 Queens 1 Cup, with lighting, video, props, and choreography, but no one was making any money.

"There was no mic, you didn't have to tell jokes to keep people there, there was no 'tip your bartenders'; it was an art show for an hour and a half, and I was like, 'You need to make money,'" Thorgy recalled telling Krystal.

No bar was going to be able to pay six people for a performance, but "the tips could be fierce," Thorgy would exhort. "Have somebody walking around with a huge garbage pail, make it a joke."

While getting paid was one of Thorgy Thor's talents, backSpace— professionally trained Ohio transplants with a Midwestern aversion to begging strangers for money—believed that the hustle was in the hard work and poured all their energy into choreographing and performing shows.

They developed a coherent aesthetic: black and white stripes and prints, minidresses, fishnets, crop tops, and torn shirts. They painted their faces with neon geometric shapes. Krystal glued massive poufs of hair onto her head, instead of wearing actual wigs, and put strips of brightly colored paper on his eyelids in lieu of lashes. Charmy strutted in thigh-high boots, sometimes wearing two mismatched heels. They wrapped themselves in chains and let their body hair grow long.

Mary Jo Cameltoe had a lisp that made her s's sound like "th," so Krystal Something-Something and Charmy gave her a list of s-words to read on the mic. Interaction with the audience was also essential. On her birthday, Whiskey Dixie performed the song "Pour Some Sugar on Me" while the other peformers and audience members emptied sugar packets onto her, themselves, and the rest of the crowd. The sugar created a clumpy paste on the sweaty, mostly naked dancers, and everyone had to wash off in a kiddie pool outside.

In Columbus, drag pageants, modeled after Miss America and beauty pageants of the straight world, were a fixture in the local gay community. Spectacles with a competitive edge, they offered cash prizes with bragging rights and were serious business. The goal was always flawless female impersonation, and contestants spent months sewing gowns and perfecting their gait, posture, and wigs. National pageants like Miss Gay America and Miss Continental kept drag scenes alive and competitive in places as far-flung as Birmingham, Alabama, and Tulsa, Oklahoma, but pageants represented the kind of zealous, unironic drag that Krystal abhorred. The best way to skewer them, Krystal realized, was to make a pageant of their own and take it extremely seriously. They named it Little Miss Mierce—a portmanteau of "mega" and "fierce"—and held it on the fourth Sunday of every month. The competition had three parts: performance, question and answer, and final look. They'd blast the theme song Krystal wrote and invite up that month's three or four contestants. Unlike the Columbus pageants or the contests in Manhattan, at Little Miss Mierce, there was no cash prize. Instead, every contestant walked away with something—maybe pudding cups or slap bracelets. The winner received a photo shoot styled by the group and shot with Whiskey Dixie's expensive camera.

·····

After peeking her head into Sugarland, Aja looked up the bar online and saw a Facebook event posted by Krystal Something-Something. Aja sent the older queen a message, and Krystal responded with an invite to Little Miss Mierce. Aja and Esai were terrified and captivated by backSpace. These unhinged, dark, and ferociously committed performers weren't just dipping and splitting, telling tired jokes, or turning corny pageant looks. They were artists. They could be mean and arrogant, but their style was that of Midwestern weirdos, not hardened New York City kids. They danced as if they'd been classically trained, which, of course, they had. They were never afraid to be weird, creepy, or ugly. Being weird and creepy and ugly was, in fact, the whole point. It inspired Aja and Esai to let loose and to consider what their own drag styles could be.

When the pageant arrived, the teenagers kicked and split and tore their clothes. The night's theme was the 1990s and they gave the judges a show, but they didn't win and, for once, it hardly mattered.

CHAPTER FIVE

The First Annual Bushwig Festival

For a boy who'd fled his grandmother's house and spent years scraping and scrimping to afford a menial existence in the shadow of greatness, DragNet—even with the drama at the finale—was a triumph. Merrie Cherry was no longer just some bored office worker—she was a drag queen with a party to promote and, during the summer of 2012, every time Merrie Cherry left her house, it felt like she was stepping into a parade. She tried to hit a different party every night. Whenever possible she danced till 6:00 a.m. at The Spectrum, an unlicensed Bushwick club with mirrored walls, a stripper pole, lasers, near-constant bathroom drug use, and body paint. So much body paint. At Bathsalts, a party held in the back of a Mexican restaurant, she watched a revolving cast of drag queens create stunning outfits using trash bags and the garbage inside them. During gross-out acts, performers bathed in kiddie pools filled with canned goods or squirted lemonade out of hoses to make it seem like they were peeing on the stage and audience. One of the hosts was known to wear high heels wrapped in layers of duct tape. The wild but talented local kids had joined forces with gay nightlife devotees, and performers who were driven but too strange or countercultural to be content working in Manhattan. For the people at Brooklyn bars and parties who showed up with faces painted, wigs askew, carrying handbags bought on Knickerbocker Avenue, the scene was new and surprising. There had been very little dress-up in the outer boroughs in the early aughts, and nothing else in New York City had the same punk look or sweaty, back-room stank. In Brooklyn, Merrie had finally found a new crew, and they weren't like those rich kids she used to hang out with, who had plenty of money but no sense of art or adventure.

One night, while drinking at Metropolitan out of drag, Merrie met another party promoter named Matty Mendoza. Matty had soft brown eyes and a septum ring. In drag—and, increasingly, in life—Matty went by the name Horrorchata, a pun on horchata, a sweet Mexican rice-based drink, and Matty's love of horror movies. Horrorchata was a Goth girl who worshipped Tejana pop princess Selena Quintanilla-Pérez. Matty, who had moved from Austin, Texas, to Brooklyn two years earlier to work as a stylist, had a penchant for thick eyeliner; big, brightly colored wigs; black ankle boots; neon animal prints; and studded vests. Horrorchata, the drag persona, was sassier and more daring than Matty. Horrorchata loved to shout "okurrrrr" into the mic during a show or toss off a shady comment followed by a quick disclaimer—"Just kidding," she'd giggle. During performances, she would jump into a split when the beat hit. She was like a friend's cool older sister who cut class and slept around but was kind enough to buy you booze.

For money, Horrorchata worked as a barista at a queer coffee shop and threw parties. Lots of parties, mostly at grimy, hole-in-the-wall bars in Bushwick, several train stops farther into Brooklyn than Metropolitan and Sugarland. Party promotion was in Horrorchata's blood. Her mother was an event planner and was always organizing quinceañeras and wedding receptions. Horrorchata had trailed behind her on countless trips to the party store, set tables, hung streamers, helped pick out cakes and color schemes. Horrorchata's father was a literal clown—white face paint, curly blue wig, big red nose—a real entertainer who could always charm a crowd.

For Merrie and Horrorchata, it felt like something magical was taking hold among the queers and the artists and the party kids. Like, how you'd be walking past your friend's house and yell up the window that you were going to Don Pedro's for Bathsalts and they'd come running down to join you. Or the way people would show up at a party for the first time, wide-eyed and in civilian clothes, and then, two weeks later, they'd be back in full paint and lashes, wearing heels three sizes too small and begging to perform, and then, three weeks after that, Merrie or Horrorchata would be holding their props onstage or helping them with a mix as if they'd always been friends and always been drag queens.

While Horrorchata and, increasingly, Merrie, could slay a lip sync and leave the crowd gagged and delighted, they threw parties, first and foremost. Their primary measure of success for an event was the number of bodies in the room and they were quickly becoming savvy promoters who had figured out how to entertain lots of gays who'd never be caught dead in a wig or high heels. In the summer of 2012, they collided with performers like Krystal Something-Something and backSpace with their professional-level choreography. Bathsalts and backSpace's outlandish parties brought art, inspiration, and weirdness to the scene. At their events, performers put on shows for one another rather than the masses. Twenty minutes of live drone singing punctuated by screams or sitting in a kiddie pool full of beans did not pack the club or curry favor with bar owners and managers.

If it was hard to market individual acts of such exquisite weirdness, then perhaps, Matty thought, you could market a festival. As a semi-closeted queer kid in San Antonio, Horrorchata had obsessively watched *Wigstock*, the 1995 documentary about a Manhattan drag festival founded and run by New York City drag icon Lady Bunny. By the time Horrorchata arrived in New York City, the AIDS epidemic and rising rents had devastated the community those queers lovingly built. But now, Bushwick—relatively cheap and far from the prying eyes of developers and elite New Yorkers—felt like it had the potential to become a similar enclave. Like the East Village in the nineties or San Francisco's Haight-Ashbury in the sixties, "Bushwick" meant art and creativity, and it was increasingly gay. It needed its own massive event, like South by Southwest in Austin, Texas, but in Brooklyn and all about drag. A way to show those in the scene—and the wider world—what had been quietly bubbling up over the past few years.

One spring afternoon in 2012, on the way to the subway, Horrorchata passed a beauty supply store. She loved these stores, with their bright, block-letter signs. Inside, the shelves, bins, and baskets overflowed with chunky plastic jewelry, makeup for every skin tone, and most especially, Day-Glo wigs in all shapes and sizes. Beauty supply stores were the perfect mix of practical and campy. As Horrorchata turned the corner, a massive Big Bird yellow Afro in the window caught her eye. She gasped. "Bushwig," she whispered quietly.

•••••

Bushwig. The idea and the name became an obsession. Now, to make it a reality, Horrorchata found a collaborator, a recent transplant from England who went by Baabes Trust, and a venue, Secret Project Robot, a poorly drywalled gallery space with a gravel backyard. They invited performers and started promoting the event online. There would be eight hours of shows. Tickets would cost ten dollars for civilians and five dollars for anyone who showed up in drag. There would be a stage, a bar, and legions of Brooklyn drag performers and fans. If Bushwig was a success, it would put all of Brooklyn drag on display and the result would be greater than the sum of its parts. The borough would become a destination—maybe *the* destination—rather than a way station for New York City drag.

A flier with the Bushwig lineup appeared online, and hopeful performers started to post and comment on Facebook. The response was overwhelming. "Is there room for another performer? I have a killer act and so want to participate," a recent transplant from Washington State asked. People were hungry for an ambitious, high-profile event. Even though Horrorchata and Baabes weren't paying people to give shows, they easily booked thirty performers and even found a few sponsors. But not everyone was included.

"Wait, why am i not seeing Krystal Something-Something's name??" the new boy Krystal was dating posted.

"um . . . there are most definitely some names missing . . . ," Krystal added. Krystal hadn't applied to perform—she thought her participation would be a given. But these weren't her close friends, and their corner of the scene didn't revolve around Sugarland or backSpace.

At this point, Krystal had lived in Brooklyn for three years, and in that time she and the rest of backSpace had leveled up. With Sugarland as their unofficial home, they were also getting regular bookings at Splash nightclub in Manhattan's Union Square and Santos Party House, which was farther downtown and co-owned by the rock singer Andrew W. K. They'd been featured in *Time Out New York* magazine and landed a nomination for Best Duo or Group at the Glammy Awards (New York's nightlife awards before the organization behind the Grammy Awards took legal action and stopped them from using the name). backSpace even performed at the ceremony. Krystal's mom made her a massive giraffe-print dress. It felt like they were at the Oscars.

Krystal's shows were unhinged. She broke her arm while hanging from a rafter at a club performing a Marilyn Manson song. She lip-synched to fifteen-minute mixes that were so frenetic and random they felt like original compositions. She played the keyboard with her dick. Because Krystal understood that she could get other people excited about things—like nineties teen TV shows or dubstep remixes—just by liking them and being committed, gay kids living in far-off small towns would sometimes discover the group online and show up at backSpace events. But for Krystal, dominating the local scene, even one as big and beautiful as Brooklyn's, no longer felt like enough. There was a new show—not in town, but on TV—that had the potential to bring drag queens national, even international stardom. *RuPaul's Drag Race*, a reality TV show on an LGBT-oriented cable channel with an audience of around 100,000, was putting drag queens—people Krystal knew and had performed with—on television to compete for a cash prize and a title. As its fourth season aired, the *Drag Race* fandom was small but mighty. After appearing on the show, even the queens who lost had a chance to tour the world earning serious money and respect as performers.

Now that some drag queens were on TV and making real cash for doing the same thing Krystal did every night for not much more than free, Krystal wanted a chance to join them. She had already upset the dance department at Ohio State and turned the New York City drag world inside out. While she loved the Brooklyn scene, she understood that a performer had to innovate, reach bigger audiences, and pull in bigger paychecks. Over the past year, she had started to imagine herself doing just that on the biggest—well, the only—TV platform for drag queens.

•••••

On the morning of Bushwig, Horrorchata, Merrie, and a gang of volunteers inflated balloons, hung streamers, arranged seating, and tried to make the shaggy wooden stage full of jagged nails less hazardous. It was a DIY venue for punk performers, so they'd have to put up with some sharp edges. The crew had painted an open mouth with red lips underneath the word "Bushwig" in bubble letters on a six-foot-wide canvas banner, and hung it at the back of the stage. The space had room for nearly one thousand people. If they filled it, Bushwig would be the biggest drag event Brooklyn had ever seen.

At around two in the afternoon, the performers began to trickle in. Those in heels stumbled on the gravel, and everyone greeted one another with air-kisses. Clinging to the shoulders of friends and nearby strangers, they made the wobbly trek across the backyard. Not Merrie Cherry, though; she had on her trusty flip-flops. That afternoon, people would refer to Merrie as "she," "her," "them," "monster," "creature," "crazy," "hooker," and "mama." As long as no one called Merrie "him," which would have ruined the fantasy and been rude, it was all good.

Krystal showed up in the early evening. The yard was cooler now, and the crowd had been drinking and dancing for a few hours. She nodded to Merrie Cherry, who was standing by the DJ and wearing a big black Afro wig. They weren't friends, exactly, more like vaguely competitive colleagues who knew better than to engage in any direct conflict. For Merrie, backSpace had been a revelation. The way Krystal commanded a room, the group's creativity and energy, it was everything Merrie hoped for when she got dressed up in drag. She'd even asked Krystal to judge DragNet. Krystal, though, had declined. She had been curious about Merrie—who'd quickly found her way to the center of this pulsing scene. But there were rumors that Merrie had been trying to cut the line at Sugarland on Saturday nights, announcing that she worked at the bar. Merrie denied this—she barely even went to Sugarland, believing that it had a dark, unwelcoming energy. But it didn't stop the backSpace dancers, who could be territorial and cliquish, from judging Merrie. They also griped that the newer queen sometimes looked like a lost gay on Halloween. Krystal loved messiness but only when it was part of an otherwise coherent aesthetic. But mess, along with absurdity, camp, and humor, had become Merrie's calling cards. For her Bushwig performance, she dressed as a "tribal person" and lip-synched to "Circle of Life" from the Disney movie *The Lion King* as she pretended to give birth to a white baby doll that she'd hidden inside her skirt. She then had two of her white friends come onstage, pretend to beat her up, and steal the baby away from her. The mix changed to "Sometimes I Feel Like a Motherless Child," by Lena Horne, and she broke down onstage, bereft at the loss of her baby. Merrie's mother had died when she was a teenager and this performance was about how white supremacy had alienated Merrie from her. "I was a Black child, but I had issues with my race because of the fact that I was inundated with nothing but whiteness," she said.

By sunset, there were hundreds of queers prowling the venue, most of them in some sort of drag. After being initially overlooked, Krystal had been given a prime spot. Charmy and some of the other backSpace dancers were out of town, so Krystal planned a solo act with two backup dancers and a few cameos from other Sugarland queens. From across the yard, she noticed Jiggly Caliente, the headliner that night. *Ugh*, Krystal thought. Jiggly was a sweetheart and a crowd favorite who had appeared on the most recent season of *Drag Race*, but Krystal had no time for her Beyoncé song, miniskirt, and carefully styled wig.

Basic and awful, thought Krystal. Beauty, fashion, or dance skills alone don't make a performance worthwhile. If their art was going to matter, drag queens needed to be different.

And doing something different, as Bushwig was finally making clear, was what Brooklyn drag was all about. By the early 2010s, drag could sometimes feel as rigid as the professional dance world the backSpace dancers had left behind. At the very moment when drag was finally beginning to go mainstream, Brooklyn drag, as represented by the audacious experimentation on display at Sugarland and Metropolitan, was all about creativity and abandon. If Manhattan represented polished conventional drag, the kind that entertained tourists and emphasized beauty and femininity above all else, in Brooklyn the point was to unnerve people and shake things up. Krystal wanted to overdose on absurdity and take advantage of all the diversity and strangeness that New York City had to offer. To prove she could do anything and do it better and bigger than her friends and her enemies.

It was dark when Krystal took the stage. Everyone had moved inside, and the room was packed. Krystal was wearing a poufy black-and-white-checkered skirt. Her hands were painted black, and her wrists were red. A black splotch oozed down her forehead like ink in a glass of water. Before the stage lights went up, two dancers crawled under Krystal's skirt. The music started: the song was "Kick Out the Epic Motherfucker," a screeching electronic track by Dada Life about rejecting the status quo in favor of partying and keeping it real. The lights went on, and the dancers in Krystal's skirt were hidden from the crowd as the tension built to the end of the song's first verse—"In a world full of lies we live to tell"—the dancers poked their arms through the holes in Krystal's skirt. They had finger lights on their hands, and they wiggled them as she lip-synched emotionally, careful not to trip over their legs.

Though Krystal had long resisted the impulse to find any sort of meaning to her drag, in this number, she had a clear message. At a key line—"For all the years that you've been feeding us all that trash"—Miz Jade, another professionally trained dancer and frequent backSpace collaborator, launched herself on stage and jumped into a split. Krystal had enlisted her help, instructing her to act like a basic-ass "queeny" drag queen—unoriginal, boring, and pretty. Krystal's number was a manifesto: an explanation of what Brooklyn drag should be. It was time for all the so-called weirdos and artists and freaks to rebel against traditional drag, to keep doing these strange, awkward, inconvenient performances, even if they were ugly or offensive or if no one understood them. For the first time, it felt like if Krystal disappeared the next day, the scene would continue. It was scary and thrilling to see how far Brooklyn drag had come since her arrival three years before. Yet one more reason to move onward and upward. She ripped off her skirt, and the dancers crawled out. The audience howled as the music reached full pitch and Krystal began to dance.

CHAPTER SIX

Supermodel of the East Village

DragNet, Bushwig, and raucous parties at Sugarland marked the arrival of something special. In 2012, everything seemed new, and drag performers floated through North Brooklyn high on inspiration, new friends, and drugs. However, though Thorgy Thor, Merrie Cherry, Horrorchata, Aja, Krystal Something-Something, and backSpace could claim to be stars of this nascent scene, *drag* itself wasn't new. It had been a touchstone of the gay community for a century as it changed and evolved, moving in and out of the national consciousness according to popular whim and political climate. Throughout its history, drag has offered gay people a sense of community and provided the wider world with evidence of that community. It helped people form queer identities and then presented mainstream America with a version of gayness that was both fascinating and frightening. Though drag has often been fringe and maligned, at points it has also been massively popular. Everyone from housewives to newspaper columnists has oohed and aahed over men in wigs and gowns. Raunchy, hedonistic, and underground, the art form was also the aspect of queer culture most likely to reach the inner sanctums of the straight world. As these Brooklyn performers painted their faces and threw themselves on the floor of dingy gay bars, drag was poised to become a national—and eventually a global—phenomenon yet again. Though some Brooklyn queens would be at the center of this explosion, the spark for the twenty-first-century drag eruption was the self-described Supermodel of the World, a very tall, very loud, freckled Black man born in San Diego, named RuPaul.

In 2009, *RuPaul's Drag Race* debuted on LogoTV with RuPaul Andre Charles at its helm. On the show, RuPaul, also known as Ru, hosts and judges as a slew of emerging drag queens compete to become America's next drag superstar. Over the course of more than a dozen seasons, *Drag Race* has become a cultural phenomenon watched by, at its peak, more than a million people. In front of this increasingly fervent fan base, RuPaul, the original drag superstar and arguably the most famous drag queen in the world, offers snappy commentary as a cast of hopeful queens walk the runway, sing, act, model, and lip-synch for their lives.

Without RuPaul, and without *RuPaul's Drag Race* more specifically, the Brooklyn drag world might have been little more than a tight-knit community of chaotic self-expression that burned brightly for a few years. But *Drag Race* gave Brooklyn drag a path to twenty-first-century commercial success. It also gave emerging queens a reason to keep going, something to strive for when the free drinks and piles of dollar bills lost their allure. A common goal and a little competition can fuel a scene as well as camaraderie and creativity. RuPaul's career would show just how expansive drag's impact could be.

Born in San Diego, California, in 1960, RuPaul was a precocious, itinerant kid with a volatile mother, an absent father, and a sister who would be his childhood salvation. He started smoking pot when he was ten and was voted Best Dancer and Best Afro in ninth grade. He developed an encyclopedic knowledge of pop music and culture and, at an early age, realized that self-invention was the secret to a good life. Ferocious femme, Afro punk, Diana Ross—as long as *he* bought whatever fantasy he was selling, he figured other people would, too.

In the early 1980s, RuPaul and a group of rough-around-the-edges queers he'd met go-go dancing in the Atlanta gay clubs arrived in Manhattan, taking a trust fall onto the shoulders of a city that was barely standing. They hit the downtown club scene—hard. Especially the Pyramid Club, a claustrophobic East Village bar full of artists and outcasts. The Pyramid acts were messy and unhinged.

"It was a basement dump and a fabulous hangout," said Linda Simpson, who became a drag queen in the 1980s, inspired by the people she encountered in the East Village bars. Linda went out almost every night with a camera and, by the mid-1990s, had taken thousands of pictures of New York City nightlife. The Pyramid Club hosted punk shows, burlesque, and performance art, and was an incubator for innovative, unconventional drag performers. It was gayer than the other East Village punk clubs but looser and more artistic than the Hell's Kitchen, Chelsea, or West Village scenes, where gay men dressed as macho men with mustaches *or* hyperfeminine drag doyennes. The Pyramid Club crew were the queers who rejected gym bodies and nightclubs full of shirtless men who sniffed poppers as the strobe lights flashed. Shut out by the world at large, RuPaul and the Atlanta crew found an incubator for their energy and talent.

The Pyramid Club's star players—people like Ethyl Eichelberger, an accordionist who wrote and performed plays about the grande dames of history and mythology, and Tabboo!, a painter who rapped in a nasal whine—"were all very individualistic," said Linda. "Before that, drag was more anonymous."

Drag's reputation among many artists and punks was "fuddy-duddy and square"—gay men making studied impersonations of glamorous, old-school starlets or dressing up to put on hackneyed comedy shows. This older generation of drag queens loved pageantry—and pageants—and aspired to be unclockable female impersonators.

"The East Village was unique because queens were creating their own personalities," said Linda.

RuPaul was one of the most distinctive of these East Village personalities. During his early years as a performer, he shaved the sides of his head, used the bald space as a canvas for multicolored "tribal" stripes, and let the top of his hair grow into a free and natural Mohawk. He released an album called *Sex Freak* with synthesizers and a drum machine. He rapped, "I like it in and out, round and round," and made cooing sex noises.

Sweet and baldly ambitious, RuPaul took long strides across Greenwich Village, from the shabby penthouse of the Jane West Hotel to the bandshell at Tompkins Square Park. In the 1980s New York City was broke, blighted, and often on fire. The population declined from almost eight million in the 1970s to just over seven million by 1980. In 1990, more than 2,200 people were murdered in New York City. Crack and heroin use were rampant. Below Fourteenth Street, amid vacant and vandalized buildings, it sometimes felt like the adults with starched shirts, shiny cars, and mortgages to pay had gone out and left the punks alone on a rusty playground covered in splinters and loose nails. Music, art, and gay life flourished. For the weirdos who were about as likely to have a house in the suburbs as a trip to the moon, it was hell and paradise.

Activism and organizing after the 1969 riots at the Stonewall Inn nurtured sexual freedom in the 1970s, but by the 1980s, a mysterious and deadly virus was decimating the gay community. Young, healthy-looking people suddenly developed lesions, cancers, and life-threatening flus. Someone would be dancing at the Mineshaft or sipping drinks at the Limelight one night and then bedridden a week later. A conservative national climate prevailed, and in the early years of the plague, the government and media paid little attention.

Andy Warhol, Keith Haring, and Madonna attended Pyramid Club fundraisers for beloved regulars battling AIDS.

Ru and his compatriots were semi-homeless, always loud, and had no money or plan. They were also shameless self-promoters who could turn any room into a party. So that's what they did, with one eye out for a good time and the other scanning for a mirror to check their makeup. Among the Atlanta crew that migrated to this downtown haven of drugs, violence, and broken windows was Lady Bunny, a giggly queen with a foul mouth and a quick wit, who modeled her persona after a *Laugh-In*–era Goldie Hawn. Bunny had been a self-described "flamer" since childhood and had been dressing up and going to gay bars since she was a thirteen-year-old in Chattanooga, Tennessee. Underneath a dumb-blonde exterior was a crass iconoclast. Drag was more than an act for Bunny. She loved to walk, dress, talk, and act like a woman and refused to be filmed as a boy. She once told a documentary filmmaker that most queens like her do drag "because they like women's clothes, and they like to put them on and wear them. It's a tribute to women."

After the Pyramid Club closed for the night, Bunny and the other drag freaks would sometimes scurry to Tompkins Square Park with a case of beer, high heels scraping the pavement. In the park's bandshell, they gave impromptu shows to ten or fifteen homeless people trying to sleep on park benches. The al fresco after-hours parties gave Bunny an idea. *Why not throw an outdoor festival?* Right there, but during the day. They had a scene going in the clubs, and this would be a way to get everyone together and bring their art to a bigger audience.

In 1984, Bunny got a permit from the city to use the Tompkins Square Park bandshell over Labor Day weekend and named the festival Wigstock. Like Woodstock, but for the downtown freaks. Wigstock would be a mad-cap parody of that smugly celebrated countercultural sacred cow. As a bonus, a daytime, outdoor show horrified those uptight queens who didn't want their makeup to be seen in direct sunlight. "Sic-adelic" was how Bunny later described it and she got the Pyramid Club to foot the bill. In addition to emceeing that first year's festival, she sang what she described as "a jazzed-up version" of "I Feel the Earth Move," by Carole King, in a fringe jumpsuit and blond wig with bangs that kept falling into her face. "Stop the pigs and give them wigs," she shouted into the microphone at one point during her daylong emceeing. Though it got very little press and the crowd barely topped one thousand people, many of whom happened to be living in the park or were grannies in babushkas who occasionally heckled the performers, Bunny deemed Wigstock a success.

"There's so many housewives and children that can't make it to the nightclubs," Bunny cooed into the microphone, promising to put on Wigstock for as long as the Pyramid Club would let them.

For a few years, Wigstock was a cute show for a ragtag local crowd. People goofing, building acts around inside jokes, experimenting with costumes and characters. One rising star of the Pyramid Club, a drag queen named Lypsinka, who could deliver unerringly precise lip syncs to classic Hollywood monologues, regularly stole the show. As the event got bigger and more popular during the late-eighties, the line between crowd and audience blurred. Wigs, feathers, platform heels, and sequins scattered throughout the park as thousands and then tens of thousands of people, often in drag themselves, attended. Like in the nightclubs, anyone could be anything, which meant boys became girls, audience members became performers, and nobodies became stars.

"We weren't thinking about being transgressive while we were putting on our pantyhose," Linda Simpson said. The point was a bit of revelry, some unhinged fun for a group of oddball extroverts and the locals who adored them. The East Village queens had been enamored with Andy Warhol superstars like Candy Darling and Holly Woodlawn. They were inspired by Divine, the poo-eating drag queen and muse to the gleefully trashy filmmaker John Waters. Just like these queens, the Pyramid Club crew wanted to have fun, act out, and get attention for it. They were classic rebels out to skewer anything serious or conservative in their midst.

Though what Lady Bunny, RuPaul, and the Pyramid Club were doing seemed new, drag is surprisingly old. Some historians will argue that the art form began when men dressed as women in ancient Greek theater. Others believe it originated with the term "drag," first used in the late nineteenth century to describe female impersonators—usually queer men—working in vaudeville theater. Whether drag began with a man playing Helen of Troy's sister Clytemnestra, or a girlish boy acting as the ingénue in a minstrel show, reinvention has always been a part of the art form. Every new generation of drag performers inevitably rebels against the previous stars. The serious and studied glamour that queens like Linda Simpson, Lypsinka, Ethyl Eichelberger, and Tabboo!, had rejected—the pageants, the pomp, the ornate and elaborate costuming—was once the height of transgression. The spirit of rebellion makes drag a refuge for outcasts. And it has brought marginalized show-offs a community and recognition for over a century.

On a snowy night in 1934, a diverse crowd of thousands, including much of Harlem high society, eagerly waited in line to enter the Faggots Ball. One attendee described the party, also known more demurely as the Hamilton Lodge Ball, as a scene of "effeminate men, sissies, 'wolves,' 'ferries,' 'faggots,' the third sex, 'ladies of the night,' and male prostitutes" gathered "for a grand jamboree of dancing, love-making, display, rivalry, drinking and advertisement." Inside, Black and white men dressed in elaborate, fanciful interpretations of starlets and showgirls dripping in satin and beads, danced, flirted, and jostled for attention. They got it. In a page-one write-up of the event, the *New York Amsterdam News* described the ball's queen, Mickey Dell, as "a pretty creature adorned by a jeweled brassiere, silk loincloth, rose-colored high heeled shoes, and a creation of white feathers which trailed like a train behind 'her.'" Calling Mickey "a jetsam and flotsam of humanity," the reporter nevertheless described the way "'she' blew kiss after kiss from the tips of her dainty fingers. 'She' spun gracefully on the stand, displaying 'her' beautiful calves, 'her' shapely hips, 'her' well-proportioned breasts, 'her' sensuous lips. 'She' bent her knees in repeated curtsies." In an interview after the crowning, Mickey Dell stressed that "'she' was a genuine article. 'I have been a sissy all my days,' 'she' said."

This sort of gender transgression was at the heart of early-twentieth-century gay life. At the time, all types of men had sex with other men, but masculine men were known as "trade." Gay men were those who couldn't or wouldn't butch up. Gay was a way of being in the world, and gay life was defined by a camp sensibility—a theatrical sense of irony, play, and subversion—flashy clothing and droll girlish mannerisms. "Coming out" meant joining the gay community for the first time, the same way a debutante comes out into high society. Back then, announcing oneself as gay to coworkers, family, or the wider straight world was largely unheard of and would have seemed ridiculous. Rich and middle-class gays camped it up in the privacy of their homes, and working-class, flamboyant gays congregated in red-light-district dives—brothels, sleazy hotels, and sex shows. This world of sodomy shows, cross-dressing, and prostitution was a target for anti-vice investigators and violent predators. Constant surveillance, policing, and public hostility toward visibly gay men made it difficult for them to gather and organize in a meaningful way.

Prohibition changed all that. During the 1920s, all nightlife—gay and straight—was forced underground and anyone looking for a good time had to find it outside the law. Counterintuitive as it seems, this gave queers more freedom to pursue their distinctive, sparkling brand of illicit fun and helped urban gay culture thrive. During the twenties, the Greenwich Village and Harlem neighborhoods of New York City were home to numerous gay bars, tearooms, brothels, speakeasies, and cruising grounds. But it was at the drag balls that "the gay world saw itself, celebrated itself, and affirmed itself," wrote historian George Chauncey in *Gay New York,* his groundbreaking study of early-twentieth-century queer life. "In a culture hostile to gay men, the balls confirmed their numbers by bringing thousands together."

Just as drag allowed Thorgy, Merrie Cherry, Krystal Something-Something, and Horrorchata to see themselves as part of a scene that was expansive, communal, and unequivocally gay, and the Pyramid Club scene created a queer art movement, the early-twentieth-century gay world was shaped by the experience of doing and watching drag. Known alternately as masquerade, faggot, or pansy parties, these balls established gender-bending as an integral part of queer life in the city and put it on display for the wider public.

The best drag balls were in Harlem, where Black gay men had a thriving network of restaurants, nightclubs, speakeasies, and apartment gatherings. Drag queens, including people who today might identify as transgender women, sometimes walked freely in the streets there, and they performed openly for both gay and straight audiences at popular clubs. At balls like the one where Mickey Dell was crowned queen, hordes of queers pranced and paraded in wigs; big, billowing skirts; or slinky, skintight gowns, as straight people gawked and grappled with anxiety over the era's rapidly shifting gender roles. It was illegal in New York City to wear a disguise or masquerade on the streets, but ball organizers avoided raids by having local fraternal orders sponsor the events and hiring cops to work security. Two men could sometimes even get away with dancing together or being sexual on the ballroom floor if one of them was dressed as a woman. In this way, a drag queen was simultaneously defying gender and complying with the broader cultural expectation of heterosexuality. The relatively conservative local media stopped short of celebrating the event, but the press couldn't resist the spectacle. By calling a queen "jetsam and flotsam," a curious, buttoned-up newspaperman could indulge in the excitement without getting any glitter on his hands. Late at night, after the party had ended, emboldened queens would walk the streets intoxicated, both literally and figuratively, by the freedom they'd found. In drag, some were droll and defiant in their encounters with cops or angry crowds. Like the time a pissed-off queen who'd been taken to the police station shocked a newspaper reporter by asking him for a powder puff.

After Prohibition ended, clubs and bars that were considered reputable—i.e., not gay—were permitted to operate openly, and those that served or employed queers were shuttered. This meant that during the 1940s and '50s, gay and lesbian bars were Mafia-run and regularly raided by police. The repression spread through the culture. Plays that depicted homosexuality were banned. Nightclubs weren't allowed to employ known "degenerates," meaning anyone who'd been arrested for something associated with homosexuality. If these gays worked at a nightclub, it lost its license. Not all these laws and regulations were new, but during the 1940s and '50s they were enforced with unprecedented zeal, a reaction to the apparent excess of the Prohibition era. Police often raided bars and arrested men for wearing women's clothing. No more pansy acts, no more drag shows. Just tolerating gay patrons was enough to get a club shut down and, for the authorities, "gayness" didn't simply mean having sex with men—it meant wearing makeup, jewelry, or even discussing stereotypically gay topics like opera. Bar owners started policing homosexuality themselves, excluding or banning gay patrons in order to stay in business. One bar owner in Times Square asked the police and the military for help getting gays out of his bar and the authorities suggested putting salt in their drinks or refusing service. When gay men were arrested, they often spent months in workhouses or jails.

However, even though gays and lesbians were frequently arrested, their names and addresses printed in the newspaper, drag continued to thrive as a way for queers to build a secret language that challenged the hierarchies, tastes, and moral authority that cast them as criminals and crazies. These performers weren't always men, either. Butch lesbians often worked in male drag, as chorus boys or tuxedoed waiters. Buddy Kent, whose given name was Malvina Schwartz, earned piles of cash doing a strip show at the mob-run 181 Club in Greenwich Village—one of the few clubs that managed to survive the regulatory crackdowns. Billed as Bubbles Kent, Buddy would take the stage in a top hat and tails and dance elegantly while removing his pants and shirt to reveal female attire underneath.

"Then I went into a girl strip," Buddy told historian Joan Nestle in an interview in 1983. "When I finished, people didn't know if I was a boy or a girl because I was quite slim and very flat." It was genderfuck—twisting the expectations and norms of male and female until someone's "gender" is not only impossible to determine, but utterly beside the point—forty years before the term was coined.

During this repressive era and well into the 1960s and '70s, drag sustained and insulated itself through the presence of camp. A touch-stone of gay culture, camp is the earnest celebration of all things fake and false. Camp reveres style over substance and revels in exaggeration. Joan Crawford, Bette Davis, and Mae West aren't simply gay icons, they're camp royalty, beloved for their deeply sincere performances of over-the-top rage, sexuality, and girlishness. In *Mommie Dearest*, when Faye Dunaway as Joan Crawford shrieked and howled at her young daughters for using wire hangers, tearing apart their bedroom and beating them mercilessly with the offending objects, the moment was at once legitimately scary and obscenely cruel and melodramatic. It was classic camp: real emotion taken to surreal places. Camp meant knowing something was bad, or overly sentimental, or painfully sincere, and liking it both because and in spite of this. Camp's absurdity, and how foolish it seems to take camping seriously, made it a secret language. Through camp, drag performers—and other gender-nonconforming queers—could communicate desires, attitudes, and opinions that were too dangerous to speak openly.

At a drag show in Kansas City during the 1960s, a drag queen named Stacy Lane waddled onto the stage in a messy wig. A dowdy dress covered her protruding stomach. "The girl is a pitiful slattern who has been 'knocked-up' and left," wrote anthropologist Esther Newton in *Mother Camp*, her seminal ethnography of 1960s drag clubs. With a grim look on her face, Stacy began to lip-synch to the Timi Yuro song "Hurt." As the song wailed, "I'm so hurt, to think that you, you lied to me / So hurt, way down deep inside of me," the queen's belly exploded with a *pop*. Stacy Lane, the scorned "slattern," had given birth to a "foot-long Norwegian troll with wild hair and a blank expression," wrote Newton, who saw the act as part of her field research. Stacy scooped up the gruesome doll and "with resignation" held it to her breast. "The desertion now takes on a more serious and realistic form that is, at the same time, ludicrous," observed Newton. The act, which was done for a mostly straight audience, killed. While seeming self-deprecating, Stacy Lane, abandoned and desperate, skewered the sacred cows of heterosexual life: romantic love, pregnancy, and motherhood. It was classic camp, the gag—that a man could be a scorned woman—eclipsed by a joke at the expense of traditional family values.

Through appropriation and parody, camp wrests power from the dominant culture and bestows it on the marginalized, if only for the duration of a song or dance. "All of life is role and theatre—appearance," wrote Newton. The difference between a drag queen in thick makeup, eyelids weighed down by fake lashes, and a movie star painted, plucked, and pouting is that the drag queen knows that glamorous appearances are unnatural. The fun is in the role-play. Conversely, the movie star's job is to convince audiences that pomp and elegance are real, rather than delight in their artifice. To lull onlookers into accepting a sort of falsity as truth.

For the downtown performers, transgression meant gender-bending—mixing masculine and feminine influences to unnerve and excite audiences—and camp provided a salve and an outlet in a world that was both discriminatory and cruel. In 1987, the year the Pyramid Club celebrated its eighth birthday, the legendary AIDS Coalition to Unleash Power (ACT UP) formed; flamboyant, closeted performer Liberace died of AIDS, then reported as "congestive heart failure brought on by subacute encephalopathy"; and in New York City a reported ten thousand and a likely one hundred thousand people were living with HIV or AIDS. While Bunny go-go'ed across the stage, RuPaul vamped and styled his Mohawk, and Lypsinka memorized every gasp and screech of classic cinema, thousands of people checked into the hospital and died.

Gay people in this moment "were eager for prominent queer figures, and there weren't many," Linda Simpson said. "It was unusual for an actress or actor to be out. Drag queens became popular because they were up front, dramatic personalities that people could count on to be visibly gay." Linda Simpson said she and the Pyramid Club performers started to feel as though they were "on the front lines providing entertainment for the troops."

RuPaul quickly became a star of this scruffy, resilient scene.

He perfectly embodied both the raunchy, hedonistic, underground aspects of drag *and* the humor and beauty that made drag appealing to straight audiences. His life could be messy—he had struggled with drugs and alcohol during the eighties, and he was adrift and broke much of the time—but by the early 1990s, thanks to his charisma and work ethic, he had started to attract real attention from mainstream America. On Geraldo Rivera's show in 1990, RuPaul and a group of what were known as "club kids," including Michael Alig, a toxic, drug-addled party promoter, giggled and preened while the mustachioed talk show host attempted to scandalize at-home viewers with questions about sexuality and the club drug ecstasy. Ru was unflappable, on a mission for recognition, and tossed out catchphrases at every opportunity.

"Everybody, say 'love!' " he commanded.

"You're born naked, and the rest is drag," he explained to Geraldo.

To Linda Simpson and others in the scene, Ru seemed poised to succeed. He'd known he was a superstar since he was five years old. But what would success look like for a loud, Black drag queen? Madonna's 1990 hit single "Vogue," as well as her 1991 *Truth or Dare* tour documentary and the 1990 film *Paris Is Burning*, which profiled New York's ballroom scene of Black and Latinx dancers and drag queens, had all brought attention to feminine men, drag queens, trans women, and gender-fluid queers. They tied drag to opulence, elegance, and fashion. But a spot as a backup dancer or in a documentary wasn't going to cut it for Ru. Fame meant Radio City Music Hall, Madison Square Garden, *The Tonight Show*, and a Top 10 single. He wanted to be Diana Ross. He stripped his persona of any outward punk influences and embraced a platinum-blond wig, lace corsets, and gowns, thinking that a glamazon—a portmanteau of glamour and amazon that implies massive elegance—look would be more appealing to the masses. He partnered with B-list producers to make dance tracks with inspirational messages, gambling that the world was finally ready to embrace a diva who was also a man.

In 1993, after years of Herculean effort, constant nightclubbing, go-go dancing, an endless willingness to do anything, go anywhere, and talk to anyone, just to get a photo in *OutWeek* or a mention in the alt weekly *Village Voice*—Ru's efforts finally paid off. He had a hit record. The single "Supermodel (You Better Work)," reached number forty-five on the pop charts and number two on the US dance charts. "Supermodel" leaned into the tropes of the ballroom and the fashion world rather than the dive bar. "Work" or "werk," or "werq," was a ballroom exhortation of fierceness. "Do your thing on the runway," Ru sang. The *New York Times* labeled him a descendent of "gender benders" like David Bowie and soul divas like Donna Summer and called "Supermodel" "a frisky house ditty that gently spoofs the fashion industry and added a few new catch phrases to the contemporary lexicon." Of course, the catchphrases like "sashay, shantay," and "work it, girl" weren't new if you'd been to drag balls, or seen *Paris Is Burning*, but Ru made them his own—and popularized them for the masses. The song was infused with that combination of eleganza and cheerleading that had become his trademark. "It don't matter what you wear," he belted confidently. Just be yourself, Ru encouraged, because as he explained to the *New York Times*, "what really, really counts is what's inside."

During the 1990s, RuPaul, sometimes along with Lady Bunny and Lypsinka, made the rounds on the talk show circuit and served middle America his brand of irreverent, glamorous empowerment. The gay rights movement and a growing awareness of the AIDS crisis meant people were curious about queer lives.

"People have realized gender isn't destiny," Lady Bunny told *Washington Post* journalist Paula Span in 1993.

In a moment when middle Americans were anxious to break

free of Reagan-era conservatism, drag offered glamour and a sense of possibility. At Lady Bunny's Wigstock festival the year "Supermodel" was released, twenty thousand people watched RuPaul perform in a silver bodysuit with a shiny blond wig piled high on her head. The crowd stretched all the way to the edges of Tompkins Square Park.

"My name is RuPaul, Supermodel of the World. You know, when I started out, right here in this neighborhood, they told me I couldn't make it." In the speech, which was immortalized in the 1995 documentary *Wigstock*, Ru sounded almost folksy as she addressed the crowd. "They said, 'Wasn't no big Black drag queen in the pop world, and you ain't gonna do it.' And look at the bitch now! That's right, I had a dream. I never faltered—ever. . . . Hold on to your dream, 'cause if it can happen for me, it can happen for you. Can I get an amen in here? Everybody, say 'love!' "

The crowd shouted, "Love!"

"It's in to be gay in the nineties, did you know that? Who would have thunk it?" Ru squealed.

An audience member at the bottom of the stage shouted a question.

"What'd I do with my dick?" Ru shook her hips back and forth, showing off the flat front of her crotch, the impossible-to-detect "tuck" she'd achieved by forcing her dick and balls between her legs. "Whoomp there it is, whoomp there it is," she said, her voice deep and playful.

As treatments for HIV and AIDS improved and the Clinton administration replaced Reagan and Bush with a more compassionate facade, the club kids and drag impresarios who'd managed to survive the brutality of the eighties had arrived on the national stage to show the straight world that gay people were fun. Far from unloved outcasts mired in tragedy, gay entertainers came to teach and inspire audiences. Thorgy Thor, then a middle school orchestra nerd with undiagnosed attention deficit disorder and prurient thoughts about the neighborhood boys, voraciously consumed every moment of media coverage about this downtown New York club scene. The lesson he took from these creative attention whores was that he could be a party animal but survive. As drag artists had done for more than a hundred years, the now-famous performers were a touchstone for lonely, isolated gays in search of community and inspiration but on a bigger scale than ever before.

That same year RuPaul released "Supermodel," he recorded "Don't Go Breaking My Heart" with Elton John. The year after that, he published a memoir, and then he toured the world. "Be yourself! Love yourself!" he implored with the reliability of a Rolex watch, which he could afford now that he was the most famous drag queen in America.

"Everybody wants to be loved. . . . Everybody, say 'love,' " he instructed the audience at *The Arsenio Hall Show*.

At last, Ru was comfortably ensconced in American popular culture. She'd been buffed and bronzed, much of the East Village grit long gone. What remained was striking and sassy but also palatable. A good-natured queerness that had mass appeal. On *Arsenio*, Ru explained that, for her, drag was about self-expression, not sex or deviance. "I'm a regular Joe," she told Hall. "I just have the unique ability to accessorize."

CHAPTER SEVEN

A Reality TV Show Is Born

By the mid-1990s, drag's footprint was massive. In 1995, The Samuel Goldwyn Company released a documentary of Wigstock composed of footage from the 1993 and 1994 festivals and candid film of performers living their day-to-day lives. The poster featured a drawing of the Statue of Liberty with a massive beehive of blue curls and bright red lips and proclaimed the film to be "a celebration of life, liberty, and the pursuit of big hair!" Fifteen years before Jason Daniels would call himself Merrie Cherry, he was a young, lonely gay boy, watching a VHS tape of the movie at his grandmother's house in Berkeley, California. He saw Alexis Arquette and Jackie Beat camp it up in front of a giant fern and knew that New York City was where he wanted to be. He felt, in some deep-down way, that these were his people. He thought that maybe, if he lived in New York, they'd all become friends.

The biggest-budget, highest-profile drag-related cultural product of that decade was the 1995, Steven Spielberg–produced, feel-good film *To Wong Foo, Thanks for Everything! Julie Newmar.* Starring the unassailably heterosexual actors Wesley Snipes and Patrick Swayze, *To Wong Foo* is the story of three New York City drag queens who find themselves stranded in a one-stoplight town and attempt to pass as bona fide women while offering the drab, depressed locals makeovers and life lessons. More than *Paris Is Burning* or the 1995 *Wigstock* documentary, *To Wong Foo* told a family-friendly story of empowerment through quirky self-expression. Lady Bunny and RuPaul landed bit parts as premier New York City drag queens, but the crux of the film is a cloying fish-out-of-water story line in which these "drag queens" stay in makeup and full drag even when sleeping. Snipes and Swayze—all muscles and breathy exasperation—appear to be impersonating women, rather than gay men in drag. The film made fifty million dollars. It felt like this boom time, what Linda Simpson has dubbed "the drag explosion," could only get bigger.

Except it didn't. Instead, after a decade of visibility and influence, drag faded. In the early 1990s, clubs like the Limelight and Area had supported a bustling drag economy by paying the most interesting and well-connected queens to party. The appetite for drug-fueled freak shows had seemed bottomless. But in 1996, Michael Alig, the notorious, social-climbing party promoter who'd mingled with the Pyramid Club crew, murdered his friend and drug dealer Andre "Angel" Melendez. The story became national news, and the grisly details—pouring bleach down the victim's throat, shoving his dismembered torso into a trunk, and dumping it into the river—poured gasoline on then mayor Rudolph Giuliani's yearslong crackdown on "quality of life" crimes. Invoking a 1926 "cabaret law" that prohibited dancing in any bar or restaurant that didn't have a specific license, police had been raiding notorious clubs and searching for drugs and building code violations. With Alig's crime splashed across the headlines, high-profile club owners were investigated for tax evasion and drug trafficking. Hot spots, recast as dangerous public nuisances, sputtered and shuttered. The adults were back, and they were breaking up the party.

When queens couldn't get paid to be in the clubs anymore, they struggled to sell their art form to the wider culture, which was also shifting. More gay people were coming out and prurient tales of gay debauchery gave way to wholesome stories of gay assimilation. TV shows like *Will and Grace* and *Ellen* featured gay characters who, despite some quirky friends and campy punchlines, mostly shared middle-American values and desires: steady jobs, monogamous relationships, and tight-knit families. Members of the LGBT community who wanted to show the world that they were no different than straight people distanced themselves from the public art of gender bending.

· · · · ·

On September 2, 2001, light winds off the Hudson River teased wigs and tousled ponytails of the eight thousand or so people who'd come to watch the seventeenth-annual Wigstock festival. The sun was shining, and Lady Bunny was doing what she did best—charming and teasing a captive audience.

"When I was just a little girl, growing up in Chattanooga, Tennessee," she cooed before interrupting herself. "Any Southerners out there? You Yankees better watch your fuckin' wallets." Bunny nodded knowingly at the cheering crowd and continued: "I used to enjoy draping a sheet between two trees and putting on a show and inviting the neighbors over"—her blond wig wobbled as she spread her hands—"and I think that after seventeen years I may have gotten it out of my system."

"Wigstock Curls Up and Dyes," an article in gay magazine *The Advocate* proclaimed. Ticket sales had lagged thanks to two consecutive years of rainy weather, "turning it into Wetstock, featuring Lady Runny," Lady Bunny told the magazine. As the festival had gotten bigger, it was more expensive to produce, and the higher costs meant bigger losses.

A week after Wigstock 17, two planes flew into the World Trade Center towers. Grief and fear paralyzed New York City. Manhattan nightlife was already in decline. Many people who would have been experienced promoters, performers, and managers by the early 2000s hadn't survived the AIDS epidemic of the 1980s and '90s, and Giuliani's quality-of-life laws and aggressive policing had bankrupted more than one club owner. After nearly a decade of popularity, drag was no longer an exciting new topic for culture reporters and magazine editors. The terrorist attacks turned the city's already chilly scene to ice. Entertainers were shell-shocked, and clubs and promoters were risk averse. Wages, ticket sales, and venue revenue stagnated as the overall cost of living in New York City climbed. Gay bars closed and, at least publicly, gay identities seemed to revel in masculinity and normativity. At Manhattan nightclubs, the freaks, in their sculptural outfits, with pockets full of powders and pills, were out, replaced by Wall Street types and minor royalty paying thousands of dollars for bottle service. In the gay bars, shirtless go-go boys and thumping dance music were de rigueur once again.

Drag queens were abandoned and overlooked in the high-profile clubs, and in the underground New York City queer nightlife scene they were no longer on the cutting edge of cool. Some queens "left a sour taste in my mouth as I suffered through mediocre performances (if lip-synching is your craft, then fucking learn the lyrics already!), predictable characters (how many Judys and Barbras can one sit through?), and too many moments of misogyny, wherein femaleness wasn't performed, but stereotyped, denigrated, and ridiculed," confessed sex educator and feminist author Tristan Taormino, writing in the *Village Voice* in 2001.

The Manhattan drag queen scene wasn't dead in the early 2000s, but compared to that nineties boom, it was dormant. Even self-proclaimed Supermodel of the World, RuPaul, took a break from drag during the Bush years to spend time with his Australian then boyfriend, now husband Georges LeBar on Georges's sixty-thousand-acre Wyoming ranch. When Ru launched his comeback, it was as much to be on reality TV as it was a return to drag. In the early 2000s, *Survivor* was the highest-rated show on television—and this form of heated reality-based competition, for better or worse, brought in ratings. Randy Barbato and Fenton Bailey, old friends who had been managing RuPaul's music career since the 1990s, ran a production company called World of Wonder and made their own pop-culture-inspired reality TV shows and documentaries. They asked Ru to host a drag-themed competition, but at first he was reluctant, worried that reality TV as a genre was too nasty and backstabbing.

"I wasn't interested in doing anything that was going to cast drag in a negative light or ridicule it," RuPaul told *New York* magazine. In 2008, however, "the winds of change changed my mind," RuPaul said, and he put aside his misgivings. Believing the World of Wonder team understood his voice and sensibility and wouldn't make fun of the drag queen competitors or humiliate him, he signed on. When it premiered, *RuPaul's Drag Race* appeared to be a send-up of the wildly successful franchises *America's Next Top Model* and *Project Runway*, with RuPaul serving as a sort of mash-up of the show's respective stars, supermodel Tyra Banks and fashion guru Tim Gunn. It was that perfect mix of familiar and boundary-pushing that had defined Ru's career and image. In carefully tailored suits, he doled out encouragement and caution as contestants cut, glued, and sewed garments in the workroom; in full female realness, he offered snappy commentary as the queens walked the runway.

Though RuPaul was America's best-known drag queen, the show hadn't been an easy sell. The producers pitched every network they could, but drag was simultaneously too edgy to be mainstream entertainment and too familiar to be seen as boundary-pushing. LogoTV had previously aired several short-run reality TV shows about groups of gay and lesbian friends, as well as the dating show *Transamerican Love Story*, in which transgender woman Calpernia

Addams dated and eliminated a series of men. A reality drag competition made sense for the network, and the stakes were low enough that the show could survive with only a cult following. Plus, it was the only channel interested.

RuPaul believes the health of his career—and the state of drag more broadly—is heavily influenced by whatever presidential administration holds power. He struggled and hustled through the repressive Reagan years, first peaked when Bill Clinton was president, and laid low during the George W. Bush administration.

"We are living in the fifties," he told a journalist in 2005, explaining his temporary break from show business. "New ideas and liberal, open-minded thinking is frowned upon." Less than one month after Barack Obama's 2009 inauguration, a headline announcing the premiere of *RuPaul's Drag Race* crowed, "Bush Is Out, RuPaul Is In."

"I thought it was time after these eight years with the Bush administration, these eight years of fear, that a new generation be introduced to drag," RuPaul said.

Drag had been out of the limelight for more than a decade and seemed like a relic to some. "Where Have All the Drag Queens Gone?" writer Thomas Rogers asked in an article *Salon* published just before the show's premiere. Citing "generational shifts that have taken place since drag's heyday," Rogers claimed there was nothing shocking about drag now that gay men could live more openly and assimilate more easily. "While generations of gay men before me spent their teenage years yearning to escape to big cities—and discover what urban gay life was about—I had Sally Jessy Raphael, reality television and Internet search engines as a guide since my early teens." Rogers even quoted Lady Bunny explaining that in the 1990s "people got used to the idea of the drag queen" and "I don't think it's that freeing for gay people anymore."

On the first season of *RuPaul's Drag Race*, nine queens vied for the title of America's Next Drag Superstar, with Ru at the helm, accompanied by regular and guest judges. Not much money was spent, and not many people tuned in, but what Rogers and others failed to predict was how deeply the audience would respond not just to the competition on *Drag Race* but to the well-edited portrayals of gayness. Those who did notice—mostly gay men, often watching at gay bars—could see that something magical was happening on-screen. A TV show by and about gay people made *for* gay audiences was a rarity. Even the 1990 documentary *Paris Is Burning*, which was groundbreaking and continues to influence popular culture and inspire adaptations, was intended to appeal to straight audiences. *Drag Race*, a corny show that appeared to be about petty squabbles between vapid glamourpusses was, at its core, a compassionate and reverent portrait of their art, pain, and beauty. It was not only relatable, it was also pitch-perfect camp.

The format would change very little over the years. In each episode contestants were assigned a challenge that required them to showcase a drag-related skill—fashion design, choreography, comedy, or makeovers, to name a few. At the end of every episode, the queens each turned a look on the runway according to a theme: "Faux Fur Realness," for example, or "Club Kid Couture" (alliteration abounds). The show alternated between footage filmed in the workroom and on the main stage and commentary from interviews with the queens.

Early in the very first episode, Ru presented the contestants with their first "she-mail" video message (likely a nod to "Tyra mail" on *America's Next Top Model* and a play on a nasty slur against transgender women) in which RuPaul delivers an explanation of the day's challenge. "Welcome to the starting line of *RuPaul's Drag Race*. To win this competition you're gonna need to be more enterprising than Donald Trump, to give bigger than Oprah, and be hotter than Tyra wearing a fat suit in July. But when it's all over, only one of you can drive away with the fierce title of America's next breakthrough drag superstar. *Mmm-hmmm*, so put your stiletto to the metal and let's take this mother from zero to fabulous in three point five seconds." Hiding in all that camp was a strong dose of reality. As the season wore on, the queens painted, tucked, tripped, argued, wrestled, pole danced, got soaked by fire hoses, and revealed their personalities, struggles, loves, and losses in heartwarming confessional interviews and group chats while painting backstage.

Despite all the artifice that goes into being a drag queen, contestants on *RuPaul's Drag Race* were anything but contrived. Drag queens were expected to show their humanity as well as their fierceness. The queens who were the most successful were the ones who were able to be truly vulnerable in front of the judges and the cameras. During an episode of his podcast *What's the Tee?* Ru would later tell aspiring contestants, "You can't root for someone that you don't really fall in love with and you don't see that vulnerability. At its core, *RuPaul's Drag Race* is about the tenacity of the human spirit and how everybody wants to be seen, they want to be heard, they want to be recognized."

In the fourth episode of the first season, the queens were instructed to create an advertising campaign for M·A·C VIVA GLAM, a lipstick whose proceeds benefit AIDS research. Ongina, a Filipino American queen from Los Angeles, broke down on the main stage after learning she won the challenge. "I've been living with HIV for the last two years of my life and this means so much to me," Ongina said, ugly-crying as the other queens rubbed her shoulders. "I didn't want to say it on national TV because my parents didn't know."

"Ongina, you are an inspiration. You are a survivor and, baby, you are still in the race. I love you, sweetheart," RuPaul announced from the judges' panel.

Then, in what would become Ru's characteristic response to

heightened emotion, she used the moment to advocate for community support and corporate sponsorship. "You are all sisters, we are all family, and if one of us is in pain, we are all in pain. We are all in trouble, so let's be joyous so that we can all be joyous. That's what VIVA GLAM is really all about."

With the inaugural season of *Drag Race*, RuPaul established herself as an authoritative and sassy guide to drag superstardom. She had refined her message of self-empowerment and acceptance. To her previous mantras, such as "Everybody, say 'love,'" and "Every time I bat an eyelash it's a political act," she added, "If you can't love yourself, how in the hell you gonna love somebody else?" and the notion of "CUNT," also known as "charisma, uniqueness, nerve, and talent," the attributes she believed every successful drag queen must possess.

Audiences and onlookers commonly assume that any man can turn a look, feminize, walk in heels, put on a face, and style a wig. Many bystanders believe the real challenge of drag is rejecting masculinity and enduring the shame of appearing feminine in a deeply misogynist world. While performing femininity can be a social liability, *RuPaul's Drag Race* made it clear to the uninitiated: getting in drag is a skill and often an art. On the show, RuPaul and the judges promoted their notion of "good drag" and passed these standards onto the viewers. Instead of punk, they urged polish and projected a sense of connoisseurship. They clocked contestants' nails, their walk, the fit of their gowns, or the shape of their waists. When the judges spotted a wig line or a crooked brow, they were correcting flaws and promoting "good drag." An aesthetic emerged. Hourglass shapes, heels, long nails, big wigs, femininity. All fixtures of RuPaul's own drag aesthetic. These were men dressing up as women, and for the first decade of the show they were always men; drag kings, out trans people, and female-assigned women were not cast. The queens might be divas, tough girls, or skanks, but genderfuck and androgyny were discouraged. Funny was OK, but sexy and funny was preferable. There were occasional opportunities for stand-up comedy, dance, or live singing, but performance usually meant lip sync. Polish was rewarded and encouraged. Fans, contestants, and drag queens watching at home all took notes. Drag queens were supposed to be jills-of-all-trades, well-rounded entertainers with strong personal brands. If the show had been nothing but a profile of drag or a portrait of some queens in their finest wigs and gowns, it's unlikely that people would have cared. But nothing legitimizes art like a seemingly objective hierarchy. The fun of *RuPaul's Drag Race* was that a winner always emerged—someone who was the best. In front of the camera, this came off as natural and inevitable, but it was a serious departure from RuPaul's Pyramid Club days, where self-expression and sense of humor overshadowed sloppiness, and hard work never got in the way of a good time, and it was not, at least at first, a place where the values of Brooklyn drag held much sway.

PART TWO

CHAPTER EIGHT
Vote Krystal for *Drag Race*

ALRIGHT, HELEN HUNTIES . . . . I'M ABOUT
TO BE ALL UP IN YOUR GRILL LIKE A JEHOVAH'S
WITNESS+++++BECAUSE I WANT MY ASS ON
RUPAUL'S DRAG RACE, AND YOU CAN HELP!!!! :-)

STARTING AT NOON . . . . VOTE VOTE VOTE
VOTE.

Krystal Something-Something was dressed for attention in all green. Sitting at a small table with her laptop, she filmed herself lip-synching to the RuPaul song "Glamazon" and explaining why she wanted a chance to be America's Next Drag Superstar. Then, while editing the video, she added a photo in which she'd painted a neon orange heart across her face, glued a scrap of white paper with black patterns across the bridge of her nose, and glued a puff of orange and white hair to the top of her head. She looked like a radioactive zebra clown. Once Krystal was satisfied with the video, she banged out the all-caps Facebook post. It was April 2012, season four of *RuPaul's Drag Race* was airing, and the show had announced an online "fan favorite" casting contest. Though some Brooklyn queers had trouble reconciling *Drag Race* queens' sparkling gowns, shaved bodies, and intense femininity with the local aesthetic of torn fishnets, smeared makeup, and gender anarchy, it was a show about drag, and many saw it as a natural next step toward a bigger audience and higher booking fees. Krystal, founder of backSpace and an architect of the Brooklyn drag aesthetic, was throwing her spiky, bright green wig into the ring.

On one hand, things seemed to be going well for Krystal. After breaking up with her boyfriend of eight years, she lost twenty pounds and was getting a new kind of attention, in and out of drag. Boys shot flirty looks across the bar. Their hands grazed Krystal's back as they walked past. She lapped it up. As Krystal's profile in New York had grown, she'd found that, in addition to performing, she loved being hired to host parties. This basically involved dressing up and hanging out in exchange for money and drink tickets. ("Just say hi to everyone who looks cool or sexy, and then keep circulating," a more experienced queen had coached.) Making out with hot strangers in the back corners of loud clubs felt incredible, and getting paid to socialize and look fabulous was an ego boost. It was also easier than choreographing a ninety-minute performance for six dancers every week.

On the other hand, Krystal was tired. Not of drag—she always had energy for choreography or performance, and she could still go out until 4:00 a.m. every night of the week—but of everything else. Living in New York City meant walking dogs for money, picking up odd jobs, saving crumpled dollar bills in dresser drawers. It was a different kind of hustle and it wasn't fun. Being picked for *Drag Race*, she hoped, would both validate the quality of her drag and offer her an escape from the grind.

It was a long shot. Despite New York City's centrality to drag, just a handful of queens from Manhattan had been cast, and no Brooklyn girls had yet made the cut. Many locals expected Krystal

Something-Something would be the first to break through. The queens who had been chosen so far didn't just mastermind and execute their own unique visions of drag but also tended to serve as representatives of their regional drag scenes. Queens from West Hollywood, the Los Angeles gay enclave, were polished, witty professionals, with sculpted eyebrows and skimpy outfits. Queens from Texas and the Deep South—pageant country—were poised and old-fashioned: big hair, sequins, legs for days. Las Vegas queens were showgirls, favoring headdresses piled with glitter and fluff, smiles plastered on their heavily painted faces. Puerto Rican queens, who often resided in Florida or California, were wildly charismatic but, at home, often relied on a cadre of helpers to put together their looks, leaving them at a disadvantage on the show, which demanded they do almost everything solo. Krystal, with her irreverent, heavily curated, ultraprecise mess, seemed the perfect ambassador of Brooklyn.

However, some local queens saw no point in distinguishing themselves from their Manhattan counterparts. "I don't fucking care," Thorgy Thor would say when asked to compare the boroughs' respective scenes. A good show was a good show, and a true professional could entertain anyone who walked through the door, on either side of the East River. But although she thought pitting Manhattan drag against Brooklyn was so *boring*, she couldn't deny there was a difference. Manhattan bars were run by professional queens, musical theater devotees, makeup artists, accomplished seamstresses, and trained dancers. The attitude of the quintessential Brooklyn queen, on the other hand, as Thorgy once explained with a maniacal laugh during a panel about Brooklyn drag, was: "Oh, gurl, I'm gonna go out there and cut my dick off, gurl. Brooklyn drag! I'll bleed myself to death and then when the ambulance comes, I'll be like, 'I was the chic shock tonight. Brooklyn drag, girl! I'm gonna die, but you'll never forget it.'"

Though Saliva! was in Manhattan, the spirit of Brooklyn drag ruled. On any given week, half the crowd was in some kind of look. Queers in skimpy bodysuits, thrifted prom dresses, and crowns of fake flowers piled into the club hoping to do an open set. Even the bar goers who showed up in street clothes stood a good chance of ending up shirtless, smeared with makeup or fake blood. Once a month, Thorgy, Veruca, and Azraea hosted the Our Lady of Saliva! pageant. "Thorgy was a money-grubbing monstress and I love her for that," Veruca said. "I'm pretty sure she started doing the pageant so we didn't have to pay another entertainer." It was also a way to bring fresh talent to the stage and a crowd of their friends to watch, buy drinks, and hopefully tip.

On March 27, 2012, spirits were high. Krystal was that night's guest performer and backSpace dancer Mary Jo Cameltoe was competing. Two other backspace members, DiBa, one of the ballet dancers Krystal met smoking behind the dance building at Ohio State University, and Charmy, the bro-turned-drag-queen, were also there to cheer on Mary Jo. The competition would have three rounds: question and answer, performance, and runway. In addition to a guest performer, Thorgy and cohost Azraea typically invited a few celebrity judges to critique the contestants, though "celebrity" was a relative term. Most of the time, these judges were past Our Lady of Saliva! pageant winners or more established drag queens. Tonight, however, the guest judge was a bona fide star in the rapidly expanding landscape of mainstream drag. She was fierce and frightening. When Thorgy introduced her, the room cheered. Though she lived in Pittsburgh, Sharon Needles had friends in Brooklyn, including her drag sister Veruca, and had been doing shows at Sugarland and the Ritz for years. However, most of the people in the room that night knew and loved Sharon because she was a contestant on season four of *RuPaul's Drag Race*.

Sharon Needles was the rare drag queen who made sense to

Brooklyn performers and the mainstream, middle-American television audience that RuPaul sometimes referred to as "Betty and Joe Beercan." Sharon was as dark, funny, and misanthropic, as her name implied. Inspired by Elvira, Vincent Price, and people she met getting drunk under bridges in Pittsburgh, Sharon delighted other freaks and creeps with her love of blood and her ghoulish looks, and she offended people by wearing a Confederate flag bathing suit. On the show, surrounded by living dolls, Sharon was a self-described "ditzy zombie." The other contestants were openly weirded out by her. Chad Michaels, a Las Vegas–based professional Cher impersonator, described her as a "whack job" on their first day in the workroom. Going down the runway in that first episode, Sharon looked like a postapocalyptic princess, and when she bit a blood capsule, the judges gasped as red-black liquid oozed down her chin. The move has since become a cliché, but in 2012, it was shocking.

"People in New York loved Sharon," said Veruca. "But it was because of New York that Sharon looked so good. She wouldn't have known how to dress herself if she hadn't spent a year and a half running around with Thorgy." Sharon was out of drag that night at Saliva! Her bleach-blond hair was styled into a fuzzy mop and her T-shirt had a picture of a Ouija board on it. Season four was almost over, and she'd thrived during the competition, winning the most challenges and provoking the ire of a fiery pageant queen named Phi Phi O'Hara. At Saliva!, Sharon watched from the sidelines as a queen named Honey LaBronx did a number inspired by the movie *Carrie*, in which a telekinetic teenage reject gets a bucket of pig's blood dumped on her at the prom. Then, wearing numerous blond wigs, one on top of the other, a bikini top, and a sarong skirt over jeans, backSpace member Mary Jo Cameltoe performed her "Shaqueera" act portraying "the number one Shakira impersonator in Tennessee, also the only female-born Shakira impersonator." Her lip sync to the song "Whenever, Wherever" incorporated all the gyrating, stomping, and hair tossing from the blond Colombian singer's original video, plus Hula-Hoops and an interlude in which Charmy squeezed a bottle of chocolate sauce onto Mary Jo's chest and stomach. Mary Jo had previously learned the hard way that chocolate sauce is much harder to wash off than fake blood. She wouldn't have attempted a stunt like that anywhere but the Ritz. At the Ritz, VIPs were allowed to use the shower in a fourth-floor apartment above the bar. After her number, she ducked out of the club and went upstairs to wash off the chocolate before it dried into a sticky coating.

In a black vest over a black-and-white-striped shirt with a light blue contact in her left eye, Krystal's look that night was an homage to the Prodigy singer Keith Flint. He'd painted black dots around her green spikes of hair and drawn a black squiggle around the top of her head. Krystal had first met Sharon at Sugarland before the season four cast had been announced and, for the past few months, had watched in awe as Sharon succeeded in being fashionably creepy on television. Out of drag, Krystal shaved his head bald and waxed his eyebrows and chest. He looked like a goblin who might seduce you and then eat your face. In drag, Krystal resembled a skinny, crazed Teletubby. It was exciting to watch Sharon freak out people while looking awesome. She was slaying the game and it suggested there was an audience for Krystal's drag beyond these sweaty, chaotic bars. As they talked near the DJ booth after Mary Jo's performance, Krystal offered her congratulations.

Mary Jo reappeared, having showered and changed into her runway look—a different white tank top and a pair of jean shorts—and found Sharon and Krystal chatting.

"You were great," Sharon told Mary Jo, "but I hate it when real girls don't do extreme makeup."

Mary Jo rolled her eyes, but criticism from one of the most provocative and offensive drag queens she knew stung. Sharon was not one to hold back an opinion or spare someone's feelings. More than once she had described RuPaul as "a Black man in a blond wig." A photo of her in a T-shirt with a swastika on it had recently made the rounds online and she'd been called out by several people for using "the n-word" during performances. In response to the criticism, Sharon said she'd never meant to cause harm with her language. "As a transgressive artist, I and a lot of my idols use language and shock imagery to juxtapose certain images and words . . . to mock and shine a light on things that scared the shit out of me when I was young." Years later, an article published in the *Daily Beast* would document accusations that Sharon choked an underage fan, encouraged them to self-harm, and sent them child pornography. (In response to the claims in the article, an attorney representing Sharon said that she "vehemently denied the allegations against her, and is prepared to defend herself against this individual to the fullest extent possible.") Though some reportedly turned a blind eye or made excuses for the queen, viewing the alleged behavior as an extension of her irreverent and edgy persona, those who made public accusations that they were on the receiving end of the hostility felt differently. Mary Jo went to sit with her boyfriend, and tried to enjoy the rest of the night. Petty slights like this were common. Even though the women of backSpace were turning looks—dressing memorably for their shows and nightclub appearances—and usually beating their faces, they often weren't seen as drag queens and felt overshadowed and ignored in the gay bars.

That night at Saliva!, Mary Jo came in second to Honey LaBronx, who clinched a win after she shit out an apple she'd hidden in her ass, used it to make fruit salad, sampled the salad and then served it to the audience. Thorgy, much to the delight and disgust of the crowd, took a bite. "It's very slippery," she announced. Mary Jo loved nights like these, when everyone was together, getting drunk, and taking an inside joke too far. Lately, though, it felt like there were less and less of them. To her, the best shows were often the ones with only four people in the audience, like the night Mary Jo gingerly pulled a string of anal beads from Charmy's ass while lip-synching to "Cheer Up, Charlie" from the original *Willy Wonka & the Chocolate Factory* film adaptation. Yet, at some point, backSpace's love of chaos had come into conflict with Krystal's perfectionist tendencies. For Mary Jo, the drag scene had lost its novelty. She was exhausted from endless rehearsals, late nights, too much alcohol, and too many arguments with drunk gay boys. She was sleeping poorly, and she worried that her friends and family who weren't in nightlife thought she was a failure. "Your brain never stops, never shuts down, and you're just feeling guilty all the time" was how she explained it.

While the backSpace choreography was always tight, the inter-personal dynamics were messy. Since college, they'd argued, gotten wasted, hooked up with one another, and then argued about who had gotten wasted and hooked up. But this division within the group had deepened recently. Though Charmy and Krystal were creatively in sync, Mary Jo and Krystal, it had become clear, had fundamentally different ideas about art and performance. For Mary Jo, national politics, the state of the world, and broader social issues were urgent and important. Krystal, however, insisted that queers and petite danc-ers in schoolgirl outfits or bondage collars wasn't a commentary on anything, it just looked cool. To Mary Jo, this was bullshit.

"It's a statement on femininity and masculinity and discipline," she'd insist. "Even the fact that it looks cool is a statement."

Nope, Krystal insisted. Any whiff of meaning was incidental. And, whereas Mary Jo used to believe that drag performers and comedians should be allowed to do and say anything onstage in the name of art or jokes, these days she wasn't so sure.

I hope Shaqueera isn't offensive, Mary Jo had thought to herself as she got ready that night. The character had a Southern accent, but Mary Jo wasn't from the South. Was it OK to do an act like that? She used to think it was funny when Krystal would lip-synch to Lil Wayne or she'd perform "Slow Motion" by Juvenile. Increasingly she believed that two white kids performing hip-hop and rap songs in gentrifying Brooklyn was not cool.

The dissonance could be crippling. "I couldn't get through a number without thinking, *Is this against women? Is this racist? Is this cultural appropriation? Am I sexually exploiting myself?*" Mary Jo said.

Krystal, brimming with ambition and addicted to nightlife, had none of these reservations.

With backSpace splintering, *Drag Race* seemed like a way for Krystal to successfully break free of the drama. For the next month, she attacked the *Drag Race* fan favorite contest with the enthusiasm and single-mindedness she brought to her choreography. Krystal lived on Facebook, uploading a new video to promote herself every few days. In one, she made and ate a sandwich. In another, she lip-synched to clips from an episode of the Disney Channel show *That's So Raven*, in which child star Raven-Symoné and her friends try to win a contest by making locker deodorizers. The pop culture references and ironic detachment coupled with manic fervor—it was all quintessentially Krystal. As she went about her day job walking dogs in Manhattan, Krystal harangued other nightlife devotees, friends from Columbus, and even her family in Circleville, Ohio.

"Can you even imagine how awesome the viewing parties would be??????? VOTE VOTE VOTE for Krystal Something-Something NOWWWWWWWW," wrote Charmy on Facebook.

The comments and posts poured in.

I love you so much omg if you don't get on drag race i'll go to ru's house and worship satan in her front yard.

I voted for your sexy ass and I am making ALL my friends vote for you!! The next season would be FUCKING PHENOMENAL with you in it!

i can't describe how absolutely amazing i think you are! i just voted again. we have to win this!!

Krystal inched up the rankings. From tenth to eleventh and then into the single digits. As she climbed, she watched Sharon continue to kill the competition on TV and imagined herself on the show alongside her doing the dance challenge, making garments out of piles of trash, and creating a political campaign for the "Frock the Vote" challenge. Much of the activity and action on *Drag Race* took place not onstage but in the pink-walled workroom (or Werk Room), where the contestants sewed, crafted, argued, rehearsed, and painted and dressed for the runway. Most of the time, queens were out of drag when in the Werk Room, but at the beginning of every season's first episode, each queen made a dramatic Werk Room entrance in full drag and introduced themselves with a pithy catchphrase. Krystal decided that her workroom entrance line would be "Hello, America, my name is Krystal Something-Something and this is my entrance."

"DEAR FRIENDS, FAMILY, FANS, AND FREAKS, you are seriously so amazing, i can't explain! . . . . . slow and steady wins the race . . . . . i've been moving up!!! let's try to get me in the top 6 tomorrow, think we can do it?!" Krystal wrote in April as season four came to a close. In the final episodes, she watched Sharon lip-synch to an ensemble number dressed as a skanky dog, walk the runway at the "Bitch Ball" serving "heroin-chic, hungover party-girl realness," and land herself a place in the season's top three. Sharon stumbled through some music video choreography but redeemed herself by wearing gloves with tentacle fingers on the runway. After the episode, Krystal gushed about it Facebook:

> in every artistic world, there is always a person who can open doors for other creators, someone who speaks to a new generation . . . sharon needles is helping us breathe a new life into the art of drag. . . .

The last episode of the season was the crowning. In front of a live audience, onstage with RuPaul, Sharon advised all the "gay kids and weird kids" watching at home, "when in doubt, freak 'em out, just go ahead and do whatever the fuck you wanna do, and if anyone ever boos you off stage, that is simply applause from ghosts." Then, this controversial queen of the underbelly and the underground won it all.

On May 1, 2012, a week after the season four finale aired, the online contest to choose the season five fan favorite ended. "i am so overwhelmed with joy and excitement," wrote Krystal in her last Facebook post about the competition. The person who'd gotten the most votes would compete on *RuPaul's Drag Race* and have a chance to win one hundred thousand dollars and the title of America's Next Drag Superstar. That person was a thirty-nine-year-old drag queen from Cincinnati named Penny Tration, the self-described "nice, fat, funny one" with an old-school campy drag style. Krystal had come in eighth place. She had run a terrific campaign and won the hearts of hundreds of savvy, discriminating New York queers, but she had not been cast on *Drag Race*. In her Facebook post, she tried to put a positive spin on the outcome and thanked people for supporting her.

it means more to me than you'll ever know that you
appreciate my art! it says a lot about the future of drag
that i have been able to reach so many different kinds of
people from all over the world! i promise i'm not going
anywhere :-)

Pop culture is full of examples of strange, challenging, awkward performers who got famous when mainstream tastes shifted or norms caught up to their aesthetics or ideas. But pop culture is also full of trailblazers who inspire a scene but never find mainstream success or attention. The most innovative or deserving creative people don't always have the biggest platform, especially when that platform only has room to launch a dozen or so people a year. Krystal would later say that she never expected to be cast on the show. But whether they loved Krystal or loathed her, many of the people who'd watched back-Space dominate the New York drag scene just assumed that someday she'd end up on TV.

"I thought Krystal was going to be on *Drag Race*—I really did," Mary Jo later said. "Krystal has both incredible artistic skills and is also a great performer. A lot of drag queens have either, not both." Mary Jo and her boyfriend at the time, Mor Erlich, stopped watching the show after season four.

"I was like, 'I'm not watching these homely *Drag Race* girls anymore.' I was livid," said Mor. "Me and Krystal weren't even that close. I think Krystal didn't even like me. But I wanted her to be on *Drag Race* so bad. They are stupid motherfuckers that they didn't put her on. I feel bad for them. I knew *Drag Race* was a mainstream show, but even if Krystal would have been eliminated the first week—which would never have happened—she would have left a long-lasting impression."

Not everyone was this outraged. One queen, in particular, took Krystal's disappointment as an opportunity. Thorgy Thor believed that Krystal was "fucking brilliant," that she had "unstoppable, undeniable brilliance," but clearly that hadn't been enough to get her cast on the show and this, like so much of Thorgy and her friends' lives, became fodder for a drag number. One night at Saliva!, when Thorgy knew Krystal would be in the audience, Thorgy stood still, in baggy print pants and black leotard, facing the crowd. An upbeat, synthy remix of the British belter Adele's "Set Fire to the Rain" began. The song, about heartbreak over a deceptive lover, had a raging chorus and when it hit, backSpace dancer DiBa and a drag queen named Miz Jade emerged from the crowd and danced behind Thorgy. It was an ambush. Thorgy, DiBa, and Miz Jade knew that Krystal loathed the song, and they had perfectly choreographed the dance to run through backSpace's signature moves—the shimmies, dramatic arms, and body rolls. A violinist friend of Thorgy's from college who had toured with Adele was also in the crowd and had been drinking steadily for hours. When the chorus hit, she took off her top, "her tits were pouring out," Thorgy would later say when telling the story. She wasn't part of the ambush of Krystal, "she just thought that's what you did at a drag show. I'm like, 'I can't shame you at all. Yeah! What are you doing next week?'"

When the song reached its climax, the music paused. "Vote for Krystal on *Drag Race*," Thorgy's voice-over had been mixed into the track.

The crowd—recognizing the joke—erupted, and many of them turned to look at Krystal, sitting stunned, out of drag in the back corner.

"Oh wait," Thorgy's voice-over continued, "didn't she come in eighth place?"

Krystal was mortified and delighted. Being passed over for the show had stung, but she wasn't going to sulk about it. She knew Thorgy loved backSpace, so Thorgy could get away with making fun of Krystal publicly. Not like there was anything Krystal could do to stop the ridicule. She and Thorgy were kindred spirits who ran their shows like mildly sadistic camp counselors. They both loved to lip-synch to their own prerecorded voice-overs, they both took themselves very seriously, and they enjoyed making fun of other people who took themselves very seriously. The song's outro played, and Thorgy rushed to the back of the room and launched herself on Krystal. The crowd looked on as they made out with sloppy abandon.

With Krystal losing steam for life in New York and Mary Jo growing increasingly worried about the content and impact of their shows, old, unresolved tensions in backSpace began to reemerge. Mary Jo and DiBa had slept together during college and now, as roommates, their friendship was turbulent. They would drink, feel resentful, and argue about DiBa's bar tab at Sugarland, where Mary Jo was a bartender. One night, Mary Jo got locked out of the apartment and DiBa ignored her phone calls. She ended up having to sleep in the park, and she and DiBa didn't speak for three weeks.

When the women in backSpace were getting along, they were less and less interested in performing in bars. This reticence upset Krystal, who had committed herself to nightlife. The members of backSpace would snipe at one another, grow frustrated and fight, and then get over it, perform, and argue again. Krystal didn't know how to resolve the conflict permanently. In the sweltering heat of July, about a year after she'd lost the fan-favorite contest, she walked down the street, a dog trailing behind her, and realized that even though she loved Brooklyn—her friends, the bars, the fast pace, and the chaos—she didn't want to live there anymore. Now that there was no casting, no runway, no reality TV prize money, or tour to look forward to, Krystal wondered, *Is this the farthest my star will rise?* She didn't want to keep auditioning for *Drag Race*, waiting patiently for someone she didn't know on the other side of a computer to recognize her. She didn't want to keep hustling like this. Krystal called her mom and, when she picked up, she told her, "I think I want to come home."

"i've decided to get away from this beautiful bitch of a city and hide away for a while, to prepare for krystal 3.0," she wrote on Facebook later that day.

backSpace would have to end. DiBa and Charmy pushed back. They wanted to keep using the name and the momentum for their own drag performance.

"I uprooted my life and shaped my schedule around what we were doing, and you're going to leave?" DiBa wailed. She'd taken an early-morning bartending job at John F. Kennedy Airport to make ends meet and have time for backSpace, and Krystal wouldn't even let them keep the name. But deep down DiBa knew that backSpace had been Krystal's creation. It couldn't happen if Krystal wasn't a part of it. And Krystal didn't want to be a part of it anymore.

"This is probably the biggest thing i've ever done for myself," Krystal's goodbye post continued. "it's horrifying and strangely comforting at the same time." She was sick of living in the same city as her ex-boyfriend, sick of arguing about costumes or choreography, and sick of being broke and working a dead-end job.

"Krystal just didn't get it," Thorgy would later say. "She couldn't survive in New York; she needed people like me who said to her, 'Your show is the best show I've ever seen, oh my God, you should be passing around a garbage pail full of tips.' That's how you pay and stay in New York. She was like, 'I don't want to do tips,' 'cause she was so proud of her work."

Krystal convinced herself the move wouldn't be permanent—it made it easier to leave. However, with the exception of a few trips back, it was. In that goodbye post on Facebook, Krystal left her friends and followers with a promise and an exhortation.

> i will be back, i have to, everything about this city makes
> sense to who i am and who i've become . . . .

> don't worry, you'll still see my face . . . it might just evolve
> in ways i didn't know possible . . . who knows, right? . . . .

> . . . . just don't forget me.

CHAPTER NINE

The BK to the *RDR*

Krystal's return to Columbus was the beginning of the end for her corner of the local drag scene. Sugarland, backSpace's home bar, was also coming apart. For years, performers had tolerated the low pay—the budget for entertainment on a good night was about two hundred dollars total—for the pleasure of working someplace with no "adult" supervision. Sugarland patrons were broke, but enthusiastic. Too poor to tip, they'd sometimes drop handfuls of napkins from the balcony to make it seem like dollar bills were raining down on the stage. One night, a woman who couldn't afford a five-dollar cover charge was so desperate to see house music legend Crystal Waters sing that she snuck in by climbing the patio wall. That had always been part of the bar's charm. It was the reason that the members of backSpace could experiment and cause chaos without ever considering cover charges or drink sales.

But by 2013, the crowds were sparse, the business was floundering, and the neighborhood was changing. The dirty streets and abandoned warehouses of North Brooklyn were now a developer's dream. Condos and luxury apartments sprung up in the previously vacant and overgrown lots. A six-story building shot up to the left of Sugarland, and then another appeared on the right. That's when the noise complaints started. Bartenders and managers would later recall that, for years, the bar's owners had been largely hands-off, trusting the staff to run the place. They'd made verbal arrangements regarding pay, schedule, and bookings. No one had a job contract or paperwork. As the citations piled up and the books dipped into the red, one manager described how the owners sent someone to hang out at the bar and take notes on everything that was happening.

One night after work in the late fall of 2013, Mor Erlich, who had been a manager at Sugarland for four years and had been instrumental in booking and supporting backSpace, was eating dinner at the bar with Mary Jo Cameltoe and another coworker. They were chatting about all the parties they'd thrown and the ways they'd all changed and grown over the years.

"One night we won't all be together eating fried chicken at Sugarland," Mor remarked wistfully.

Later that week, as he was heading into work, he got a phone call. "Whatever you do at the bar, we don't need that anymore," Mor recalled Sugarland's owner telling him.

A few weeks later, another manager was fired, and Mary Jo quit in solidarity. Some former employees claimed they'd been accused of stealing. The bar had become a source of hurt feelings and ruined friendships. On Mary Jo's last day, she, Mor, and another employee got tattoos. Mor and Mary Jo's read "TA DA," like a magician's flourish after pulling off a trick.

"I knew it couldn't last forever," Mor said, but they wanted to commemorate the good times.

By December 2013, rumors that Sugarland was closing had been circulating for months. It was Untitled Queen who broke the news online: "Sugarland Nightclub is closing. We need to send this place off with a blast of champagne and a toast to the dark hidden secrets it has provided us that we tell only when we're high and intoxicated." Not long after, Saliva! Tuesdays ended, too.

Not everyone was sad. Merrie Cherry, who identified with Metro and had long felt uncomfortable with the sometimes cliquish atmosphere at Sugarland, felt indifferent about the news. But she still went to the final New Year's Eve blowout and danced in a cloud of confetti and glitter. Soon after the bar closed, backSpace dancers DiBa and Charmy left New York. First back to Ohio, and then on to Los Angeles, to try to start a moving company with DiBa's boyfriend. Mary Jo, Whiskey Dixie, and the remaining members of backSpace kept making solo work. Sometimes they'd collaborate as they tried to cross over into the broader New York City art and performance scene. Krystal came to visit them a few times, but her tenure as a New York City drag queen was over. Columbus had a vibrant gay scene and a gay pride parade that rivaled Chicago's. For a smaller, often-overlooked city, the appetite for and caliber of drag was top-notch and bar goers and performers welcomed Krystal back into the fold. A massive local drag family who called themselves the Wests was respected in drag circles across the country, and their shows kept a number of local queens booked and blessed. People in Columbus liked and understood Krystal's drag whether they'd known her before she moved to New York City or not. Within a year, Krystal had won the Miss Axis pageant at Columbus's most popular gay bar—her first time actually competing for a title—and had fallen in love with a new boy. Occasionally, she'd send Mary Jo or Charmy a wistful text with an old video or photo from the backSpace days. Their all-consuming, debauched life was now something the backSpace dancers looked back on fondly. Their stint as the pinnacle of Brooklyn coolness reduced to a warm memory, like their years spent in dance classes at Ohio State University, or watching reruns of *Full House* in middle school. This could be painful. They missed one another. They'd text late at night—"Remember that time when we thought Krystal was making out with a lesbian?" "Yea, and then the guy lived on my couch for a year?"—or someone would stumble across an old photo online and share it around.

Through it all—the dissolution of backSpace, Krystal's move, Sugarland closing, Saliva!'s end—Thorgy Thor persisted. Thorgy could publicly tease Krystal about not getting cast on *Drag Race* because they were friends but also because Krystal knew Thorgy had taken every opportunity to send in an audition tape and had watched for years as queens she knew got on the show.

What do they have that I don't have? Thorgy wondered.

She saw them booked across the country after the show—the winners and the losers. As attention shifted to *Drag Race*, the regulars at Metropolitan were more excited by the girls on the show than the hometown performers who busted their asses at the bar every night. They'd buy tickets for a Ru girl's show or tip generously when it was a cast member and, as these "sub-lebrities"—people who are well-known in a subculture but hardly stars in the wider world—entered the atmosphere, their gravitational pull left less room and fewer dollars for the local girls. The growing popularity of *Drag Race* also presented a dilemma for some. As the seasons piled up and the TV show gained fans and followers, the values and aesthetics presented on the show began to trickle down to queens and audiences alike. Suddenly, the bars were filled with people who had opinions on wig lines, face contour, and song choice. This was great if your song choice, wig lines, and makeup conformed to *Drag Race* standards but less ideal for those who couldn't or wouldn't measure up. To many, it seemed like there were only two career paths: they could follow convention in the hopes of leveling up, or they could stay true to their artistic impulses and content themselves with being a niche act.

"*RuPaul's Drag Race* has sort of killed drag for queens who are not on the show," Thorgy told the online publication *Queerty*. "We're begging and begging for bigger budgets for the clubs and trying to find more money to do better shows in New York."

Increasingly, the only way to ascend was to get cast.

In March 2015, there was yet another call for audition tapes. Thorgy told herself that this would be her final attempt to land a spot on the show. She'd watched for years as the queens she booked at Saliva! and Sugarland were cast. She vowed that if she didn't make it onto season eight she'd move to Los Angeles and enroll in cinema makeup school. Being passed over year after year "felt pathetic," she later said. "So I was like, 'Fuck them. They don't get me.'" She put her all into that tape and told the producers about her talents, her fears, her strengths, weaknesses, hopes, and dreams.

"I wanna conduct a forty-piece orchestra. In a tuxedo. And have Rufus Wainwright wheel out on a piano to do a song. I could make this happen. I could really do this," she pledged. "I can sing, I can do choreography very well. I'm a very good dancer. I'm a good stylist."

Later in the tape, she showed off her "Fu Manchu snow-beast look," an outfit made up of an oversize shaggy white coat and a wig of thick white yarn.

"The biggest hardship I've ever faced is me being my own critic and getting down on myself—being so neurotic about having something so perfect," she said as the tape showed clips of her playing the cello and lip-synching to songs from *The Lion King*. She was exhausted and, despite her firm belief that she deserved to be on the show—*far, far* more than a lot of the other queens they cast—she was beginning to lose hope that the producers would realize it.

When Thorgy finally got the call telling her congratulations, she'd been cast on season eight, her reply was matter-of-fact: "Thank you, yes, finally. When do I leave?" She was ready. So ready.

The producers gave Thorgy a list of vague runway categories like "retro," "movie premiere," and "neon" and told her to get together appropriate looks in the two weeks before they started filming. Thorgy was especially excited to make a couture look out of vintage library books. Thorgy's mother, who had died of cancer when Thorgy was twenty, had been a librarian. This would be an opportunity to pay homage to her mom while doing her favorite thing in the world.

"When I get there, I'm gonna be myself, and everything I say on TV is gonna be real to me," Thorgy told Out.com. "If I go home and watch something I faked or was contrived, I'm not gonna like me." Then, she checked a hundred pounds of luggage and boarded the plane for Los Angeles.

On the set of *RuPaul's Drag Race* everything was both more boring and more magical than the queens could have ever expected. Thorgy walked into the workroom in a frizzy red wig and a gold-and-red ice-skating costume and shouted, "Whoo, Thorgy with a 'TH' and 'ORGY,' and I feel in-cred-i-ble." She soon saw two familiar faces: Bob the Drag Queen, a bald, Black, riotously funny queen who was a regular at Saliva!, and Acid Betty, another New York queen who used makeup, glue, glitter, and cardboard to transform herself into dreamlike interpretations of animals and mythical creatures. While Acid Betty lived in Brooklyn, she worked in Manhattan, and would often jokingly refer to Brooklyn queens as "poopy diapers." Bob lived in Harlem, and some of her first bookings had been at Saliva! back when she called herself Kitten with a Whip. Except for a few appearances at Sugarland, Bob was a Manhattan queen through and through. She was hilarious, quick-witted, and warm. Seeing her sisters on the show, Thorgy felt at home. New York City was finally getting its due, but only one queen was going home with the crown.

The days went by in an anxious, sleep-deprived blur. Thorgy had moments of triumph—like when she dressed up as Michael Jackson for the "Snatch Game," the show's beloved celebrity impersonation challenge and had RuPaul giggling uncontrollably. At one point, Ru told her, "With your auditions, I've seen every video tape, and I felt like you were most ready this year because you seemed more relaxed."

Thorgy didn't necessarily *feel* relaxed, but she was glad to know that's how RuPaul saw her. She battled her perfectionism and obsessive need to be the best—and be *known* as the best. Though the edit would suggest otherwise, she laughed and joked with the other queens, kiki-ing as they called it, including Bob, who was consistently slaying challenges and being complimented by the judges. Did Thorgy wish she were getting that level of praise? Sure. But did it annoy her? Not nearly as much as what aired on TV would suggest. She was Thorgy Thor, and she was an entertainer, and this was a stage. Granted, her audience had been replaced with a panel of judges that included RuPaul, and she was getting by on significantly less alcohol than she did during a typical drag show. But drag was her art, and drag queens were her people.

In episode seven, during the "Black and White" challenge, she put on a satin collared shirt with geometric black and white print, parachute pants, and a long white wig under a black bowler hat. "I'm giving you Mae West meets Carrie Bradshaw," Thorgy said in a prerecorded voice-over that played alongside a video of her storming the runway. Most of the queens that week had painted their faces white, but Thorgy's looked gray under the lights.

"She looks a little ashy," RuPaul joked as she went down the runway. "Lotion up, girl. Lotion up."

Every episode of *Drag Race* ends with the queens assembled on the stage in front of RuPaul, in full drag, and a panel of judges that includes one celebrity guest. The judges offer critiques and choose that week's winner. During Thorgy's black-and-white runway critiques, one judge said she looked like "a dead Boy George." RuPaul criticized Thorgy for not knowing how to edit her ideas, and she stammered, "I always just keep going and going; it is difficult for me to shut my thought processes down." During the judges' deliberations, when the competing queens were waiting backstage, Michelle Visage, a veteran of the 1980s ballroom scene, a longtime *Drag Race* judge and RuPaul's best "squirrel friend" called Thorgy's runway "a swing and a miss."

"I know she's wacky and different," she said, "but it should be cohesive."

Thorgy's aesthetic sensibility had made her stand out in New York City. The way she'd created a distinct character who wasn't always glamorous, who didn't have to be polished or beautiful, had made her the quintessential Brooklyn queen. Someone cool enough to be stupid or look messy. But on the runway that day, the judges weren't awarding points for originality.

Every episode, the two queens with the worst critiques of the week, also known as the "bottom two" (or simply, "the bottoms;" the winners are "the tops") were instructed to "lip-synch for your lives," battling it out in front of RuPaul and the judges in a final push to save themselves from elimination. "Shantay you stay," RuPaul told the winner while the loser was forced to "sashay away." That week, Thorgy ended up in the bottom with a lovable Louisiana drag queen named Chi Chi DeVayne. The song was "And I Am Telling You I'm Not Going" from the musical *Dreamgirls*. Thorgy knew the lyrics perfectly. She shook and swayed; she collapsed on the ground, got back up, and, dodging beads that had fallen off Chi Chi's dress during the song's climax, Thorgy cartwheeled across the stage. Chi Chi, on the other hand, went to a place of deep emotion, parked it, and took everyone to church.

After the song ended, Chi Chi and Thorgy stood silent on the stage, panting and awaiting Ru's verdict. "Chi Chi DeVayne, shantay you stay," RuPaul announced. The lip sync had been a moment for sincerity, not spectacle, and Thorgy, with all the sass and energy of a city kid used to throwing every prop, kick, squeal, and sequin at the audience, had misread the room.

RuPaul turned to Thorgy. "Thorgy Thor, you brought the BK to the *RDR*, and, girl, I ain't gon' l-i-e. We loved every minute of it. Now, sashay away."

"Thank you, Ru, so much." Thorgy bowed slightly and walked

across the runway to the exit. "Bye, guys. Witty catchphrase, you know what I mean?" she said before ducking offstage. She'd been eliminated the episode before the "Book Ball" and wouldn't get a chance to wear the look inspired by her mother.

Thorgy flew back to Brooklyn and waited six months for the show to air. She tried to keep the fact that she'd been cast a secret, but it was impossible. Months before, *Drag Race* fans on the social media site Reddit had managed to sleuth out the entire cast by cross-referencing bookings and cancellations for pretty much every prominent drag queen in the country. The world was about to learn what Thorgy, Merrie, Horrorchata, and dozens of others already knew—that New York was the biggest city in the world, home to Broadway, Wall Street, and the Empire State Building, but Brooklyn was an idea, an aesthetic, and a way of life. Grimy new bars opened regularly—yes there were nails in the ceiling snagging people's wigs, and light fixtures swinging on loose cords—but a baby queen could walk in at two thirty in the morning knowing no one and nothing and be onstage by three. Brooklyn had the numbers, it had the attitude, and partly because most bars stayed open until 4:00 a.m. every night, it had the opportunity. Thorgy Thor had taken those opportunities, she'd worked and hustled and performed, and she'd gotten cast on a reality TV drag competition hosted by the most famous drag queen in the world.

But what Thorgy discovered was that, on *Drag Race,* brilliance, talent, and experience are only part of the package. "The producers have an ideal winner that they want, and everyone else fits into how they get kicked off and how they're depicted," Thorgy later realized.

She had not won, and she was not one of the top three finalists. Bob, of all people, ended up taking the crown after winning the most challenges and proving herself to be one of the funniest queens to ever appear on the show. But Thorgy had showed up and showed out. When her season aired, she kind of hated watching, knowing she wasn't going to win, but she maintained she had no regrets. She had been herself, and now the world—or at least a few hundred thousand drag fans—knew her name. Brooklyn, too, would benefit from Thorgy's turn in the spotlight. She had kicked open the doors to RuPaul's workroom, and now everyone was waiting to see which local queen would enter next.

As the show was airing, people often approached Thorgy in the bars, certain she had made it to the end of the competition. "You're top three, I know it," they'd tell her.

From a New York City perspective, this made sense. Thorgy was one of the most well-known, talented, and established queens in the city. One of the few who regularly worked in Brooklyn and Manhattan. She was nominated for Glammy Awards every year. In multiple categories. Thorgy was a queen with talents beyond lip-synching who could give you a damn good lip sync. She had wanted a bigger stage, more money, and a national platform for Brooklyn drag. She had worked for it, and she had gotten it.

Yet, appearing on, but not actually winning, *Drag Race* presented a new set of problems. Though a spot on the show felt like the reward for years of often thankless work, Thorgy knew that if she wanted her career to continue for years, let alone decades, she couldn't stop there. She'd been given a shot, but it was another staircase to climb, not an elevator to the top floor. Now was time to make this relatively quick turn in the spotlight into a bigger, badder life: the kind she dreamed about and thought she deserved. The possibility that this was the peak of her notoriety was always looming. At some point, every entertainer's career reaches its apex—the point at which there was no next big gig, role, or opportunity. Was this hers? She'd just have to figure out how to keep climbing higher.

CHAPTER TEN
Mr(s) Williamsburg

While Thorgy was auditioning (and auditioning, and auditioning) for *Drag Race*, Aja—who had dropped Injektion Marie Von Teese from her name for ease and simplicity—was hustling. She was still a teenager, living with her mom and Esai after he'd had enough of his own dysfunctional family. The young couple spent their days sleeping, splayed out on couches and beds covered with clothing and costume jewelry, or playing Pokémon and chatting with boys online, and spent their nights in the bars. They mopped makeup and lied to their parents about where they'd been or where they were going or whether they'd been to school that week. They memorized song lyrics and chatted with other queens on Facebook; this headlong plunge into a new life felt like being reborn. They could dress up, beat their faces, and jump through a trapdoor to a world where all the annoying, frustrating, hurtful, and scary facets of their lives couldn't touch them.

Drag gave Aja an outlet for her love of fashion and her eccentric sense of style. Once she was dressed up, her social awkwardness and anxiety made her seem outgoing rather than weird, so most week-nights at around ten, Aja and Esai would begin to paint their faces while practicing their lip syncs. They'd arrive at the bar at 1:30 a.m. and wait until around 3 a.m. to perform in the third and final set of the night. If they scowled and mean-mugged as they walked inside and then acted like they belonged there, bouncers and bartenders would usually let them stay.

In May 2012, just weeks after she'd won the very first round of DragNet, Aja competed in Thorgy's Our Lady of Saliva! pageant at the Ritz. During her lip syncs she went off. She shuddered and shook like a woman possessed; she crouched down and spun around. She vogued, her arms darting out like clock hands. She bounced across the floor, crouching, and leaned backward dramatically, her leg jutting in front of her at an impossible angle. She dipped and spun in a dervish of limbs, and then she won.

"I don't know how you won," a queen told her later that night. "You were flailing around like a fish."

"I won because I'm fierce," Aja barked back.

Aja was talented and she owned the room when performing, so, a few months later, Thorgy booked her for the all-stars edition of Our Lady of Saliva!, where Aja performed a vogue sword fight with Esai.

Winning contests was a way to earn some quick cash, but without regular bookings, Aja knew she would never be able to make enough money to help her mom and support herself once she turned eighteen. The stress of losing the fifty-dollar prize at the first DragNet had been part of the reason Aja popped off at Merrie Cherry. Even after several months, Aja and Esai were still hopping subway turnstiles in drag to get to their gigs and, when they didn't make enough coin to afford the trip back, hopping turnstiles home. They began to hear rumors that Merrie Cherry was telling people not to book them, saying they were crazy, ghetto, and unreliable. Aja worried that people secretly hated her and it was hurting her bottom line.

A few months after the DragNet finale, Aja and Esai walked into Metropolitan and saw Merrie Cherry sitting on a stool by the bar.

"What the fuck, Merrie?" Aja demanded. "What have you been telling people about me?"

Esai glared. "Why are you trying to ruin Aja's dreams because you're upset about something so stupid?" he asked.

Merrie, the older, taller queen, rose slowly from her stool in order to stare them down.

"Girl, really?" Merrie replied. "I didn't do shit to you." Merrie sighed. "You're always acting crazy."

From Merrie's perspective, Aja and Esai had appeared on the drag scene out of nowhere and were strange and confusing. They were always trying to read tarot cards for money and had once passed a hat for a "charity fundraiser" that felt absolutely not real. Now, Merrie sized them up, wondering if they were seriously going to try to fight her again.

"We're cool, you need to relax," she assured them. "Aja, I'm not telling people not to book you. I'll book you." And even though Merrie *had*, in fact, been shit-talking them all over Brooklyn, she recognized that they weren't going away and that Aja's performances more than made up for the drama that seemed to follow everywhere she went.

"Perform at the DragNet Halloween show." Merrie looked at them, eyebrows raised in annoyance, as if to say, "Are you satisfied now?"

Aja and Esai looked at each other, their righteous anger rapidly deflating. Fifty bucks plus whatever tips they could hustle was worth squashing the fight.

"Fine, Merrie, yes. I want the gig." Aja exhaled, annoyed but placated.

In those late months of 2012, after Aja and Merrie Cherry declared their fragile truce, Aja's gigs began to pile up. Charisma is a strange virtue. Perhaps the most egalitarian of all traits, it is bestowed irrespective of class, race, age, or appearance, and it is hard to define, except to say that people know a charismatic person when they see one. The pull of charisma makes it difficult to look away, makes others want to throw money or applause at a stranger. It is the singular trait of being watchable, living and acting in the moment. It's rare and virtually impossible to cultivate or learn. Even in Brooklyn, true charisma made a difference, especially when paired with hard work, luck, and some of those more tangible assets like beauty, kindness, and intelligence. Much to the chagrin of her detractors and the people she fought at the bars, Aja *was* charismatic, especially onstage. She sometimes made bad performance choices, her looks could be messy, and she said dumb things on the mic, but she had a run-on way of talking and a cuteness that made her hard to ignore. She instinctively knew how to fill the space and let the music move through her as she gave the crowd a fantasy of a bad bitch, or a banjee queen, a tough girl on the block living her best life. Put simply, she was extremely fun to look at.

In the year after she and Merrie made peace, Aja got more comfortable in the bars. Not everyone liked her, but slowly she got attention. Besides being charismatic, Aja worked hard, showing up night after night. She started to make friends with other performers, posing in dressing room photos with their arms draped around one another. They tagged her in Facebook posts and shrieked "Yaaaass, werk" when she performed. People she'd never met followed her on social media and liked and commented on her posts. She could tell that when she entered a bar, people she did not know recognized her. Merrie, who'd spent 2013 building her own career in the borough, even hired Aja to style some wigs. It was a peace offering and a flex, since it suggested Merrie's drag gigs were lucrative enough to allow her to pay someone for help.

Merrie, though, was trying to make drag into a career. Most people in nightlife either have rich parents or a side hustle. It was outrageous to think you could pay rent and survive in the city just by being a local drag queen, let alone hire other people to do things for you, thereby putting money back into the drag economy. But Merrie, who was sick of working a dull nine-to-five at a nonprofit, thought that maybe she could do just that. Merrie was ten years older than Aja, and she wanted to be the boss: in charge of the shows, booking the girls, holding the mic every night. And a big part of that power came from publicity. In New York City, good entertainment doesn't stay underground for long. Merrie knew that freelance writers, photographers, and filmmakers frequented the Brooklyn gay bars and you could never predict when someone with the power to put you on-screen or in a magazine might walk through the door. Bushwig had become an annual event and a guy Horrorchata met in a coffee shop had made a crowdfunded documentary about the first few years of the festival. An editor at the *Huffington Post* was attempting to publish a Q&A with every notable Brooklyn drag performer. No one was making national news like the *Drag Race* girls were, but the attention helped members of the scene feel important and like they were part of something bigger. While queens like Aja and Esai took any and every gig they could, Merrie wanted to be able to make an event successful just by being involved. So, when Dominic Andolina, known in drag as Alotta McGriddles, decided to throw the definitive Brooklyn drag pageant, Merrie jumped at the chance to help organize the event.

A beefy former high school football player with a thick New York accent, Alotta had spent four years at SUNY Purchase hanging out with Thorgy Thor, singing opera, and doing cocaine. Alotta never did drag in college. When she first moved to Brooklyn, she'd openly criticize queens for busted looks and weak performances. "I love you, but you can't read people unless you have the balls to do it yourself," Thorgy told her. "OK, I'll do it and I'll do it better," Alotta vowed. Alotta believed that people became drag queens because they'd failed at their true passion. According to this philosophy, Thorgy was a failed classical musician; Miz Jade, a SUNY grad and frequent backSpace collaborator, was a failed dancer; Untitled Queen was a failed visual artist; and Merrie Cherry was "a failed coat check girl." Alotta decided to call the competition Mr(s) Williamsburg, a nod to the fact that no one ever knew what gender pronoun to use when referring to local performers and the desire to make the contest especially inclusive. In addition to the usual retinue of drag queens, Alotta also invited burlesque performers, drag kings, and queer performance artists to participate.

Brooklyn drag had always been collaborative *and* competitive, and, as co-organizers, Alotta and Merrie butted heads from the beginning. They argued about how much cash to award the winner, who to invite to judge, and what the categories would be. A trio of Williamsburg bars hosted the qualifying rounds. People jumped at the opportunity to represent their local bar and rule their neighborhood. In 2014, Aja, now twenty years old, with two solid years as a drag queen under her belt, signed up to compete at Metropolitan, the first Brooklyn bar she'd ever performed in. Aja's choices of music had always been eclectic and suggested taste beyond her years. Some favorites included "Bang Bang (My Baby Shot Me Down)" by Nancy Sinatra and Eartha Kitt's version of "Come On-a My House." When performing contemporary tracks, she loved Nicki Minaj and Azealia Banks. For the competition's first round at Metropolitan, Aja came dressed as a deranged nun and lip-synched to the Annie Lennox song "Money Can't Buy It." She stripped off her habit and revealed a harness and a chain mail jockstrap and then led Esai and another dancer across the stage by leashes. These hijinks and the pure joy she displayed during her second number—a lip sync to "Jungla" by the Peruvian coloratura soprano Yma Sumac, performed in a V-shaped monokini covered in bright yellow fringe and accessorized with a feathered headdress and cha-cha heels—secured Aja a spot in the pageant's finale four weeks later.

Competing against Aja in the finale was a drag queen named Charlene, a stoner from the South with a fierce intellect and a habit of stripping down to her underwear—or less—during her numbers. In the first round of the pageant at a gay bar about a mile west of Metropolitan, Charlene lip-synched to the bouncy, yet vaguely dark, club track "Til It's Gone," by Britney Spears. Charlene's onstage confidence was so otherworldly it could have been beamed into her body by a passing satellite. While Britney's voice echoed over galactic sound effects and keyboards, Charlene gave the song a maudlin gloss. In black panties and a bra, she threw herself onto the stage, lurched and stomped, her body wracked with grief. A slideshow of her childhood photos played in the background. When Britney sang the bridge, "Holding on my heart is breaking / Can't let go," Charlene touched her bulge suggestively, reached for a pair of scissors she'd hidden on one of the bar's rafters earlier in the night and, before most people in the audience realized what was happening, a bright red stream of liquid squirted between Charlene's legs. As Charlene furiously hacked inside her underwear, the beat hit and Britney shouted, "You'll never know what you've got 'til it's gone." Stripping out of the underwear, drenched with fake blood, Charlene swung from a beam on the ceiling and crashed onto the stage, red smears down the insides of her thighs.

The terms had been set, the gauntlet thrown. As the audience screamed, Charlene writhed on the floor like a sexy fetus.

It was Brooklyn drag at its finest: shocking, emotional, and a little gross. "Oh my God," Alotta screamed into the mic. "Who wants a hot dog?"

•••••

On May 3, 2014, Aja and Esai, who had changed his drag name yet again to Momo Shade, shuffled into Lulu's in Greenpoint, another dingy bar with exposed brick and a rickety balcony. Momo was carrying a giant cardboard box that had been painted black and covered with silver glitter, and Aja dragged a battered black suitcase. They headed for the backstage area. That night was the finale of the Mr(s) Williamsburg pageant, and every Brooklyn drag devotee would be there. Eliminated competitors who'd swallowed fire, performed in mascot costumes, stripped off their corsets, and shown their dicks onstage, had come in civilian clothes to watch the show. Merrie Cherry was hosting. She'd painted her face red and her lips blue, darkened her brows and had on a black tunic with embroidery around the neck and sleeves. Thorgy was judging, her blond frizzy wig in a head wrap and a giant fake gold chain around her neck.

Krystal Something-Something had even flown in from Columbus to be a surprise guest judge. "i wanna see something i've never seen before . . . . i wanna see something that makes me stand up in the middle and cry . . . i wanna hear music that cuts at my brain in the most delicious way possible . . . i wanna see a face that isn't yours . . . at this stage in the game a cheering audience means nothing—it's all about your talent . . . . sheep take a seat—make way for the shepherds," she wrote on Facebook just before the competition.

There had been nearly fifty contestants and now there were four. Aja and Charlene would be competing against burlesque performer Miss Cherry Delight and a drag artist named Chris of Hur, who once described her looks as "a lot of accumulation" and was known for wearing stacks of wigs that flopped and flapped around her expressive face. During Chris of Hur's number, she wrestled with a giant ball of hair and fabric in a dress with long pink sleeves. As her curls and twists swung back and forth, she resembled a baby stomping through the house with a blanket draped across its arm. Charlene, wearing a G-string and electrical tape X's over her nipples, lip-synched to an original recording and managed to get the room to sing "Charlene is Miss Williamsburg" in three-part harmony. As the track ended, she took the microphone off its stand and flailed on the ground, bicycle kicking her legs and belting, "I'm a star." Though Charlene was out of tune, she wasn't wrong. She was a star, able to project energy to the back of any room.

All were local performers, but Aja was the only one who'd grown up in Brooklyn. Aja thought she was talented, but that didn't mean it was easy to show up and have this attitude among queers who seemed so much richer, more experienced, and whiter than her. For all these competitors, being chosen as the winner by a panel of their peers would signal to the rest of the community that you were a force and an influencer. But for Aja, it would be an incontrovertible sign of acceptance.

When it was Aja's turn, the sounds of an organ cranking blasted through the speakers. Esai, now Momo, in a red wig with a clown face of white foundation and black triangles painted above and below her eyes, scurried down the balcony stairs holding the cardboard box she'd carried in earlier and opened it onstage. Yellow smoke poured out. One of the judges gasped. Aja appeared at the top of the stairs in a yellow-and-black jester costume. She descended, peered into the box, and a beat began to slap. "Danger danger" a voice growled. Aja looked up, feigned surprise, took off her jester's hat, picked up the box, and tossed it to the side of the stage. She walked slowly toward the crowd, crouched down, and began to lip-synch "I want to be free" as the music reached a crescendo. The song was "Yung Rapunxel" by Azealia Banks and the vocals were all distortion and bravado. Aja, kneeling on the floor, rapping along, became controlled chaos. A coiled spring of energy and rage. Cameras flashed around her. Unbridled enjoyment spread like the smoke through the room, and the audience began to scream. Aja, buoyed by their excitement, walked back up the stairs, slowly took off her yellow dress, and turned around to reveal a yellow-and-black-checked bodysuit underneath. At the top of the stairs, painted like a white-faced clown, she straddled the railing, crouched seductively as she clung to the banister, and launched herself toward the floor, landing in a perfect split.

"Yes, yes, yesssss, go, go," the shrieks from the audience were as loud as the track.

The song had changed again to "Whip It" by Nicki Minaj, a fast, upbeat dance track that felt like it had been made for Aja to lip-synch. Aja mouthed, "'Hey stranger over there / I'm really liking the way you whip it, whip it'" into the adoring face of a young drag queen named Lady Simon. Then Aja twirled back around the stage and slammed into another split.

There was no question. When Aja put her mind to it, when she let herself have fun, embraced a dumb idea, and went wild onstage, she was unstoppable. It looked easy and instinctive because it was. She knew when to turn, when to dip, when to fall onto the ground. The music and the crowd lived inside her. They were her steering wheel and her motor. It was a far cry from the way she'd been received as a seventeen-year-old with a ratty wig, a bad attitude, and duct tape peeking from the sides of her underwear. Aja had kicked, split, dipped, jumped, and done the damn thing. She'd won the five-hundred-dollar prize and she was Mr(s) Williamsburg 2014.

A few days after the competition, much to everyone's delight, the *New York Times* published a short article and photo spread about the event, calling it, "a nine-week extravaganza where anything goes." The article singled out "a performer named Charlene pretending to wound herself with a scissors, finishing up with fake blood sloshing down her legs," and the contest's winner, Aja, described as a "twenty-three-year-old" Williamsburg native, "who said she never expected to see something like this in the old neighborhood."

Overnight, Aja had gone from being a local teenager to a prize-winning drag queen lauded, if somewhat inaccurately, by the most reputable newspaper in the world. In the final days of 2014, Aja celebrated her accomplishments online and looked forward to her future in drag: "I can truly say I'm blessed and ready to accept anything that comes my way! #2014 was phenomenal! #2015 will be even better!!" The taste of victory whetted her appetite for success. She was more determined than ever to dominate the small scene that she'd crashed into nearly three years earlier. With the validation of the win like armor protecting against any doubts, at least for a little while, Aja felt unstoppable.

CHAPTER ELEVEN

Call Me Mother

As the reigning Mr(s) Williamsburg, Aja had ascended to the inner circle of Brooklyn drag. She and Esai were booked and blessed. They even got their own show appropriately titled *Shit Show* at This N That, a newish bar in Williamsburg also known as TNT, and finally had money to take an Uber or a car service to the gig. They'd arrive swathed in neon spandex or dripping with fake diamonds and give rambling, chaotic, and celebratory shows until four in the morning. In the early months of 2015, as Aja was performing "Look at Me Now" by Chris Brown and rapper Busta Rhymes and showing off her ability to lip-synch to the complicated, double-time lyrics, a big, bearded Dominican boy named Kevin Candelario walked in, took a seat at the bar, and watched, captivated.

"I was like, *Who are these two men in wigs just going off onstage?*" he would later tell the hosts of the *Grizzly Kiki* podcast. Kevin had a raspy voice, cute chubby cheeks, and had grown up in the Bronx in a strict Mormon family. "Yes, there are Dominican Mormons," he'd explain when people looked surprised. Sad and overweight, he'd been quietly obsessed with drag for years, ordering wigs and heels online and hiding them in his closet. He'd recently taken a drag name, Kandy Muse, after the Warhol superstar Candy Darling, and started to think of himself not as a lonely boy who was good at makeup but as a performer worthy of a stage. He was out that night in search of drag queens. After their set, Kevin sauntered over to Momo Shade, formerly known as Esai. As Kevin was complimenting Esai's hair and his heels, Aja interrupted.

"Let's go, Momo," the older queen demanded. "I've gotta get up early."

"Hey," Kevin said. Now that she was standing next to him, he recognized Aja. Years earlier, they had traded dick pics and chatted over Facebook and AOL messenger. They'd hung out at the park once but had no chemistry. "It was the most awkward half hour of my life," Kevin would later say when telling the story to the *Grizzly Kiki* hosts. But Kevin and Momo were chatting like old friends, so Aja sighed and agreed that he could come back and crash at the apartment. After that night, Kevin just started showing up. He raided their closets, rifled through their makeup, and transformed into Kandy Muse. When they were going out in drag, so was she. Aja joked that being friends with Kandy was like "when you feed a stray cat on your street one time and it never leaves."

Aja and Momo Shade introduced Kandy Muse to another boy who was calling himself Dahlia Sin in drag. Aja, Momo, Kandy, and Dahlia started going out together, swapping bodysuits and heels, giving shows at bars across Brooklyn, and occasionally getting fall-down, puke-in-a-taxi drunk. Mostly, however, they hung out at Aja's house doing makeup and insulting one another. They spent hours online, posting and commenting on photos, chatting with boys on messenger, watching videos, and live-streaming themselves getting ready for gigs. By 2015, a red lip and a smoky eye wasn't going to cut it. YouTube made it possible for drag queens to create makeup tutorials demonstrating what products and techniques they used to create their signature looks. Several influential YouTube makeup queens had been cast on *RuPaul's Drag Race*, and their advice and style had made extreme makeup the norm. Everyone was expected to have a distinctive face that complimented their features and made them instantly recognizable in a photograph. Contouring had become an essential part of a drag beat.

"I gotta contour, but in my country we call it 'cunt-tour,'" Aja joked, spreading a clay-colored foundation around the perimeter of her face. Softening a masculine face, contouring and blending it to look traditionally feminine, is a feat of artistry, but it also shows just how easy it is to manipulate the perception of gender. Drag queen makeup tricks the eye to make brows look higher and thinner, eyelids bigger, chins and foreheads smaller, and cheekbones more pronounced. For all the ways that drag subverts gender, embraces fluidity, and complicates our assumptions about what it means to be male or female, drag makeup often takes an essentialist approach to an otherwise mystical transformation. Of course, faces often have both masculine and feminine features, and plenty of men wear makeup as well, but historically, a painted face is a female face. Drag queens are painting for the stage and increasingly for the camera. Bright lights—stage and studio—can mask flaws in a well-painted face or expose them when the makeup doesn't work, but a face without highlighter, contour, glitter, and overdrawn lips risks fading into the shadows. It wasn't always this way. In the 1980s and '90s, drag makeup was simpler—a bright lip, a smoky eye, some severe blush to create the illusion of a sharp cheekbone. Little that resembled the carved-out, baked-in, contoured and highlighted faces that Aja and other queens painted. Even during the "Supermodel" era of the 1990s, RuPaul didn't contour her nose or cheeks (though she did shave her eyebrows and draw them higher) instead relying on makeup to emphasize her natural features.

Contour can soften a jaw, make a wide nose or flat cheeks seem pointy. Depending on how contour is applied, it can also make a drag king—or someone with a more stereotypically feminine face—appear more masculine. Before blending the contour, however, it looked as though Aja had painted a whitish upside-down triangle on the center of her face and drawn a red ring around it. "If you don't blend, you're gonna look like painting by numbers," Aja joked while pressing the sponge methodically across her face.

The jigsaw puzzle of lines and triangles became a complexion. Once the foundation was well distributed, she "cooked" her makeup, applying powder with a round puff so that it would stay relatively dry and creaseless. There was only one lamp in Aja's room, but if one of the other girls painting beside her complained, Aja snapped, "You have to *earn* the light."

As they worked, Aja, Momo, Kandy, and Dahlia talked shit.

"We're transitioning, slowly," Aja might say, pausing to cackle. "Turning from a caterpillar to another caterpillar."

Momo liked to sing along to whatever song was playing. As she painted, she talked to herself approvingly—"These eyebrows look mad nice, they be looking awesome"—and Aja would heckle her from the other side of the room.

"OK, bitch, you flattering yourself."

"Don't be shady, be a lady," someone would admonish as Momo waved off the snide remark.

A new dynamic had emerged now that Aja had an audience for her barbs and insults and her stories about Momo's drunken exploits, her bad outfits, her mother trying to wheedle cash out of Aja. They could both be incredibly shady, but Aja's meanness was performative. She had been the older, more-knowing and capable one for so long that no one, not even Momo, questioned her eminence. The disparity in their relationship was firmly established. The undercurrent of resentment was almost imperceptible amid the everyday chiding and teasing common among gay kids with big imaginations and even bigger attitudes—but it was there, and it gnawed at Momo while she beat her face alongside her best-friend-boyfriend-mother-tormenter.

The deeper into the paint, the crazier things would get. "I think the chin should be pink, looking like balls be hittin' the chin," Aja once said. "I got those 'bitch, I took a Xanax when I was pregnant' cheeks."

By the time their faces were set, they'd be sucking in their cheeks and angling their heads from side to side to inspect their beat. "I'm feeling cunt, feeling my fantasy," someone would announce.

"Girl you look like Cinderella tonight," Kandy might tell Aja. Cinderella or Cindy was their word for a face that was flat and square like a brick, because "what's heavier than a brick? A cinder block."

As Aja examined herself in the mirror she'd pucker and purse her bright red lips. "These lips are Wi-Fi lips," she'd once said to the room. "I sucked a dick from fifteen feet away. You mad? Only a real bitch could give a man orgasm without touching him."

Momo would occasionally lean over to inspect her own, much simpler beat in the light. Her baby face was more feminine, and so it took less makeup to transform it. Momo painted a comparatively thin line of black above her top lashes and contoured lightly. She'd finish the look with silver eyeshadow and a fat red lip. It never took that long, especially since she rarely glued down her brows or contoured her forehead and chin. Once they'd used makeup to create the illusion of cleavage, daubed perfume behind their ears and along their clavicles, glued down their lace-front wigs, and teased their hair as high as it would go, they went out in a cloud of hair spray, feathers, insults, and translucent powder. Piling into cabs, with their phones "on live" streaming their rides to the bar, they burst through the doors with a "hey, hey, love," and a double kiss for every acquaintance and queen and sweet-looking boy they encountered on their way to the back of the room.

"Oh, are y'all the Haus of Aja? Look, it's Aja and her daughters," people would joke when they came in. Aja, Momo, Kandy, and Dahlia would get annoyed. But it kept happening, people joked that they were the Haus of Aja, and the four young Latinx New Yorkers who hung out together and shared a love of drag and a sense of humor started to think, *Why not form a house?* Aja already called Momo her drag daughter; what's a few more children? In the drag world, performers who work together or are especially close call one another sisters or brothers. "Give it up for this queen; she's my sister," is a vote of confidence and a sign of affection. Aja did drag at gay bars to make money, but she had never lost the sense of chosen family she'd found on the piers among voguing and ballroom queens. While white queens were seen as unique and allowed to flourish as individuals in the scene, locally born Black and Latinx queers were often lumped together whether they wanted to be sisters or not. Aja, Kandy, Momo, and Dahlia decided that there could be strength in numbers. As Aja later put it: "You want to call us the Haus of Aja? OK, we'll be the Haus of Aja and make money off of it, thank you!"

·····

A drag house made them seem legitimate, a force to be reckoned with. Legitimacy was increasingly important because Aja, having turned twenty-one on January 4, 2015, was now eligible to audition for *RuPaul's Drag Race*. Not every artist wants mainstream celebrity, and there were certainly drag performers in Brooklyn and beyond who had no desire to be on TV. However, drag, even the messy, inclusive, artistic kind that was practiced in Aja's backyard, was a commercial art form. Performers were paid in tips and small fees from the bars—a couple hundred dollars a week if you were really booked; their job was to pull in crowds who'd buy drinks and pay cover charges. Doing drag was expensive. Even if you shoplifted your makeup, made your own clothing, claimed hand-me-down shoes and jewelry, the bits and bobs—tights, glitter, Elmer's glue sticks for covering your brows—would add up. Drag wasn't grant funded or included in highbrow cultural events—it was popular and accessible. For any queen who didn't have a day job or parental assistance, cash was king, and the best way in 2015 for a drag performer to get paid was by appearing on *RuPaul's Drag Race*.

Not everyone in Brooklyn was happy about this. *Drag Race* prioritized and extended its platform to a narrow style of drag—cisgender men dressing as hyperfeminine women—and excluded the trans people, women, drag kings, and gender-nonbinary performers who thrived in Brooklyn. RuPaul further alienated some queers when he defended the show's refusal to cast openly trans women and embraced the word "tranny," a slur against transgender people. (While some trans-identified people have reappropriated the word, most view it as deeply offensive.)

"I love the word 'tranny,'" said RuPaul, who has never publicly identified as trans, in a 2012 interview with the *Huffington Post*. "No one has ever said the word 'tranny' in a derogatory sense."

This statement was not only defensive but wrong. The very fact that some trans activists reclaimed the word was an indication of its cruel history. Trans people have long been a punch line in popular culture, derided and dehumanized as they experienced some of the highest rates of violence in the country. Trans people are frequently discriminated against by doctors, employers, and educators. Family rejection, lack of access to health care, and harassment all contribute to higher rates of homelessness, suicide, and self-harm than the general population. If any group needed and contributed to the life-changing power of drag, it was the people who'd fought to live outside gender binaries full time, the people who'd defied social expectations and suffered mightily because of who they were.

As the pushback over RuPaul's comments persisted, he continued to defend the playful use of these terms. "I can call myself a nigger, faggot, tranny all I want to, because I've fucking earned the right to do it," he told the podcast host Marc Maron in 2014. "I've lived the life." RuPaul later denied that it was the transgender community that was even criticizing him. This, too, was wrong. A number of former *Drag Race* contestants had spoken out against RuPaul's use of the term, including some who had come out as trans after appearing on the show. Yet RuPaul continued to insist that his critics were "fringe people . . . looking for story lines to strengthen their identity as victims." This put him at odds with transgender queens and activists, including many Brooklyn-based performers, who resented the way *Drag Race* seemed to gloss over drag's rich history as a refuge for gender-nonconforming people. At the bars and in group texts and social media posts, Brooklyn performers dragged Ru with more sarcasm and less restraint. As the most famous drag queen in the world, some of this was to be expected. The show could feel out of touch with the community.

"Ru is going to die of old AIDS," one especially sharp-tongued queen drunkenly slurred into the mic.

"*Drag Race* is for straight housewives," a drag king complained.

While some people defended RuPaul as an icon from a different generation who couldn't be expected to have all the most progressive political views, many of the Brooklyn queens who auditioned understood that *Drag Race* wasn't perfect—but it was the best opportunity out there. Ideals were great, but so was one hundred thousand dollars and a chance to tour the world.

Aja had gotten used to the attention and the income that came with being regularly booked. She watched *Drag Race* religiously, and she understood that a spot on the show would bring validation and financial security, even to those who only survived for a few episodes.

She knew she was talented, and she wanted to share this talent. She was young and she was hungry—both metaphorically and literally. She assumed that if she got cast, she'd excel, just like she had at the Mr(s) Williamsburg pageant. Like so many other queens in Brooklyn, her attitude toward the show was one of pragmatism and convenience. If *Drag Race* was willing to embrace her, then she would embrace *Drag Race*.

Aja made an audition tape for season nine of *RuPaul's Drag Race* in early 2016. In the video, she lip-synched to the RuPaul song "U Wear It Well" while walking along the Bushwick streets at night. She performed against the black iron gate in front of her mother's house and in front of a shuttered store, a junkyard, and while climbing on scaffolding. She showed off the looks she'd made over the years: baby-doll dresses, catsuits, ruffled skirts.

A few months after submitting the tape, Aja, Momo, Kandy, and Dahlia booked a trip to Los Angeles for RuPaul's DragCon, a three-day convention centered around the show and the polished, camera-ready drag it portrayed. The hope was that the producers would meet Aja, like her, and cast her on season nine. After paying for the flights and an Airbnb a thirty-minute drive from the Los Angeles Convention Center, they were "some broke-ass bitches," Aja later recalled. At the airport, Kandy discovered that her suitcase was thirty pounds over the weight limit. As the people in line behind them at the ticket counter sucked their teeth and fidgeted impatiently, Kandy opened everyone's bags and began piling dresses and shoes into Momo's and Dahlia's suitcases to avoid paying extra.

"Weigh it out, ma, weigh it out," she said, handing the bag back to the worker behind the counter and beaming when it weighed in under fifty pounds.

On their first morning in town, they got a free Uber ride to the convention after they complained that the driver had called them "faggots."

"We lied to get credit," Aja would later admit. "In all fairness, we were walking to the car and the driver sped away." Aja hadn't heard him utter the slur, but she'd seen an opportunity in that moment of likely homophobia. When the next car came, it was economy-sized and they all piled in. It was "a car full of clowns, and it didn't fit any of us," Aja said. She had on a red-and-gold crown that dipped down to her forehead and a gauzy red floor-length jacket over a red bra and pants with a thick gold belt. She'd worn two chestnut brown wigs, one on top of the other. As she was getting out of the car's back seat, the hook for hanging dry-cleaned clothes caught on her wigs and yanked off her hair. Wigless and stunned outside the convention center she began to fall apart. She had no money for food and had barely eaten in two days. She'd staked everything on this chance to meet the *Drag Race* producers and convince them to put her on the show.

"I'm not going inside, get me a car home." She collapsed on the ground.

"Girl, we don't got money for an extra car so you can't go nowhere," Kandy snapped.

Aja was spiraling. The rest of the Haus of Aja stood in a semicircle around her shouting for her to "get up, bitch" and "go inside." Aja was the undisputed leader, the most experienced drag queen among them, and the most successful, and she felt the pressure of their expectations and needs. The only way out was through those convention doors and onto *RuPaul's Drag Race*. She took a deep breath, stood up, dusted off her wigs, and fixed her crown. "I'm not going to let the wig fool me today. I'm going in."

In early July 2016, two months after their trip to LA, Momo Shade was shopping on Knickerbocker Avenue. Her phone buzzed with a call from Aja. "What's up?" she asked.

On the other end of the line she could hear Aja sniffling and gasping for breath. For years, Momo had depended on Aja for survival. They'd both dropped out of high school partly because drag was so consuming, but also because, in Momo's words, school was "a waste of time." When people asked why she'd left, she'd wave her hand dismissively and say, "I don't need a piece of paper to tell me I completed, you know, a course." They'd built their strange careers together through sheer energy and charisma, but at some point, Momo had gotten tired of the arguing and the bossiness. Though Momo had lived with Aja off and on since she was fourteen, it was still Aja's mother's house and she would always be the friend crashing because her own family wasn't fit to take care of her. Now that they were the Haus of Aja, Momo felt even more trapped. She had always been the ride or die, but in the end it was a teenage relationship, and increasingly she wanted her own life.

Standing in the store on Knickerbocker, Momo was, as she'd been for so long, Aja's first call in an emergency. "What's wrong? Is Gizmo OK?" Momo asked, worried Aja's elderly pug had died.

"No. They called me," Aja replied.

"Werk!" Momo shouted in the middle of the store. *RuPaul's Drag Race* had asked Aja to do a psychiatric evaluation. This was the final step before a queen was cast on the show. Momo had butterflies. This was it. Momo knew that if Aja got on the show, it could help her own chances when she was finally old enough to audition. The show liked to cast previous contestants' drag daughters, sisters, and mothers. Momo resolved to hold on, keep her mouth shut when Kandy told her she looked like a thumb and Aja told embarrassing stories about Momo's family on Facebook live, secretly hoping that Aja would get cast, go to LA, "and leave me the freak alone."

Aja completed the show's mandatory psychiatric evaluation, and, on July 26, 2016, her phone rang while she, Momo, Kandy, and Dahlia were in line at Walgreens to buy contact-lens solution. Aja had been cast on *RuPaul's Drag Race* season nine.

"It was equal parts excitement and fear," Aja later said. "I had no money to get nice things; I went home for the next three weeks and made whatever I could."

As Aja got ready to leave, she got sick, her body aching and feverish, but she kept sewing. When her machine broke and she couldn't afford to fix it, a designer named BCALLA, who'd been making looks for drag queens for as long as there'd been a Brooklyn drag scene, invited her to take clothes from his archive.

Aja entered the workroom in a floor-length black vinyl BCALLA cloak covered in cushy black vinyl spikes over a plum-colored minidress decorated with rows of similar black vinyl spikes. It was a dark anime fantasy, designed not for women but for drag queens, and it was perfectly suited to Aja's playful video-game-inspired aesthetic. She was the last queen to enter the workroom. "Your edges are officially snatched," she announced as she dropped the coat. She posed at the workroom door and the rest of the season nine contestants responded with a chorus of "yaaasss."

Aja looked to her left. *Who is this bald-ass bitch?* she thought, and then screamed so loudly the producers made her stop and repeat the entrance. When she successfully kept her shit together on the second try, she rushed over to the group and pulled a tall, bald queen in a felt crown and black vintage sequin dress in for a sincere and enthusiastic hug.

"I'm so happy to see you," Aja exclaimed, and the other queen, who had a low voice and a jagged unibrow, wrapped her arms around Aja. Brooklyn, drag, and mutual respect were most of what Sasha Velour and Aja had in common. But any local sister was a welcome sight when you'd flown three thousand miles to change your life and hopefully become a star.

"I love Aja," Sasha said during a one-on-one interview in that first episode of season nine. "She is the number one name in Brooklyn that people are talking about right now."

Aja greeted each of the other queens in the workroom with double air-kisses and gentle hugs. She had packed up her life and said goodbye to her drag daughters. It felt like "for the first time in a long time, I didn't have to fight someone or defend myself," she said later. In the workroom, she looked around, giddy, certain that this now-global platform would bring admiration, success, and adventure.

Aja put her hands to her face, overcome with excitement. "I feel like I'm at home with so much talented girls," she said. It felt like maybe the hard part was over and she was finally going to thrive.

CHAPTER TWELVE

"Wear a Crown, Fuck with Gender."

Sasha Velour's path to reality TV was unconventional, even for Brooklyn. Born Alexander Steinberg in Berkeley, California, Sasha, who was assigned male at birth but is gender-fluid and uses the pronouns "she" and "her," grew up in a southern Illinois college town, dancing to *Swan Lake* in the living room. Sasha's mother, an editor of the journal *Slavic Review*, was an encouraging playmate, dressing Sasha up as the Wicked Witch of the West, making her a Dracula cape, and sitting for hours at her "beauty shop" as she contemplated how to best style her mom's fine, curly brown hair. After studying modern literature at Vassar College in upstate New York and landing a prestigious Fulbright scholarship in Russia, Sasha went out in drag for the first time to the local gay bar during a visit home. Later that year, she moved to White River Junction, Vermont, to get a master's of fine arts from the Center for Cartoon Studies. It seemed like an odd choice for a twenty-four-year-old intellectual with a love of costumes and dress-up, but Sasha was no stranger to small-town life, and she wanted to take all the academic obsessions she'd developed during her adult life and render them accessible and beautiful to the uninitiated through comic books. Sasha vowed that all the comics she created would be about queer people and worked hard to incorporate complex ideas about gender, sexuality, race, class, and history into the work.

A picturesque stop on Amtrak's Vermonter line, White River

Junction has a population of less than three thousand, and a ramshackle, vaguely historic air. Surrounded by rolling hills and sixty-foot spruce trees whose branches grow heavy with snow in the winter, the town has one of the only music venues in the region and several quirky cultural centers exhibiting local art and hosting fashion shows. Aging hipsters escaping the pressures of the city, cool kids who've found solace in northeastern small-town life, and the people who never left formed a small, enthusiastic community. Here, Sasha made a semifictional comic about the 1969 Stonewall riots, critiquing the way white gay men were often given credit for starting the riots, when it was actually Black and Latinx trans women, drag queens, street kids, and lesbians who were the driving force in the historic standoff with the police. Another comic was "deeply queer and firmly anti-corporate," with a "kind of a meta-narrative about white masculinity," Sasha explained in a Q and A on her blog. Her work could be heady and esoteric, but the overly saturated color and inviting shapes drew readers into the stories.

In White River Junction, Sasha also began assembling a crew that would carry her through the next five turbulent, heartbreaking, and joyous years as a drag queen. Sasha first noticed John Jacob Lee at a local Turkish café. "It was love at first sight," she would later tell a reporter for the *Valley News*. Johnny, as he was known to friends, was an actor and dancer working the music theater circuit, in town for a production of *Annie* at the Northern Stage theater. Imagine their luck to find each other in the cold, lush environs of Vermont's Upper Valley on these narrow streets of gabled and gambrel-roofed colonial revival houses.

Of course, they weren't the only people in White River Junction with open hearts and creative spirits. Nancy, who would later give herself the surname "The Girl" and start a business selling gender-inclusive vintage fashions, had grown up a few miles from town and gone to college in New York City. She'd gotten married soon after graduating and was back working at Revolution, a local vintage clothing store. Nancy had a mass of blond curls, a wide smile, and knack for costumes and friendship. She met Sasha as the aspiring drag queen browsed the women's racks of tulle and satin at Revolution. Dress-up and costumes had always been Nancy's favorite things in the world. Trying on outfits and playing with clothing was like writing in a journal, a way to explore and express her feelings. Vermont was blessed with world-class thrifting. Its large elderly population, its remoteness, and the affordable rents made fertile ground for ambitious upscale shops and hoarding enterprises alike. Across the region known as the Upper Valley small cottages by the side of the road and multilevel houses were converted into fantastical caves of boots, jewelry, purses, silk pajamas, fur coats, and old toys.

For fashion-obsessed artists, plunging headfirst into these overflowing repositories for old people's stuff and pulling beaded frocks, cowboy boots, old dolls, and petticoats off the shelves was like being kids let loose in a candy store. These fabric-filled cocoons, brimming with evening gowns and bursting with shawls, were the perfect places for a drag queen with a classic sensibility to hone her style. Nancy's mom was the same size as Sasha, and, thanks to her job in local politics, she had an ever-growing evening gown collection and would regularly consign dresses at Revolution. Nancy would put them aside for Sasha to try on or wear.

All this dress-up inspired Johnny, too. In the spring of 2013, as Sasha was finishing her thesis for cartoon school, the couple produced a play called *Whatever She Wants: A Drag Musicale* at the Main Street Museum, a quirky cultural center in a converted firehouse known for its taxidermy collection, which included rabbits with wings and antlers and stuffed foxes frolicking alongside plastic toys. In the campy absurd revelry, "Veronica, a night club chanteuse on the downslope of her career" and "Jayne, an upstart ingénue hellbent on success" battle for the stage. As they rehearsed, blocked, and rewrote lines, Johnny and Sasha fell into a comfortable rhythm. Johnny asked Nancy to be in charge of the costumes, and then, when one of the actors dropped out, he gave her the third-largest part, that of Sugar, Veronica's biggest fan, who would wait outside of every show, shrieking and swooning.

White River Junction had some upscale restaurants and a decent amount of arts and culture for such a small town, but residents were titillated and confused by the prospect of a "drag" play. "What is drag?" customers at Revolution asked Nancy as they tried on hand-made dresses, silk vintage gowns, and nineties rompers. Nancy tried to explain, but the truth was they were all kind of winging it. While Nancy understood how an outfit could tell an entire story about a character, Johnny was a theater aficionado and talented choreographer, and Sasha had snuck out of her parents' house to do drag at a home-town bar, no one had much experience doing makeup or making a coherent drag look. The trio would gather in the basement of the Main Street Museum and google "contouring" and "drag padding" and "we tried to figure out how these faces and bodies were built," Nancy said. They bought padded bras from Walmart and Nancy followed the instructions for contouring in celebrity makeup artist Kevyn Aucoin's book *Making Faces*. Nancy discovered that by cinching her waist with a corset and pushing up her bust she could transform her own shape into a bombshell fantasy. When she was growing up in the 1990s, lithe, sinewy arms, concave collarbones, flat stomachs and narrow, almost boyish, waists dominated fashion editorials and advertising. Supermodels—women over five foot nine inches tall who wore a size zero—had the bodies many young girls coveted, but without the genes or some truly miserable dieting, there was no hope of conforming to those absurd beauty standards. Now, creating looks for a drag show, Nancy was discovering that shapes and sizes were relative. *If men can make their bodies look like this*, she realized, *I one hundred percent can.*

Dressing up, putting on plays, and expressing themselves through clothes was like being kids again. But they weren't kids, they were adults with adult problems, and they needed reinvention and release more than ever. On a trip to New Orleans for Mardi Gras in 2013, Nancy went to a masquerade ball. "Being surrounded by that many beautiful costumes, and being in one myself, made me feel happy in a way I hadn't felt in a long time," she later said. During the party she realized that her marriage was horrible and that, if she ever wanted to feel like herself again, she needed to get a divorce. The drag had reminded her of who she really was. "In trying on a character, I actually found myself again," she said. She started experimenting with her look. She contoured her face with makeup every day. She put on shapewear and padded bras to go to the grocery store. The drag—and by then she understood that even though she wasn't a man dressing as a woman, this was drag—became her armor. It had been dress-up, costumes, and partying that had finally given her the push she needed to leave her marriage, and it would be dress-up that got her through those sad, exhausted, scary first months after the breakup.

For Sasha, too, clothes and makeup seemed to be a way to show feelings without having to talk about them. As Sasha would later explain on *Drag Race*, her mother had been diagnosed with cancer soon after Sasha finished college. Like Nancy, the young queen was using dress-up—not just drawing a character but becoming one—to process the fear and pain of her mother's illness.

By the time Sasha finished cartoon school, her mother had lost all her hair after repeated chemotherapy treatments. She'd text Sasha selfies, wispy strands forming a halo around her mostly bald pate. "I look like Gollum!" she'd said. Sasha's mother was adventurous and free-spirited, but the baldness was still a burden. She refused to wear a wig—they were itchy and "she felt they were for other people's comfort, not her own," Sasha wrote in an essay on Facebook. She stopped wearing hats and allowed herself to be bald. Sasha had always experimented with her hair, first shaving it off in high school just to see what it would look like. Once Sasha started doing drag in earnest, making it a conscientious part of a larger art practice, she didn't eschew wigs altogether, but she questioned their ubiquity. "Is the idea that a drag queen must have a giant wig tied up in the same beauty oppression that correlates female sexiness with long hair?" she asked in that Facebook essay.

In July 2013, after Sasha graduated from cartoon school, she and Johnny moved to Brooklyn. In a renovated Bed-Stuy apartment with some artful prewar details on a block where the sunsets glowed cotton candy pink, they cobbled together a convincing mid-century living room decorated with Sasha's ever-expanding art collection. Everything in New York City throbbed with history and art. The graffiti on the buildings and in the subway stations, the architecture, the shop windows, even the advertising on the subway seemed stylish and fashionable. During the fall and winter of 2013, Sasha made comics, taught English language classes for money, and got dressed up in drag.

It was Johnny's idea to make a zine about their mutual obsession with the art form. Sasha had been thinking about calling herself Sasha Velour, an homage to the inexpensive fabric that looked and felt luxurious. It would be a nod to the falsity and fakeness inherent in good drag. Johnny took the Velour name as well, and the zine project, which they called *VYM*, became part of the House of Velour. In a fundraising video Sasha made enthusiastic pronouncements about the power of a drag magazine to "showcase and celebrate the smarts and the honesty and the weird campy freaky side of our community that's wonderful and that can inspire absolutely everyone on the planet."

"This could be a revolution," Sasha continued before collapsing in giggles. Their fundraising and publicity efforts drew a surprising amount of media attention to the project. For idealistic reporters it was a feel-good, erudite story of transformation and self-actualization.

Drag "laughs in the face of identity, specifically the limitations of gender," Sasha told a reporter for her hometown paper back in Illinois, the Champaign-Urbana *News-Gazette*. Their rhetoric could seem lofty, at times, like when Sasha compared *VYM* and drag to the Talmud, the ancient book of Jewish law, in an interview with the *Jewish Daily Forward*. But mostly it was affirming and engaging.

VYM's influences were legion. The old-fashioned pageant queens who called themselves "female impersonators"; the wild performance artists who used drag as a way to offend and assault the status quo; the fashion icons who walked runways for designer Thierry Mugler; the queens from Brazil, Australia, and Thailand. In addition to studying the East Village Pyramid Club scene; the work of John Waters's muse Divine; the pageant world created by Mother Flawless Sabrina and upended by the legendary House of LaBeija; Linda Simpson's drag magazine *My Comrade*; the crooning, dreamy performances of drag king Stormé DeLarverie and the queens of the Jewel Box Revue, Sasha and Johnny set out to represent and include a wide range of drag performers in the pages of their zine. If drag was about gender, it seemed natural that it be about all genders, including drag kings and people who identified as female in their day-to-day lives and did drag as "femme queens." Drag kings and queens had different concepts of glamour but both performed a campy, exaggerated version of gender meant to elicit emotion and convey a fantasy.

"Drag kings show me that you can stylize masculinity, too," Sasha once told an interviewer for the blog *Bedford and Bowery*. "It's not neutral and can be totally dramatic and silly, too, and that being a man is performative as well." Sasha and Johnny knew drag kings had to be included in their drag zine and, in June 2014, Johnny took to Facebook to see if anyone could recommend a drag king for a project he was working on.

·····

Though drag queens get most of the mainstream attention, drag kings—performers who explore masculinity and masculine culture through lip-synching, live singing, comedy, and theater—have been a touchstone of the queer world for decades. Drag kings are often lesbians who put on shows for other lesbians, but they can also be transgender men—people who were assigned female at birth and now identify and live as men—and gender-nonconforming people who are drawn to masculinity as performers. Just as some gay men experience both pleasure and shame in their own femininity, many queer women and trans men grow up struggling with gender non-conformity in a world that expects them to be not only heterosexual but girlish and demure.

By the end of the twentieth century, an unprecedented number of female-assigned people were coming out as trans masculine, taking hormones, and publicly grappling with the onus of male privilege. The drag king scene was a safe space to make fun of men and to emulate them in front of a crowd of fellow queers who were also often living outside gender norms. In the 1990s and early 2000s, kings found enthusiastic audiences at lesbian bars in cities as far flung as Columbus, Ohio; Sarasota, Florida; and Enid, Oklahoma. Where drag queens revered divas, pop stars, Hollywood starlets, vixens, and femme fatales, common drag king inspirations were icons like Johnny Cash and Elvis, charismatic sex symbols like Prince, glam rockers like Elton John and David Bowie, and rockabilly rebels, jocks, bikers, leather men, Greek gods, and teddy bears. Though they were never as visible to the mainstream or as well compensated as their drag queen counterparts, kings like Murray Hill and the Backdoor Boys stuffed their boxer briefs, clipped on their ties, slicked back their hair, and put on sold-out shows across the country for hordes of queer people eager to celebrate, lust after, and laugh at these exaggerated performances of masculinity.

In 1996, Mo B. Dick, the rockabilly drag king alias of a go-go dancer named Mo Fischer, began a weekly drag king party called Club Casanova at the Pyramid Club. "My motto was instead of being an angry woman, I became a funny man," Mo, with glued-on sideburns, skintight denim, and a perfectly styled pompadour, told an interviewer for the Addresses Project website about her early years as a drag king on the Lower East Side. "The very first time I dressed in drag and didn't get catcalled or harassed or verbally accosted, it was just amazing! A woman cannot walk freely down the street without fear and repercussions."

As the show moved to a few different bars in the neighborhood, a drag king community formed around it. "You walked in, there was a drag king at the door collecting money," Mo told the Addresses Project. "And you'd look over and see a drag king deejay, there were drag king go-go dancers, drag kings milling about in the crowd, and then a drag king show."

The show became a hit, and, after Mo was cast in the John Waters movie *Pecker*, she took Club Casanova on the road, selling out shows in dozens of cities a year and performing for thousands of people. Drag kings were on the map. There were drag king anthologies and glossy photo books. Drag kings showed up on the TV show *Sex and the City* and in documentaries. Within the queer community, drag kings broke down barriers between lesbians and gay men by pointing out all the blatant homoeroticism in straight male culture.

"So much of drag king culture is about making two macho guys be gay and wind up making out," explained one king. For many, dressing up as the jocks and boy band idols their high school crushes lusted after was fantasy fulfillment. "The Backdoor Boys go for all the fag subtext of these homoerotic groups, exploring their interpretation of the real meaning of the hit song 'I Want It That Way," explained sex educator and feminist author Tristan Taormino in the *Village Voice* in 1999. "It's all about butt fucking."

•••••

If the Velours were looking for a drag king in Brooklyn in 2014, their best bet was Saturday night at Outpost, a queer coffee shop about three miles southwest of Bushwick. Outside, a glittery hand-painted sign read, "Drag King Show! Everyone welcome!" Downstairs, amid industrial freezers and fifty-pound bags of onions, the cast of Switch n' Play, a loose collective of queer women and trans men, were getting ready for the show.

Since 2006, Switch n' Play shows had been a permeable, non-hierarchical space where fluidity reigned. Full of group choreography and lip syncs, the performances gently poked fun at masculine tropes—the bad boy, the greaser, the jock. Favorite acts featured "Macho Man," by the Village People, classic rock icons like Queen, and a gay interpretation of "Save a Horse (Ride a Cowboy)" with full choreography. Backstreet Boys' songs were a Switch n' Play staple. When they performed them, their hips gyrating, group members grinding on one another, the audience of typically mild-mannered queers shrieked and hollered like teenage girls at a stadium show. The group's goal was warmth, fun, and affirmation for everyone: all genders, all identities, all ethnicities and experiences. Years before Merrie Cherry threw the first DragNet competition or Aja and Esai walked through the doors of Metropolitan, Switch n' Play members painted on goatees and sideburns with mascara and eyeliner, wore matching striped athletic tube socks, and lip-synched to boy bands and popular country songs as a way of feeling less isolated in the big city. They were sometimes nerdy, their looks cobbled together from gym wear and suits purchased at thrift stores or borrowed from guy friends and sometimes—at least at first—not very good. The lip syncs could be sloppy, the choreography spotty, and the outfits like Halloween costumes. However, they were real, affirming, and joyful, and so they managed to find a steady following among Brooklyn's more earnest and tender queers. For the people who were looking for a safe space, who were lonely, struggling with their gender identity, overflowing with frustrated energy and searching for an outlet or a way to play with masculinity, these kings offered something deeply felt and desperately needed.

In 2006, a small, quiet recent Smith College graduate met one of Switch n' Play's founding members when he answered a Craigslist ad for a "queer/trans roommate share." In their apartment, K.James would watch the collective rehearse, desperate to play along. In the wider world he was shy, but from the very first time he got onstage to lip-synch the R & B hit "I Wanna Sex U Up" by Color Me Badd in 2008, he was a force. For the next decade, he explored and perfected a mischievously sexual and flashy persona, all traits that could be difficult to express in the regular world. It wasn't that he'd swing his hips, grind on his knees, or roll his body with the music—every moderately sexy drag king did that—it was the way he did it, with a deep, serious smoldering *Hey, girl* look in his eyes and the slightest knowing smirk. One glance from those gangly, jangly hips up to his face could melt even the most skeptical, seen-it-all queers.

In a world where objectifying men means drooling over pecs or biceps and fantasizing about sweat and dirt, K.James, with his faux hawk, his thin legs, and his sparkling costumes, somehow managed to be sex incarnate. It was the manifestation of every softly crooning boy band member, the smolder of every hormonal jock's stare, the fluttery feeling smitten preteens get when listening to *NSYNC sing "it's gonna be me" or claim "you're all I ever wanted." K.James's sex appeal was equal opportunity. Not safe, but not dangerous or dark, either. Onstage he was the natural outpouring of a gender identity and desire too complex to fit into mainstream norms. The objective, he once explained in an article for Mic.com, was "taking control of how people see me. Because trans people are objectified: We face violence and street harassment, or just being generally stared at, being objectified and pathologized by doctors in the medical community as a whole. But when you're a trans person and you get to put yourself onstage, you're basically inviting people to objectify you . . . it's like, 'I'm consenting to this, but I'm steering the story and taking control of the narrative of what you get to see.' It's basically feeling empowered in that space with people staring at you."

Not everyone loved drag kings. To some queer women, jocks and bad boys weren't cute or carefree fodder for impersonation: they were the people who had bullied them in school and shouted "dyke" from car windows. Many queers couldn't understand why bona fide lesbians who'd worked so hard to free themselves from the clutches of the patriarchy would want to embrace it—even for a night. But, for many, the fact that this was deep camp and extremely tongue-in-cheek made it easier to indulge in the guilty pleasure of watching a cute boy strut across the stage.

K.James was not only a formidable solo drag performer: by 2011, he and his girlfriend, who would come to be known as Miss Malice, were a local queer drag power couple. They met in 2008 at Smith College, in Northampton, Massachusetts, a town that boasted the most lesbians per capita in the United States. Malice's mother was a feminist who believed that fighting the patriarchy meant distancing herself from anything soft or girly. She encouraged her daughter to do the same. When Malice was ten years old, her mother dressed her as a biker for Halloween in a leather hat and studded jacket. They both have a hereditary disability that can make it difficult to walk, and Malice's mother's solution was to hide in baggy clothes so no one would notice. Malice had other ideas. To her, femininity was not reserved for straight women and it did not signal weakness, submission, or frivolity. In college, Malice had learned about the bar femmes of the fifties and sixties lionized in *Boots of Leather, Slippers of Gold*, a history of working-class bombshells who dated rough, hard-living butch women, sewed their own clothes, and made glamour from nothing. These women were tough, larger-than-life lesbians, but they were also unequivocally feminine. When Malice left an abusive relationship in college she found comfort in a hard femme exterior. She wore lipstick and winged eyeliner to her 10:00 a.m. classes and took up smoking so that when her ex-girlfriend was surprised to see her outside with a cigarette, she could say, "Yes, I smoke now—fuck you." Or at least she could think it and sneer. It was a sign to herself and others that she would no longer put up with cruel girlfriends and ugly public fights.

After graduation, Malice moved to New York City to be with K.James and promptly fell in love with the scene. In Switch n' Play, surrounded by all these different versions of masculinity, Malice fine-tuned her own sparkling, fierce, campy version of gender. She bought some wigs, some heels, and some tubes of bright red lipstick and started doing high-femme drag. In 2011, Miss Malice formally joined Switch n' Play as a "femmecee" (like emcee, but femme) and performing member. She brought what she thought of as big-dyke energy to the shows. Just because her nails were so long she struggled to pick up her MetroCard when it fell on the ground didn't mean she was in any way helpless, weak, or scared. She didn't defer to men. She hated the patriarchy with every ounce of her glitter-encrusted being. "It is really, really important to me that people understand Miss

Malice as a subversive queer gender expression," she said. "It's not regressive. This is not conventional femininity." For Malice, beauty and glamour had an edge. They could be angry, they could be strong, and they could be very, very gay.

Gay bars, though a pillar of the queer community for generations, haven't always been warm and welcoming to women, to trans and nonbinary people, or even to many gay men who were turned off by all the cruising, drugs, and heavy drinking. Malice always felt accepted within the wider Brooklyn drag scene, but for those drag-obsessed queers and drag kings who couldn't or wouldn't spend their nights in bars, pounding shots alongside cisgender boys in cutoffs and shredded tank tops, Switch n' Play provided an accessible space for gender play and camp. Other drag and burlesque performers were drawn to their kindness, the tender way they tried to be inclusive and considerate of both the audience and the other performers, and their deep organizational prowess. When she hosted, Miss Malice's setlist was an actual spreadsheet that included performers' names, gender pronouns, cues, and the text of their bios.

At a typical Switch n' Play Saturday night show, after everyone was firmly but consensually crammed into the twenty-by-twenty-foot back room, Malice would emerge from downstairs to a whoop and holler from the crowd, walk carefully down the aisle, mouthing hellos and waving to friends, and make her way to the stage. On any given night, the exact phrasing of Malice's jokes might vary—or it might not: regular audience members had been known to complete the punch lines to some of Malice's well-trod lines—but without fail she started the show with a quick rundown of how to be a respectful audience member.

"You're so smart, you're so fantastic, you're so intuitive," she buttered up the audience. "You've already identified a key way you can make this show go really well, which is to make people feel good onstage, which is by making some fucking noise."

The cheers got louder. The audience was excited, if a little impatient, and when the noise died down, Malice continued.

"There's another way you can show your appreciation at the drag show, and that's that tangible financial kind of appreciation." She scanned the room and when a volunteer inevitably produced a dollar bill, she noted that they were "subverting capitalism and rewarding the queer body," and nodded to the crowd. Malice ended her introduction with an approving smile. "It's so easy. We're not going to have any problems, but if we do . . ." The threat hung in the air, the message was clear: *Be respectful, or be thrown out.*

Though the drag kings and burlesque performers that Switch n' Play showcased weren't cast on television or rewarded with huge cash prizes, they represented the inclusivity and diversity that Sasha and Johnny revered. In their utopia, drag was heterogeneous, a display of any and every gender presentation, practiced by people of any and every gender identity. In the summer of 2014, Johnny Velour reached out to K.James with a proposition. *Be in our zine about drag?* The result was a photo shoot of K.James getting ready for a show. As he transformed from man to drag king, a photographer shot pictures of the in-progress makeup and a contemplative moment of him pulling on his shoes.

"I do queer, campy drag," read the caption under the photos, printed in K.James's own handwriting. "For me, drag is parody and not about creating an 'illusion.'"

The Velours had found their king.

CHAPTER THIRTEEN
The Velourian Scream

Initially, most of the established Brooklyn drag queens took little notice of Sasha and Johnny's efforts to build a drag dynasty. However, one fateful evening in December 2014, Scott Dennis, a drag queen who went by Madame Vivien V, or Viv as she was known to her friends, watched for twelve minutes as Sasha performed during an eclectic drag show in a converted armory in Brooklyn. Sasha's skirt was covered with Keith Haring–style figures and, with the help of a skinny, charismatic backup dancer in boy clothing, the performance told the story of the Haring drawings come to life.

After the armory show, Sasha had a stand selling her art and Stonewall-inspired comic books. Viv introduced herself to the backup dancer—Johnny Velour—and complimented the performance. Johnny explained that Sasha's goal in drag was to be one of her comic book characters.

"That's brilliant," Viv replied. Viv described herself as a "shooting star here to 'viv' her best life" and had an elegant, old-Hollywood style that she undercut with crude onstage stories about disastrous sex. She had fled to Brooklyn in her early twenties after growing up on a pig farm in Washington State. Her first gig ever had been as the opening act at the inaugural Bushwig festival in 2012, and she had been doing drag ever since. She no longer spoke to her father, but her older brother, who used to make her feel awful about being gay, now proudly showed his friends photos of Viv's looks on Instagram.

That night at the armory, Viv was looking for new acts to book at Bordello, her monthly show at Bizarre Bushwick. It was the type of creative outlet she'd dreamed about as a little kid playing in her mother's red patent leather six-inch heels. Bizarre was right in the middle of one of Bushwick's busiest intersections and had a prewar charm complete with glowing sconces and antique tin ceiling tiles. There was an actual stage with lights and a professional sound system. It had originally been conceived of as an absinthe club, and the seedy aura of that illicit, mildly hallucinogenic spirit permeated the space. Viv's monthly show was sexy and theatrical with a rotating cast of performers, many of whom came from Brooklyn's edgy circus community and did things like swallow swords, spin fire, and contort their lithe, obsessively conditioned bodies. Viv often had a packed house, and she preferred to only book one other drag queen for each show. She thought that most all-drag lineups were boring.

Sasha and Johnny Velour were not boring, however, and Viv invited them to perform at Bordello. There were plenty of reasons to be excited about the opportunity. Not only was Bizarre a few blocks from Sasha and Johnny's apartment, but it was a sit-down-shut-up-and-enjoy-the-show kind of place where a performer didn't have to fight for the audience's attention. On the night of the show, Viv, in a red angular wig and a tight mesh crop top over a gold sequin bra, introduced Sasha as "one of the best drag queens around" but also one of the best comic book artists. "So if there's any losers in this room—which I see plenty—you should be familiar with her," Viv joked before retreating out of the spotlight.

Onstage, a figure appeared from the shadows. It had a white foxtail strapped to the top of an otherwise bald head and clutched a brown fur stole. A reptilian screech rang out, and the creature began to gnaw on the stole, fangs flashing, talons gripping the swatch of fur. The sounds of an animal feeding frenzy intensified and focused into a single wail, the creature faced the audience, crouched, and showed its face. It was a meticulously painted Sasha Velour. Sasha-as-creature spun around, and a white cape decorated to look like a coat of feathers fluttered behind her. A fast-paced, synthetic beat thrummed, and Sasha licked her five-inch talons languidly. She was the perfect mix of animal and glamour, and she began to lip-synch along with Britney Spears. The song, "I Wanna Go," told the story of a bored, frustrated pop star looking for a way to escape and lose her inhibitions. In the song's video, Britney fights cyborg paparazzi before jumping into a getaway car driven by actor Guillermo Díaz, who then pours milk all over himself. In Sasha's interpretation, this lust for adventure and sex was now a desperate and animal cry for freedom. As she lip-synched, her eyes rolled seductively and the foxtail swung from her head. She dragged her talons up her thighs. Underneath the feathered cape she was wearing a simple black strappy bodysuit that evoked high-fashion bondage. Britney sang, "I—I—I wanna go-o-o all the way-ay-ay / Taking out my freak tonight," and Sasha's lip sync alternated from sex kitten to tigress. While Sasha vamped, Johnny Velour and another dancer leaped onto the stage in tan, safari-style clothes and hats and began a simple choreography behind her. Sasha picked up the moves for a few beats before the backup-dancers-slash-hunters shot her with a blow dart.

When Britney sang about being tied up, Johnny pulled Sasha's arms over her head and tied a ribbon around her wrists. The beast had been captured. He removed Sasha's foxtail and this bald, pointy-eared, snarling animal faced the audience in a plea for compassion. Sasha looked at the ground, her face in agony, her hands bound above her head.

"Shame . . . on me," Britney cooed sarcastically, "to need . . . release."

With the dancers' help Sasha, hands tied above her head, stepped into a black hoop skirt that resembled a cage and gave the audience a defiant look. Johnny placed a long, blond wig on her head, and she freed her hands. The chorus returned, and Sasha and the dancers had a moment of synchronized and energetic choreography. The fearsome hunted animal transformed into a pop star flanked by sexy backup dancers—but not for long. Sasha's character ripped off the wig with a snarl and, in between choreographed dance moves, mauled the backup dancers. She mounted Johnny's back triumphantly. The final whistles of the song echoed through the room, there was a howl—indistinguishable as animal or human—and the stage went dark.

Viv was delighted with Sasha's strangeness and her ambition. Sasha had mixed her own song, brought backup dancers, and used costume changes and reveals to tell a story about the constraints of beauty standards and the expectations placed on female sexuality. Viv hired her to work the door at the next Bordello, and Sasha met more drag performers and got more gigs while she and Johnny put the finishing touches on *VYM*. On June 11, 2015, they held a launch party at Bizarre Bushwick and sold signed copies. The Switch n' Play performers were there, including drag performer Pearl Harbor (later known as The Illustrious Pearl), who tore apart a rotisserie chicken while lip-synching to R & B singer Macy Gray's cover of the Radiohead song "Creep." K.James did an Elvis number, and then Sasha led the crowd in a toast to K.James and Miss Malice's recent wedding.

When it was Sasha's turn to perform, she hid behind an umbrella and reappeared, wigless, long-eared, and sneering. In drag, Sasha paired an often-bald head with a pair of long pointy prosthetic ears for a vampiric homage to the black-and-white movie character Nosferatu. She often painted a dark, jagged unibrow reminiscent of the Mexican artist Frida Kahlo. With sequins and shapeware, she skirted the line between fear and glamour. Building on the freak from her "I Wanna Go" number, that night Sasha had become one of the most debased, pathetic, and wretched characters in Western culture: the hateful Gollum from J. R. R. Tolkien's classic series the Lord of the Rings.

Sasha's performance suggested that an alter ego—even a monstrous one—could be a salve in trying times. As she would explain in that Facebook essay about baldness, she had watched her mother choose to be bald instead of conforming to uncomfortable beauty standards. This tension was relatable, poetic, and not that different from having a drag persona. In Sasha's portrayal, Gollum had become a sympathetic character—bald, skinny, monstrous even, but deserving of love, freedom, and fulfillment.

Sasha's drag seemed revolutionary and liberating because it provided a space to express ugliness, flaws, anger, and fear. Though the nuances of her performances were lost on some in the Brooklyn drag scene, many appreciated the cerebral, daring shows from this polite and good-tempered queen. A few of the borough's more established performers, including video artist and drag genius Chris of Hur and Zoe Ziegfeld, a snake charmer who had fled the uptight world of ballet for the sideshow and burlesque stage, were impressed with Sasha's creativity and style. They booked her for their shows. It seemed like every day there was a new idea, gig, or collaboration. Most important, Sasha had secured a date for the first installment of NightGowns, a drag performance that would showcase everything she loved about the art form and, hopefully, help put her on the map as a producer and local queen.

Then grief dropped like a sandbag from the rafters. On June 17, less than a week after the *VYM* magazine launch party, Sasha's mother died of primary peritoneal cancer at the age of sixty-four, as she would write in an essay on Daphne Chan's website. NightGowns was less than two months away. Sasha did not cancel, however. She and Johnny booked two other performers: Elle McQueen, a transcendent dancer who Sasha met at another one of Viv's shows, and a drag king named Lee Valone, who possessed a country swagger and had started to incorporate sideshow into his acts, putting out cigarettes on his arms or eating soap all while wearing pounds of facial hair and wigs.

The audience at that first NightGowns was small, but everyone in the room was passionate about weird, gender-fluid drag. The members of Switch n' Play were once again present. Madame Vivien V was there, too. She had watched Sasha's most recent version of the Gollum act, so much more developed than the Britney Spears lip sync at Bordello back in February, and continued to be impressed by this relative newcomer's vision and poise. Viv had also loved it when Sasha performed "If You Go Away," by Shirley Bassey. As the song's story unfolded—a desperate plea for requited love—Sasha held up a stack of brightly colored, high contrast, blocky drawings depicting the evolution and dissolution of a love affair. The woman in the pictures, striking, tall, and glamorous in a long black coat and red dress that matched Sasha's own outfit, is not a woman at all but a vampire. As Sasha showed the audience page after page, discarding them one by one on the floor, the story unfolded. The woman, abandoned by her lover, lashes out, crawling in his window and sinking her teeth into his neck. When the act ended, Viv stood up and announced that Sasha was selling the images for ten dollars apiece. Several people approached waving money.

"You killed it," Viv would later write on Sasha's Facebook page after the inaugural NightGowns, "literally, in every act something died."

"If you aren't pretending to murder someone," Sasha responded, "you aren't doing drag."

At the second NightGowns in September, Sasha told the crowd

about her mother's death and how drag helped ease the grief and the loneliness. When Sasha got to the hospital, her mother hadn't been able to speak. "She moved around a lot—whispering to herself, occasionally breaking into a smile so big she looked like the Cheshire cat—and she, too, was fading away," she said. Drag had taught Sasha about grief and loss. "I learned that it can be empowering to wear your mother's dress. Or power suit. At first I was worried that it was a little Norman Bates *Psycho* (but then I just embraced it, and now I'm a murderer)."

Sasha booked a third NightGowns for October and then a fourth in November. As the show built a solid core of regular performers, it further connected Sasha and Johnny to the wider drag scene. But Sasha still had to work to fill the room. She promoted, cajoled, complimented, networked, and posted. She booked Merrie Cherry and Horrorchata. "There drag goes, savin' my life again through beauty!" Sasha reflected in a January 9, 2016, Facebook post just days before the sixth incarnation of NightGowns. It had been less than six months since her mother had died. In the post, Sasha positioned herself as "the crazy professor auntie" rather than a luminary of the Brooklyn scene. She wanted conversation and communion. Her shows would be political, yet intimate, she promised. "That's why it's called NIGHT-GOWNS, after all . . . named after the dress you wear when you AREN'T going out on the town . . . the one reserved for an evening of holding court and planning revolution at home."

· · · · ·

In early 2016, soon after Sasha posted that deep outpouring of gratitude and self-reflection on Facebook, she submitted an audition tape for season nine of *RuPaul's Drag Race*. She was a long shot. But the audition was a chance to tell her story and practice putting forward a coherent sense of her drag and personality.

In late June 2016, Sasha canceled an upcoming performance. She wrote on Facebook that she was going to St. Petersburg, Russia, and would be away for the month of July, she was so sorry to bail. The *Drag Race* season nine queens wouldn't be announced for six months, but the crackerjack sleuths on Reddit had once again compiled a list of working drag queens and, by obsessively tracking their whereabouts during the weeks when the show was known to be filming, they were able to determine who'd been cast. When Sasha got back to Brooklyn that summer, everyone who cared about drag suspected that she hadn't been in Russia at all. The rumor that Aja and Sasha were both on the upcoming season of *Drag Race* spread through the borough until February 2, 2017, when the cast of *RuPaul's Drag Race* season nine was finally announced.

At NightGowns the week after, Bizarre was packed. People crowded against the bar and squeezed into every available corner. Hanging heavy in the room that night was the recent inauguration of Donald Trump as president. People like Sasha, Johnny, Switch n' Play, and Madame Vivien V, who lived with politics at the forefront of their drag, had spent the months since the election in a fever of fear and incredulity. Nothing felt certain anymore. Were gay rights improving or would the cultural and political gains eked out over the past thirty years be systematically trampled and revoked? Were their undocumented friends about to be deported? Would trans people lose their access to health care? Would the United States' numerous ongoing foreign conflicts bubble over into another world war? Any and every negative outcome felt possible, no one was safe, and in light of all this uncertainty, Sasha and her fellow drag performers clung more tightly than ever to their rarified, politically progressive chosen families. They needed to be engaged, they needed to fight back, but how? What did performance-as-resistance look like?

Sasha had some ideas.

That night, she walked onto the stage at Bizarre smiling in a pink, boxy Russian hat and a matching pink fur-trimmed coat, stepped up to the microphone, and screamed.

The amplified roar echoed off the walls, and the crowd responded with a wild cheer. "That is the revolutionary scream of the new generation of queer drag superstars. Honored to speak your"—she paused and nodded to the packed room—"language. . . . Outside in the waking world actual death eaters have taken over positions of power. But here in our necessary dream world we are living a utopian dream where we get to be in charge."

Sasha looked around the room. "Who's here for the first time?" she asked, and choruses of "whoooo" rang out. The announcement last week that Sasha was going to be on *Drag Race* had stirred interest in NightGowns and she was able and absolutely willing to absorb and inculcate this growing audience. As RuPaul noted before the inaugural season of the show, trends and priorities in drag often mirror the prevailing national mood and presidential administration. Perhaps NightGowns and the wider Brooklyn scene, with their refusal to bend to convention or expectation and their emphasis on community, were especially well suited to resistance in the Trump era.

"I can tell from your enthusiasm that you belong here, you've belonged here all along, and you've finally come home." she told the crowd. "I am going to ask you all to join me in a Velourian righteous scream." She seemed downright giddy, and her joy was infectious. "Who's ready for some shows?"

The first performer that night was Merrie Cherry. Sasha introduced her as the "critical heart at the center of the Brooklyn drag scene." Merrie took the stage, giving Sasha a smile of gratitude and a few air-kisses, and Sasha retreated to the shadows to watch her perform. At a break between sets, Madame Vivien V found Sasha. It was Viv's first night off in weeks and she would have stayed home, except she wanted to congratulate her friend. She'd brought a gift of a houndstooth hat pin to mark the occasion.

"I wish you every happiness," Viv whispered, nestling her face in Sasha's humid shoulder.

Viv had been in the Brooklyn scene for as long as Merrie Cherry. She had competed in DragNet and in the Mr(s) Williamsburg pageant but never really felt like she fit in. She had recently started working at a nightclub run by showgirls and circus performers with a decidedly heterosexual crowd; however, she was proud of her history with "*Drag Race* girls." She liked to tell people that Aja had tried to teach her to dance, "back before she realized I had no rhythm" and that she had believed the eighteen-year-old when she claimed to be twenty-six. ("Older than me!" Viv would later cackle.) Viv, who boasted that she'd been the first queen to book Sasha in Brooklyn, was just finishing her own *Drag Race* audition tape for season ten of the show, and she understood that being cast was a matter of luck as much as talent. Paying her bills as a local queen with a regular nightlife gig, however, was pure hard work and hustle. It was also exhausting. At around eleven, after watching Switch n' Play member Pearl Harbor lip-synch using an ear of corn as a microphone, Viv downed the rest of her drink and headed home.

It was a cold, drizzly weeknight. The streets were empty. Three blocks from her apartment, Viv heard voices behind her and, as she moved aside to let them pass, something blunt and heavy hit her on the back. She collapsed onto the pavement, and the concrete scraped her face. A foot connected with her side, and she felt a sharp pain in her chin.

"Faggot, fucking pussy."

Oh, she realized. *This is it*. The moment every swishy boy fears. Though Viv had always expected it, she wasn't prepared. She covered her face and tried to stand up. A hand pushed her down.

Her screams startled the attackers and she broke free just as a car cruised past, its taillights glowing. Viv limped off the sidewalk, waving her hands.

"These people are beating me," she croaked through tears and blood. The driver cringed but stared at the street in front of him, refusing to meet her eyes.

"You should probably call the police," he said, rolled up the window, and drove away.

The men dragged Viv back onto the sidewalk and hit her again, this time in the stomach.

This really is it.

Her attackers fled when another car, an Uber, pulled up and the passengers shouted for Viv to "get in." The girl inside took Viv back to her apartment, called the police, and together they rode with the cops through the neighborhood looking for the men who'd attacked her.

This was the danger that motivated queer performers to immerse themselves in the struggle for gay rights. A spot on a beloved TV show was a chance to show the often indifferent masses the magic of queer resilience in the face of growing oppression and violence. For Viv, queer resilience meant having the nerve and the courage to persist after incredible trauma, but it also meant doing it with style, beauty, attitude, and a whole lot of glamour. It meant asserting her right to not only exist outside the mainstream, but to thrive there. Two days after the attack, Viv went back to work in drag, though it would be months before she felt safe enough to go outside in civilian clothes. Her friends brought marijuana and costume masks to wear until the cuts and bruises on her face healed. They ordered Seamless and held her in bed for hours so she could sleep. Viv testified against one of the men in court. Group therapy for PTSD helped keep the panic attacks under control. Though she spent days paralyzed with fear, unable to leave the house, she never thought about quitting.

"Meryl Streep probably can't see her life without acting, Beyoncé can't not sing, and I don't feel I can live on this earth without drag," Viv said. As Viv slowly recovered from the attack and Donald Trump began to unravel the already fraying fabric of civil rights and justice in the United States, Sasha prepared for season nine to air.

CHAPTER FOURTEEN

Monsters Reign

By the time Thorgy Thor, Aja, and Sasha Velour appeared on *Drag Race*, queerness had become cool. Life for LGBT people in America wasn't necessarily better. Gay people lacked federal antidiscrimination protections, queer kids were kicked out of their houses or sent to conversion therapy by hostile parents, and gay and trans people—especially those who were poor or non-white—experienced violence at an alarming rate. But in art, music, fashion, and media the insistence that men be masculine and women be feminine had become oppressive and outdated. Gender-bending and gayness were no longer restricted to outsiders and rebels. Celebrities like Miley Cyrus proudly called themselves gender-fluid or pansexual. *Moonlight*, a movie about queer desire between two Black men struggling to find themselves amid drugs and violence in Miami Beach, won the 2017 Academy Award for Best Picture. Jaden Smith, the gender-fluid son of hyper-masculine megastar Will Smith, was a brand ambassador for Louis Vuitton's 2016 women's line, and that same year seventeen-year-old YouTube makeup star James Charles was the first male face of Covergirl makeup. Thanks to tweens and teens on the internet, "yaaasss, qween," "werk," "realness," and "shade," phrases that originated in the ballroom scene in New York City, many of which RuPaul had appropriated and popularized, were becoming household terms.

RuPaul's Drag Race, entertaining and relatable reality TV, both benefited from and contributed to this astounding boom in the visibility and popularity of gay culture. Since its inception, the show had elevated the profile of its queens and led to regular appearances at gay bars and concert venues around the world. Season eight of *RuPaul's Drag Race*—where Thorgy introduced the world to Brooklyn drag—had been a turning point. The show was now available on major streaming platforms like Hulu and Netflix, and fans could follow their favorite queens on Instagram and YouTube. The wider world was learning what many gay people had known for generations: drag was entertaining. RuPaul was en vogue yet again, gracing magazine covers both in and out of drag and gaining fans as a convivial and sometimes controversial interview subject. Celebrities, especially quirky, stylish young women, commented on their favorite *Drag Race* girls' Instagram posts, hired them for music videos and televised performances, and openly gushed about their love of the show. And in what was arguably the strongest indication that *Drag Race* had reached the mainstream, RuPaul won an Emmy for Outstanding Host for a Reality or Competition Program. After season eight, Viacom, the parent company of LogoTV, where *Drag Race* had aired since its premiere in 2009, announced that *RuPaul's Drag Race* season nine would air on VH1. This meant nearly a million people, many of whom had never seen a drag show at a gay bar, watched Aja and Sasha walk into the workroom on their first day of filming.

Drag Race's production budget had also grown, making the show more palatable to viewers who weren't predisposed to care about a campy art form dominated by gay men. The stage lights were brighter, the guest judges more recognizable, and the video quality sharper. After Aja and Sasha exchanged warm greetings in the workroom, Aja introduced herself to a Southern queen in a strappy catsuit named Trinity Taylor. Known for her flat tuck and her round, surgically enhanced ass, Trinity and Aja gave air-kisses and the show cut to Trinity's out-of-drag interview.

"Aja's makeup is just really rough around the edges, but she comes off as confident," Trinity said with a baffled look. "But does she know what she looks like? 'Cause if not, I need to tell her."

As is the case with most reality TV, viewers at home saw a heavily edited and condensed version of what happened. In the workroom, during the challenges, on the runway, and in one-on-one interviews, producers focused on conflicts, honed in on dramatic moments, spliced in reactions, and used sound effects to emphasize emotions and jokes. (A rattlesnake sound effect that played when a queen said something particularly shady had become a pop culture punch line.) The story lines weren't invented, but they were sculpted. Everyone who went on the show knew this, but most believed they would be able to present the best, most winning aspects of their personalities, do well in the competition, and come off as likable to the viewers. Contestants wanted to win but knew that having the viewers on their side was equally important to their postshow success. For some, this was absolutely what happened. *Drag Race* produced countless wonderful television moments. Like the time when season five queen Roxxxy Andrews removed her wig during a lip sync to reveal another identical wig underneath, or when season four queen Latrice "Motherfucking" Royale shouted, "Get those nuts away from my face" while playing a prison guard trying to stop a group of queens from fighting over a bag of peanuts. Many of the queens appeared delightful and lovable on television and gained legions of fans and bookings. Others received less-flattering edits. In all cases, though, queens who were accustomed to managing their public personas down to the photo filter and the punctuation in a tweet, lost that agency when they walked through the workroom door.

Sasha Velour had meticulously constructed her image to convey intelligence, history, and elegance, but once she stepped in front of the cameras she couldn't control how the judges interpreted her looks. The runway category for the second episode of season nine was "White Party Realness." While some of the queens took the opportunity to show off their perfectly padded bodies wearing as little fabric as possible, Sasha's outfit was a tailored jacket and floor-length matching skirt covered in silver crescent moons. She had on white shoes and, in a voice-over, Sasha told the at-home audience, "I've taken a classic silhouette and updated it with a commitment to showing women who are strong." Her explanation of the look was followed by judge Michelle Visage's commentary.

"You know what they say about girls who wear white pumps?" Michelle asked.

"True hooker," RuPaul replied.

·····

Not simply a venue for great drag, *Drag Race* was *a competition*, the judges and contestants continually reminded viewers.

"I consider myself very much a competitor," Jaymes Mansfield said in the second episode of season nine after being chosen second-to-last for a group challenge.

"I need to win," Trinity later explained. "I'm not here to play games; the next challenge is mine."

"This is such a high-pressure competition," Aja said early in the season. "You have to be sure of yourself."

However, though the stated objective was competition, the point was to find the best drag queen in the bunch while making the most entertaining TV possible. Queens who could accept the unreality of the situation had a better shot at weathering the incredible stress of twelve-hour days dancing, sewing, singing, and cracking jokes on a cold soundstage with a group of other professional antagonists. Those who viewed *Drag Race* as a means to an end, a way to get their faces in front of a massive potential fan base and build an international career, could often keep perspective when they got negative critiques from the judges, flubbed a challenge, or heard the other queens talking shit. The amount of self-confidence and perspective a queen had coming into the show could determine how well she handled the pressure of being judged, taunted, and sometimes undermined.

In the third episode of season nine, as the queens painted their faces together at the workroom mirrors, Alexis Michelle, a Manhattan queen and trained musical theater performer, noticed that Aja was drawing her eyebrows higher than usual. "Are you afraid of what America is gonna think of your makeup without Facetune?" Alexis asked, referring to an app that allowed people to edit and smooth out their facial features in social media posts.

"No," Aja replied.

The camera cut to another queen giving side-eye and some of the others giggling. Aja insisted she looked the same in photos as she did in person.

"Sometimes girls who come up on social media can get a lot of praise for the way they present themselves online," said another queen in a one-on-one interview.

Photos of Aja with what appeared to be flawless makeup appeared on-screen interspersed with shots of Aja doing her makeup in the workroom.

"However," the queen continued, "it's how you *apply* that makeup, because sometimes when people see you in person they can get a little bit disappointed."

She never mentioned Aja by name, and her statement could have been said about several of the queens competing that season. But for the purposes of the TV show, the message was clear: Aja's makeup was lacking.

In that week's challenge, each queen had to transform herself into a fairy-tale princess by sewing an original look and creating a fictional sidekick. Aja designed orange chaps with a matching orange tube top and a floor-length orange mohair coat, and on the runway she introduced the judges to her sidekick, Disastah, a volcano from Bed-Stuy who liked to hang out in the club with her clouds. When it came time to deliver critiques, Michelle Visage said she hadn't understood Aja's story and complained that Aja's makeup was too dark. "It's been kinda dark this whole journey," she said.

Backstage, while the contestants waited for RuPaul and the judges to decide the top and bottom queens of the week, they discussed their critiques. Valentina, a Mexican American makeup artist, had been performing well in the competition despite only having ten months of experience in drag. When someone asked Valentina about her critiques, Aja, who had just been excoriated for her ideas and her makeup, unleashed one of the most memorable rants in *Drag Race* history. In Aja's exaggerated interpretation, the judges couldn't stop praising Valentina.

"You're *perfect*; you're *beautiful*; you look like Linda *Evangelista*, you're a *model*," Aja said. "Everything about you is *perfect*; did you stone those tights? Oh, you're smiling?"

The other queens shifted awkwardly on the backstage couches.

Aja raged. "She could walk out there in a fuckin' diaper, and they'd be like 'Valentina, your *smile* is *beautiful*.'"

On the main stage, Aja learned she was up for elimination and therefore would have to lip-synch for her life against Kimora Blac, a Las Vegas queen whose main talent seemed to be wearing not a lot of clothing. The song was "Holding Out for a Hero," by Bonnie Tyler, a high-energy eighties anthem with a driving beat and frequent cymbal crashes. Aja artfully took advantage of each one, executing a high kick and a 360-degree-jump into the splits. It was as if she were back at Metropolitan, willing each member of the audience to throw a dollar or shout her name, dancing furiously to overshadow the girl next to her. She camped it up, emphasizing the urgency of the song with quick air punches. As the track ended, she fell backward onto the stage in a dip, one leg bent beneath her, and then rose in slow motion to a crouch, her eyes never leaving the judges' panel in front of her.

She won the lip sync handily, but her confidence was shaken. "I just feel like I walked into here thinking like I was unstoppable, and now I feel like I really need to reevaluate," she said in her one-on-one interview. In drag she'd gotten what she wanted by being wild. Here, she was expected to be humble and follow the rules. She'd made four pieces of clothing, she argued, and other competitors—ahem, Valentina—had on little more than a bodysuit and a wide smile.

"Aja's true colors are coming out," Valentina declared in her solo interview. "She presents herself as confident, but there's a lot of insecurity there."

Sasha, Aja's Brooklyn sister, was shocked. "For Aja, the challenge is going to be not becoming bitter, because she sees herself as a superstar, and to be told your makeup is off, your outfit isn't great, is a bit of an ego check for her," she said.

While Aja was under the microscope, squirming from the glare, Sasha was avoiding drama. She occasionally let loose during challenges in these early episodes, like when she and Chicago-based queen Shea Couleé lasciviously shared a stalk of broccoli during an on-camera cooking demonstration, but otherwise she stuck to the margins as other contestants argued, whined, and boasted. While manufactured drama can sometimes backfire, hardworking, quiet, brainy drag queens have also not historically fared well on *Drag Race*. The format rewards people who manage to seem genuine and relatable, but it also demands action and absurdity. For Sasha, being genuine meant talking about philosopher and gender theorist Judith Butler and portraying German early twentieth century film actress Marlene

Dietrich for the "Snatch Game" celebrity impersonation challenge. As Marlene Dietrich, Sasha delighted RuPaul by making jokes about bisexuality in a thick accent. Again, however, she was overshadowed by bigger, hammier personalities.

As Aja struggled to regain her confidence and Sasha attempted to move into the foreground, the queens were challenged to perform an adaptation of the nineties teen drama *Beverly Hills: 90210* called "9021-Ho" that would be directed by actresses from the original series. Aja complained about her assigned role until Shea Couleé volunteered to trade parts. With everyone annoyed, Aja realized she'd made a mistake.

"I feel so childish right now," she said.

"Well, you probably should, girl," Sasha replied curtly.

While the queens did their makeup for the runway, the conversation turned to cancer. Most episodes contain these interludes, what fans of the show sometimes call "mirror talk," when contestants reveal painful or dramatic details about their lives amid tears and hugs. Savvy *Drag Race* viewers know that queens shown discussing their lives at the mirror are often that week's top or bottom contestants. This week, sad background music played while Sasha told the other queens that she's bald because when her mother lost her hair from cancer, "she felt like she couldn't be beautiful." In her one-on-one interview, Sasha explained that incorporating her mother's experiences with cancer and chemo into her drag "was the most important thing I've ever done in my life." Back in the workroom mirror, she lamented that "the drag queen I am now is not the drag queen she got to see." Aja offered to give her a spiritual reading. While to some, the offer seemed random, for Aja, who'd been immersed in Afro-Caribbean spirituality since her teens, it was a sincere act of love and friendship.

The queens who performed best in challenges like "9021-Ho," campy parodies of pop culture touchstones, approached them with a commitment to the story and a willingness to make fools of themselves. The audience might cringe at the lines, but the judges expect the contestants to sell the script no matter how corny. Aja and Sasha underwhelmed the judges in their respective roles as class bitch and lunch lady. At the end of the episode, they stood on the runway in front of RuPaul and the other judges as dramatic music played.

"Aja, your bitch was botched," RuPaul said. "Sasha Velour, your lunch lady left us hungry."

They were both in the bottom along with Nina Bonina Banana Fofana Osama Bin Laden Brown, a queen with transcendent makeup skills and disastrously low self-esteem. The tension built, and the queens shifted awkwardly. The music stopped.

"Sasha Velour, you're safe," RuPaul decreed.

Sasha thanked Ru, sighed deeply, and retreated to the back of the stage. This meant Aja and Nina were up for elimination and would now have to lip-synch for their lives. Aja looked dejected and very young beneath her makeup and a dome of frizzy blond curls.

"This is your last chance to impress me and save yourself from elimination," RuPaul announced. "Good luck and don't fuck it up."

The song was the 1991 club hit "Finally" by CeCe Peniston. Aja made the most of Peniston's wails and "ooooh"s, falling to her knees and mouthing every syllable. Lip sync was the heart of the art form, and watching Aja do it was pure entertainment. However, because this lip sync was on TV, audiences would only ever see ninety seconds of her four-minute-long performance. Rather than displaying the powerful onstage charisma that had brought her to such dizzying heights in drag, Aja's lip sync would become a plot point in someone else's story. For a queen like Aja who was begging to be seen and accepted on the street, in the bars, and among her friends, this was a kind of erasure. This show—the holy grail for so many queens—had put her face on a million people's screens. Audiences heard her story and watched her perform, but that didn't mean they understood her. In the end, people would see only those moments a group of television producers in Los Angeles felt were necessary to create the most compelling storyline.

The final edit showed Nina Bonina Brown beating Aja on the main stage and, Aja, lips quivering, eyes downcast, sashaying away.

"Thank you so much for everything. I've learned a lot about myself here, and I really owe it to you guys," Aja told the judges.

Upon elimination, most queens offer a farewell catchphrase or joke on their way out, but Aja left the runway with no final message. Back in the now-empty workroom, she addressed the camera.

"This show is a lot harder than you think. I came here and I was like, 'I got this.' I feel extremely disappointed that I can't go further." She had become a caricature. The confident queen who was the shit in Brooklyn but couldn't hack it in the competition.

Sasha knew there was more to Aja and her drag. She was "heartbroken" when Aja left. "Aja was my Brooklyn boo, and I'm really, really gonna miss her," Sasha said after Aja's departure.

Drag Race is a competition and, like all competitions, contestants enter on unequal footing. Aja had embarked on *Drag Race* with some clear disadvantages. She lacked funds for clothes and makeup, a stable family, and, in the hustle to earn money, her craft sometimes suffered. Though the show had put her on TV and would change her life in countless ways, in that moment, being eliminated was a reminder of everything she didn't have. Sasha, on the other hand, entered the competition from a position of relative advantage. Despite grief and hardship, Sasha had a first-rate education, a growing community of creative peers, and a supportive partner and father. Moreover, due to her own combination of privilege, personality, and hard work, it was clear that, no matter what happened on the show, she would likely continue to have opportunities to perform and make art. As

Aja retreated from the competition, deprived of the validation and obvious transformation that would come from snatching the crown, it was clear that while both queens wanted to make it to the end on *Drag Race*, one of them had *needed* it more than the other.

• • • • •

Early on in season nine, Sasha seemed to flounder. Though she was approaching the competition with her trademark intellect and sincerity, the judges and other contestants often found her to be "too smart for the room." Yet, week after week, Sasha prevailed, and when the pack of fourteen had dwindled to five, the challenge was to create three distinct looks to walk in the "Gayest Ball Ever." The categories were "Rainbow-She-Betta-Do" a play on the catchphrase "Oh, no she betta don't"—where the queens showed off gay-pride-flag-inspired looks, "Village People Eleganza Extravaganza" in which each of the queens had to create a runway look honoring a different character in the disco group the Village People, and "Sexy Unicorn."

For Sasha's rainbow look, a "deconstructed" homage to the *Wizard of Oz* and "the importance of Dorothy to the gay community," she wore a canary-yellow turtleneck, an orange front-slit pencil skirt, pink bobby socks, a blue fake flower boutonniere, and lavender shortie gloves. As she walked the runway, she removed a red cylindrical hat to reveal a house—also rainbow color blocked—constructed from paper and glued to the top of her bald head.

"Careful before someone drops a house on you," RuPaul commented.

Sasha's "Village People" look was a send-up of the cowboy character for which she'd created a chic, structured crop top and pencil skirt from red calico-print fabric. Her elbow-length gloves were red leather on one side and cowhide on the other, and she wore a red rancher hat.

The judges were impressed. "There's something extremely modern about your style," actress Andie MacDowell, that episode's guest judge, told Sasha.

Judge and former *Queer Eye for the Straight Guy* host Carson Kressley complimented Sasha's "Little House on the Fairy" rainbow look and, though the judges questioned whether the outfits were drag and not just high fashion, she landed herself a spot in the top four. The final group was packed with talent and charisma. Besides Sasha, there was Peppermint, a longtime New York City club kid and fierce performer; Trinity Taylor, a consummate professional and showgirl with a sharp sense of humor, whose exciting lip syncs left nary a hair out of place; and Shea Couleé, who oozed star power and had won the most challenges that season.

For the ninth season of *Drag Race*, the producers had shaken up the finale rules. In previous seasons, RuPaul chose the three final contestants during the penultimate episode and then, in the finale, they reunited and a winner was crowned in front of a live audience. But this year, RuPaul announced that the four queens would compete at the finale in a "sudden-death, lip-sync smackdown for the crown." The finale was taped in front of a live audience, nearly a year after the queens had finished filming the previous episodes. The season had been an incredible success. RuPaul was named one of *Time* magazine's "100 Most Influential People." He was profiled in *The Atlantic, Vanity Fair*, and *New York* magazine. *Saturday Night Live* aired a sketch in which car mechanics revealed their shared obsession with the show and competed in a lip sync battle in their coveralls. Now that Donald Trump was president, feeding a stream of vitriol and bigotry to his legion of followers, *Drag Race* proved an uplifting unifier, a way of assuaging liberal America's fears over this racist, homophobic backlash. As one season nine tagline claimed, "Drastic times call for dragtastic measures. . . . We need America's next drag superstar now more than ever."

When Sasha emerged on the stage during the finale, resplendent in a floor-length cobalt-blue-and-white gown with an ornately beaded white-and-blue runner down the center and a massive lace collar, she received a standing ovation from the crowd. She and Brooklyn-based designer Diego Montoya had originally wanted the gown to be red, an homage to the character Lucy Westenra in the 1992 film *Dracula*, but the producers banned queens from wearing red, afraid their looks wouldn't stand out against the stage's set. Blue was a nod to Russian porcelain, Diego later explained in an interview with *Out* magazine. With her bald head poking out of the collar, she resembled a bejeweled Eastern Orthodox velociraptor. Sasha had never been in the bottom two, so she had yet to lip-synch for her life on television. *Drag Race* fans wondered whether she would be able to hold her own against the other queens. Sasha, however, was a confident performer and had brought some tricks with her. She believed that she was the future of drag, and now all she had to do was prove it to RuPaul and a few hundred thousand people watching on television.

That night's performances would be the most watched lip syncs in the history of drag. To determine the order of the battle, RuPaul spun an oversized wheel with the top four queens' names on it. Dramatic game show music played as the wheel went round and the arrow landed on Trinity Taylor.

"Trinity, the wheel has spoken and now you get to choose who you will lip sync against," RuPaul instructed. "Choose wisely."

"I want a battle. I choose Peppermint," said Trinity. That meant Sasha and Shea would compete next.

When it was their turn, Sasha and Shea entered holding hands. In her other hand, Sasha clutched a red, long-stem rose. Uncharacteristically, she was wearing a long auburn wig with wide finger waves and a center part. Shea Couleé, the pride of Chicago, had on a patent leather jacket with wide lapels and a cinched waist over a pair of black patent leather chaps and thigh-high boots. Sasha's dress grazed her knees and had an abstract floral print in red, gold, and pink. Her hips were padded, her waist cinched, and she wore gold elbow-length gloves. To be this understated and elegant was bold considering that, because she was never in the bottom two, she hadn't lip-synched on *RuPaul's Drag Race* before that night.

The queens had been told ahead of time which songs they'd be performing. Sasha and Shea would be lip-synching to the Whitney Houston song "So Emotional." Shea snapped along with the intro, and Sasha tore the petals off the rose she'd been carrying in time with the beat. They both moved up and down on their respective sides of the stage, lip-synching with an intense focus. Shea put her hands up to her face as Whitney sang, "I remember the way we touched / I wish I didn't like it so much," and Sasha, who'd been pulling gently at the fingertips of her left glove, removed it in a swift motion, releasing a shower of red rose petals. Though a well-timed glove peel with a surprise effect was common in the burlesque world, it sent a ripple of surprise through the unsuspecting *Drag Race* audience. Sasha's face lit up as she mouthed the chorus. She was just getting started. The other glove came off with another burst of rose petals just as the next verse was beginning.

"So Emotional" is a short, straightforward pop song with a joyous chorus. When Whitney Houston sang about the animal way her lover moved, Sasha crawled to the floor. Whitney described watching her lover's mouth, and Sasha pointed to her own. The next time Whitney let out a grunt of desire and sang "I wish I didn't like it so much," Sasha reached for her wig with both hands. Moving in slow motion, she lifted the hair, and a cascade of rose petals fell over her signature bald head. Aja, seated in the audience in full drag with the rest of the season nine queens, gasped. Sasha's father, sometimes referred to as "Papa Velour," clutched his chest in the seat next to her boyfriend,

Johnny. A wave of surprise and glee spread through the audience members as they leaped to their feet. "Ain't it shocking what love can do." It was the climax of the song, and Sasha brandished the wig triumphantly before dropping it and pounding her chest. As Sasha's show intensified, Shea Couleé, the clear favorite to win that season, faded into the background. Shea later said that when she saw the roses fall from Sasha's wig, she knew it was over. Sasha's reveals had made the crowd gasp, not just because they were beautiful but because they'd been genuinely surprising. The nontraditional influences Sasha had amassed and immersed herself in at home had given her a competitive edge few could have predicted before the finale. Technically, this was a battle, but there was no contest.

Peppermint had beaten Trinity Taylor in their lip sync face-off, so it was down to her and Sasha for the crown. Sasha changed backstage into an all-white floor-length gown with curved spikes at the shoulders and a gauzy, snake-skin-inspired bodice. It was her second Diego Montoya look of the evening and the piece de resistance was a white beaded mask made of felt and lace that covered her entire head and looked like a monstrous, toothy egg. When the song "It's Not Right But It's Okay," a song about surviving a lover's betrayal, also sung by Whitney Houston, began, Sasha removed the part of the mask covering her mouth so the audience could see her red lips as she performed. Peppermint, who was wearing an opalescent ball gown with an asymmetrical ruffled skirt and a bodice covered in beads, fat sequins, and lavender feathers, looked like a fierce and foreboding dinosaur. She had been shocked by the rose petal reveal and kept watching Sasha from the corner of her eye, expecting something to emerge from inside the mask. At the chorus, Sasha removed the entire mask, exposing her now iconic bald head. This was the final reveal of the season.

Peppermint was a classic lip sync assassin. If Sasha was going to win this whole thing, stunts wouldn't be enough. She'd have to turn out a heartfelt performance that resonated with even the most traditional drag fans. For the rest of the song Peppermint and Sasha relied on whatever theatricality they could convey with their faces and bodies. They twirled, they crashed to the floor, they stomped and shook, and, watching them move, the crowd felt the pain and triumph that Whitney Houston described.

In most art forms the creative product is easy to recognize. Visual artists make objects of beauty, musicians compose and perform songs, writers string words together to convey emotions and ideas in new and surprising ways. Considering the emphasis placed on authorship, it can seem absurd to call lip-synching—someone dressed up, mouthing the words to a song they did not write or sing—an art. But lip-synching at its best is pure performance. Untethered from the demands of having to actually sing or compose and the limitations of their particular voice, the lip sync artist is free to create a new reality for themselves, the song, and the audience. Great lip-synchers understand that songs have long and complex lives that transcend their singers. Like pastiche artists, they can see the sometimes unexpected and counterintuitive ways that music resonates with people, and when they perform they draw on these emotional connections to create something new from the familiar. The song becomes a palette for their interpretation. It's no accident that gay people love lip-synching, that they crave a rein-terpretation of the mainstream in order to celebrate something queer, effeminate, and often uncanny, and that their hearts pound and their eyes well up when they see an especially talented drag performer act out a fantasy onstage. With every reveal, every expression of shock or elation, Sasha had given this fantasy to the crowd in the theater and watching at home. She would later tell *Vice* that the lip sync battles were "a return to what drag is at its essence, which isn't about how well you can perform on television—it's about speaking and performing in a way that can captivate people and uplift them and make them feel strong and emotional."

In order to keep the actual winner a secret, the show filmed crownings for Peppermint and Sasha. No one would know who'd won until the episode actually aired. A few weeks later, the two New York City queens from either side of the river watched the finale on television, sitting together backstage at the viewing party. They seemed to be kindred spirits. Both low-drama and openhearted members of a thriving drag community. Watching the lip syncs, they clung to each other on the couch. "Oh my God, you really do look like a dinosaur," Sasha joked to Peppermint, and she laughed. When the performance ended, they embraced, exchanged whispers of encouragement, and waited for RuPaul to announce the winner. Sasha heard her name. Her mouth fell open, and Peppermint burst into genuine applause. No one could be mad about losing to such artful, beautiful performances.

It was an outcome few had expected at the beginning of season nine. But as soon as Sasha was crowned, it all seemed inevitable. New Yorkers are used to attention. They expect to see movie stars on the streets, host the most important events in the world, and be the center of national conversations about art, fashion, and music. But Brooklyn still had that small-town feel. Would a hometown queen's success on a reality TV show change that? Did her triumph mean other strange and talented queens waiting in the wings would soon get their own shot?

Back on-screen, in the previously taped crowning, season eight winner Bob the Drag Queen handed Sasha a sparkling scepter. Struggling for breath, Sasha shouted to the crowd, "Let's get inspired by all this beauty, all this beauty, and change the motherfuckin' world!"

PART THREE

PART THREE

CHAPTER FIFTEEN

Super Queens

After bringing the BK to the *RDR* in 2016, Thorgy Thor had a whirlwind few years. She traveled to the UK, Australia, and Canada. She performed across Northern Europe and the United States. McDonald's paid her thousands for some sponsored posts on Instagram. Inspired by the easy money, she contacted Poo-Pourri, a toilet air freshener, and told them, "All the queens are working with makeup companies, would you do something with me?" To Thorgy, it made sense with her brand. "This is funny, it's a way to cover up your poop smell," she later said. They agreed, and again she made several thousand dollars for some sponsored posts. She appeared alongside Jane Fonda and Lily Tomlin on a cable talk show, and backstage they all hugged and joked about doing drugs. She even performed on a cruise to the Bahamas headlined by the pop star Kesha. At the country's best and biggest gay bars, in full drag, she gave shows, the bills—not just ones, but fives, tens, and even twenties—rained down, and the alcohol flowed. She lived the dream of being a professional clown with enough money, fame, and opportunity to keep her comfortable and busy.

Thorgy and the hundred or so other queens who'd appeared on the show were the beneficiaries of a new, unprecedented drag economy. A spot on *RuPaul's Drag Race* had become a golden ticket for any queen lucky enough to be cast. For at least a year after a queen's season aired, she could show up in most American cities and get paid hundreds and often thousands of dollars to do a number or two, throw back a few shots, collect a pile of cash, and do it again the next day. She had fans in Brazil, Japan, and Australia. She sold merchandise decorated with her face and catchphrases. She landed sponsorship deals with booze brands and wore custom gowns to premiere parties and fashion shows. Previously, only queens who'd been in the business for decades or who'd had a brush with wider celebrity could afford to support themselves through drag. People like The Lady Chablis, a sharp-tongued, smooth-operating queen who played herself in the 1997 movie adaptation of the book *Midnight in the Garden of Good and Evil*, or Sherry Vine, who'd been performing since the drag boom of the early nineties, might set out on a small solo tour by car or occasionally plane to the few gay clubs in the country big enough to afford to hire guest entertainers. But being on television in the second decade of the twenty-first century brought more recognition overnight than a lifetime spent hustling within the gay community.

In addition to the bar appearances, popular *Drag Race* alumni could join branded tours—choreographed productions with meet and greets, props, stage managers, production assistants, and dressing rooms. These multi-performer stage shows were "all ages" with presold tickets and assigned seats. A few different management companies organized and promoted various tours, but they all followed a similar format and were linked to *Drag Race*. Onstage, some queens lip-synched while others sang live. The performances featured backup dancers, elaborate costume reveals, and all the catchphrases, throwbacks, and inside jokes from their time on the show. Queens would leave for tour before their seasons had even finished airing, and some would tour on and off for years, stopping only when they couldn't stand road life anymore, were no longer getting booked, or fell out with a tour manager. Touring was a fun way to meet queens from other seasons and offered a guaranteed paycheck, but it could be grueling. They traveled by bus and plane, lugging massive suitcases bulging with wigs and garments that weighed thirty, forty, or even fifty pounds. They slept little, ate poorly, and lacked privacy. Generosity, camaraderie, rivalry, crankiness, and fatigue reigned.

On a winter's night a few weeks before *Drag Race* season nine premiered, nearly one thousand people filed into Philadelphia's Fillmore theater for *A Drag Queen Christmas*, a tightly run, two-hour showcase of eight former *RuPaul's Drag Race* contestants. In the bathroom, young women inspected their heavily contoured makeup. Near the bar, gay couples held hands. When the lights flickered, everyone rushed back to their seats just as the emcee was greeting the crowd.

"For those of you who were dragged here by your girlfriends or kids and don't know who I am, my name is Bob the Drag Queen. First name 'Bob,' last name 'the Drag Queen.' " Bob's dress was a belted Santa coat that barely grazed her thighs. "Is this anyone's first time at a drag show?" Bob asked.

There were a few scattered "whoos" from the audience.

"Oh, so you've never seen this?" the heavily painted, six-and-a-half-foot-tall queen gestured suggestively to her towering frame. "Then let me break it down: we—are—men."

Between November 16 and December 29, 2016, *A Drag Queen Christmas* performed in twenty-two cities. Bob hosted and Thorgy Thor played carols on the violin in a pair of red-and-green-plaid palazzo pants. Thorgy loved touring. She excelled during the "Haters Roast," a yearly stand-up-comedy tour in which queens took turns ripping each other to shreds onstage. She was exceedingly confident in her roasting abilities.

"All these girls cannot even kind of compete with how good I am at this," Thorgy said. "I wait for the audience to be quiet, set up the joke, deliver it, and take a sip from my wine and let them laugh. The other girls all fumble through their jokes." She would tell "racist, horrible jokes," like one about Bob the Drag Queen she debuted at the height of the Black Lives Matter movement. "Bob is really funny, however, Bob's makeup is so bad it makes me question whether Black lives really matter," Thorgy said onstage. She cackled when Bob, Monique Heart, and Monét X Change retaliated by walking to the front of the stage and raising their fists in a symbol of Black power.

A Drag Queen Christmas was a coast-to-coast spectacle that brought Thorgy even more fans and followers and allowed her to perform alongside some of her favorite queens. It also brought her and the other queens a new and enthusiastic fan base: children. As Drag Race has attracted attention beyond the gay world and queens have built massive online followings, kids have also flocked to the show and the art form. In some respects, this makes sense: drag queens are big, loud, (generally) friendly characters in bright colors, covered in sparkles and glitter. The growing acceptance of gay culture has also brought drag queens to more family-friendly venues. At Drag Queen Story Hour, drag performers read books to children at libraries across the country. The event was created by queer parents looking for an activity that would appeal to LGBT families and offer messages of inclusivity and acceptance. At many story-hour events, children choose their own drag names and learn about gender and self-acceptance from a drag queen—basically, a clown-princess hybrid with above-average stage presence.

"For the kids, it's just like Mickey Mouse," said one Drag Queen Story Hour organizer. Though Drag Queen Story Hour has been a favorite target of conservative protest and fearmongering, progressive parents have embraced the event as a sassy, confrontational alternative to the kissy face, baby-voiced coddling entertainment made specifically for young children.

That night in Philadelphia, Trixie Mattel, a drag queen country singer from season seven who looked like the love child of Dolly

Parton and Pikachu, addressed the crowd while holding her guitar. "Are there kids here?" she asked wryly. A mother with a child in a pink wig on her lap waved energetically from row U. Though *Drag Race*–branded tours were typically all ages, during her set, Trixie sang updated versions of classic Christmas songs like "All I Want for Christmas Is Nudes" instead of Mariah Carey's "All I Want for Christmas Is You."

"Do you guys want to know why I started doing drag?" Trixie paused. "To not fucking fraternize with children." She was being honest, but the comment was also a self-deprecating acknowledgment of her popularity among kids. It was common on tour to see an eight-year-old girl cosplaying in a massive blond Trixie-inspired wig and heavily painted face. Thousands of teens and tweens discovered Trixie and her frequent collaborator Katya Zamolodchikova, who describes herself as "just your average run-of-the-mill bisexual transvestite hooker," through their YouTube show *UNHhhh* where they riffed, often incoherently, on broad topics such as drugs, flirting, religion, wet dreams, and hair. On their podcast, *The Bald and the Beautiful,* Trixie and Katya expressed ambivalence over the presence of young kids at drag shows.

"I do not fuck with children, but I'll take their money," Trixie Mattel said.

What Trixie loved about drag, she explained, was its sordid sleaziness, and she balked at requests to tone down her crass content. "There's kids here? Well, they're about to hear about me licking an asshole."

A parent of a four-year-old girl once told Katya, who has publicly discussed her mental health struggles, meth addiction, and sex work, that she was her daughter's favorite drag queen.

"A mentally ill, prostitute drug addict?" Trixie asked, sounding shocked.

"I'm a literal crack whore," Katya said, incredulous.

Nowhere was the presence and influence of young fans more apparent than at RuPaul's DragCon, a three-day, RuPaul-branded convention. For about fifty dollars, fans of all ages could meet their favorite queens, shop for drag and *Drag Race*–related merchandise, and gather with one another to celebrate their love of the show. Beginning at around 10:00 a.m. *Drag Race* alumni made their entrances down "Glamazon Boulevard," a double-wide runway that cut through the center of the room. Commonly known as "the pink carpet," Glamazon Boulevard was meant to blur the distinction between ticket holder, drag queen, and supermodel. The queens waved like small-town beauty pageant contestants, dragging trains behind them, their tiaras sparkling despite the convention center's glaring fluorescent lights, and fans jockeyed to get a glimpse and a photo of the arriving stars.

DragCon drew a diverse crowd. Dads wearing clear platform heels and skirt suits pushed strollers as their children scattered pretzel sticks on the floor. Siblings dressed up in queens' iconic looks tore up and down the aisles oohing and aahing over the colorful dresses, wigs, and jewelry on display. In the center of the DragCon exhibition space was a ball pit and a "kid's corner," where a rotating cast of drag queens hosted Drag Queen Story Hours. The all-ages event aimed to provide something for every drag fan, and a walk through the convention center was like scrolling a drag fan's Instagram feed but with more people looking tired and chewing gum. By the afternoon, attendees and presenters, many of whom had consumed little more than Red Bull that day, were sweating through their outfits. The atmosphere was more commercial than social, and the operative phrase overheard at booths and in the aisles was "amazing." A voguing drag queen in a massive pig's head mask and a spandex bodysuit was "amazing"; merch tables of styled wigs in neon colors were "amazing"; six-inch glittery heels with a two-inch platform were "amazing" and on sale at two pairs for three hundred dollars.

Down the aisles and in the lines that were forming in front of the queens' booths, people would quietly shove, sigh, and sulk as they waited, sometimes for hours, to get the thing they came for: a moment of connection with someone they watched and admired on TV and a photo of that moment. To take a photo with a queen, a fan had to buy merchandise from her. Merch could cost anywhere from ten to a hundred dollars. Hardly unique to DragCon, this was the modern fan convention model. Shea Couleé, another season nine finalist, required fans to spend sixty dollars in order to take a photo with her and promised "the Shea Couleé experience" a longer, more personal interaction and higher-quality photos. Sasha Velour had eight-by-ten-inch headshots for sale for ten dollars, pins available for thirty, and a hardbound, full-color book for sixty bucks. Any purchase granted a spot in the meet-and-greet line. One year at DragCon, several preteens ended the day in tears because, even after six hours in line, they hadn't been able to meet Katya.

"It's basically a giant mall," lamented one Brooklyn queen who'd worked a booth for a *Drag Race* alum. "It's so insanely frustrating that the success of an entire industry is based off one reality television show. When you do *Drag Race,* and you sign those contracts, you sign a part of yourself away. You have to constantly keep feeding the machine. You have to keep going to DragCon and putting out new merch, and if you don't keep feeding the *Drag Race* machine, then the machine spits you out, and then you're forgotten." If some queens found the demand for photos to be impersonal and vaguely demeaning, or the corporatization soul sucking, well, this was the cost of drag's arrival in the admittedly niche mainstream, and the payout was substantial. A popular queen could easily walk away from DragCon with fifty thousand dollars. Even some of the crankiest, most political performers saw no point in fighting this wave of commodification. Most of them preferred to ride it.

In addition to the young kids, *Drag Race* now had female and genderqueer fans who were old enough to recognize the inherent queerness of the art form but too young or straight to have been to a gay bar. Sometimes known as "drag girls," they were internet native, social media savvy, gender-fluid, and deeply concerned with representation, inclusion, and identity politics. To many of them, drag meant self-determination and the kind of self-love mantras that RuPaul wove into the fabric of the otherwise cutthroat competition. It was a fun, flashy way to experiment with high-femme glamour outside the context of heterosexual society. They were passionate fans of numerous *Drag Race* alums, but the queen many of them loved most was Sasha Velour. The first winner since *Drag Race* appeared on VH1, and an icon for this new era of queer visibility, the "drag girls'" devotion in the year after season nine aired helped Sasha become one of the most recognized and lauded *Drag Race* alumnae. Responding to Sasha's generous if somewhat restrained spirit online and in interviews, they showered her with praise, video tributes, and, for those lucky enough to see the season nine winner in person, gifts.

Sasha also proved irresistible to the media. Because *Drag Race* had now crossed into the mainstream, *Vanity Fair*, *Rolling Stone*, *Entertainment Weekly*, *The Atlantic*, *Billboard*, and *Vogue* all came calling for interviews, and Sasha politely and thoughtfully answered their questions about her rose petal reveal, her gay-history comic books, the other season nine queens, RuPaul, antigay political action in Russia, and the myriad ways that drag turns "darkness into power." "Sasha Velour Relies on Brains," declared an NPR article published after her crowning. Sasha illustrated the Google Doodle on the search engine homepage in honor of Marlene Dietrich, spoke at the Smithsonian in full drag about losing her mother to cancer, and made another drag-themed book with Johnny—this time in hardcover. She also used the money and notoriety to further NightGowns. In April 2017, while season nine was airing, Sasha moved her passion project to National Sawdust, a three-hundred-seat venue in Williamsburg where attendees bought advance tickets rather than paying a ten-dollar suggested donation at the door. She did another sold-out show a month later, and then again a month after that, and, by the time the season nine finale aired, fans clutching gifts and wearing her merchandise lined up down the block to see Sasha perform alongside members of Switch n' Play and several other stalwarts of the Brooklyn scene.

Political, nerdy, and unabashedly feminist, Sasha was a guiding light for fans who wanted drag to be inclusive and radical. At times, this meant contradicting the art form's most prominent voice: RuPaul. In a 2018 interview with the *Guardian*, RuPaul yet again enraged some performers and fans when he said he wouldn't allow a queen who was trans and had gender-affirming surgery to appear on the show. "You can identify as a woman and say you're transitioning, but it changes once you start changing your body," he said. "It takes on a different thing; it changes the whole concept of what we're doing."

On social media, Sasha was inundated with tweets and messages asking her to address RuPaul's comments. While she was always careful not to attack "Mother Ru" directly, she made her opinions crystal clear. "My drag was born in a community full of trans women, trans men, and gender non-conforming folks doing drag," she tweeted two days after the RuPaul interview was published. "That's the real world of drag, like it or not. I thinks it's fabulous and I will fight my entire life to protect and uplift it."

"Call me old-fashioned, but I refuse to celebrate drag without women," she said in a written speech at NightGowns a few weeks after RuPaul's interview was published. "There continues to be a very oxymoronic debate about what qualifies as real drag, yeah, so here is our official response: trans women, trans men, AFAB—which is assigned female at birth—and nonbinary performers, but especially trans women of color, have been doing drag for literal centuries and deserve to be equally represented and celebrated alongside cis men. . . . We transform ourselves into queer superheroes." She paused and looked up from her paper.

"But underneath these clothes we are just eyebrowless, fleshy beasts. All earth tones—we're boringly similar. Drag is what we use to transform ourselves into unique . . ." Sasha trailed off.

"I lost my place," she mumbled dryly. "I got really into it," she cackled, and the crowd of new and old Sasha Velour fans whooped and hollered. Sasha rarely lost composure, and her palpable frustration that evening was exciting.

Sasha knew that with all this visibility came responsibility to advocate for those excluded from the *Drag Race* family. Gender-nonbinary people, trans men, and women—both trans and cisgender—had been Sasha's closest collaborators since the early days thrifting with Nancy in White River Junction and performing alongside Switch n' Play. Now, they were also the bulk of her fan base. As she toured, made appearances on TV shows, posed for ad campaigns and photos with left-wing politicians like Alexandria Ocasio-Cortez, she would continue to have deep ties to the borough. Her friends walked with her at fashion shows, appeared in video lip sync performances, and toured with NightGowns.

Because drag stardom still flowed first and foremost through *Drag Race*, Sasha Velour levels of fame were inaccessible to Miss Malice, K.James, and the slew of other trans women and female-assigned performers Sasha considered her nearest and dearest. Though some of them wouldn't have wanted a spot on the show even if it were available, others were desperate for similar opportunities. Despite her earnest efforts at inclusion, Sasha couldn't provide the same level of visibility for her friends as *Drag Race* gave its contestants. The impression was of a happy world of queer fantasy and family operating at the highest level of drag excellence. However, the reality was that, despite all Sasha's efforts at inclusion and community, there was only one name at the top of the marquee.

CHAPTER SIXTEEN
Go, West

Merrie Cherry sat at the makeup table in her North Brooklyn bedroom naked but for a bedsheet wrapped around her. Her computer was open, and she was streaming live on Facebook to a dozen or so of her followers. "Hiiiiiiii." Merrie drew out the greeting so that the word was multisyllabic. Her eyes scanned the screen and she smiled. "I'm having, like, a little pregame moment." She gestured at two bearded boys who lounged on the bed behind her.

It was winter 2016, two days before Christmas and one month before the cast of *RuPaul's Drag Race* season nine was announced. While the Velours and the Haus of Aja were consumed with a grueling and exhilarating schedule of photo shoots, shopping, fittings, and general content creation in preparation for their season and the nonstop gigs that would follow, Merrie was also making moves. The attention paid to drag queens on TV was creating a kind of trickle-down effect in Brooklyn. Established local performers like Merrie and Horrorchata were now known beyond the borough and every few months, legit media outlets like the *New York Times* and *Time Out New York* asked for interviews. People followed their favorite performers, not just on Facebook, but on Instagram, too, where queens could create accounts with their drag names. (Facebook required users' legal names.) A video of Merrie reading at Drag Queen Story Hour published on *Vice* went viral. For the YouTube channel of *Drag Race*'s production company, she painted a garish Pinocchio look on legendary club kid James St. James. Thanks to her growing visibility in the local press and online, plus the connections she made with out-of-town queens visiting Brooklyn, Merrie had been hired to give shows in Los Angeles, New Orleans, and even Berlin. Sometimes she had to pay her own way, but twice the bar had covered her airfare.

Merrie now lived on the same block as Metropolitan, mere steps from the gay bar that first welcomed her into its fold and paid her to dress up in drag. The walls of her room were covered with posters from parties she'd thrown there. On her shelves were a dozen Styrofoam heads holding wigs she'd worn at those parties. The previous winter, Merrie had been fired from her desk job at the nonprofit after she refused to remove her nail polish and eye makeup. Instead of rushing to find another nine-to-five job, Merrie filed for unemployment and threw herself into networking. She managed to convince bars to hire her, not just to perform, but to schedule shows, book other queens, and promote them on social media. She stopped wearing flip-flops— mostly—she'd started to contour her face, she even had some custom designer looks made. She charmed bosses and bar managers with her characteristic bald ambition and airheaded sass.

"The proof is in the pudding, and my pudding is good," she told one during a meeting about a possible weekly hosting gig.

"I'm always keeping it fresh, boo. My cherries are the freshest," she'd said to another.

At first, Merri's grandmother had balked at the prospect of her grandson leaving his office job to do drag full time, especially since Merrie had delivered the news expecting—"spoiled brat that I am"— Grandma Ruth to send help in the form of cash.

"Then you better drag it out!" Merrie's grandmother had replied with no offer of material support. Merrie was shook. After six months or so, when it seemed clear that Merrie was managing to support herself, Grandma Ruth grudgingly accepted the career shift.

"How's Cherry Berry," Grandma Ruth would sometimes ask when they spoke on the phone, or she'd tell Merrie a story about seeing "the Roople" on TV. This was the first year since Merrie had moved to New York City in 2009 that she wasn't going back to Berkeley for Christmas. She couldn't afford the plane ticket home or to turn down lucrative holiday bookings.

As Merrie was pregaming that night, Beyoncé was playing and Merrie began to lip-synch as she painted. "'We like to party,'" she mouthed, waving her hand in front of her face. This was what it meant to work in nightlife. You had friends and you had followers, people who knew who you were and wanted to hang out with you. The most-booked queens in Brooklyn all had a seemingly bottomless capacity for partying, an ability to stay up until sunrise despite, or sometimes because of, the churn of inebriation. Sober drag performers existed, and some of them were fierce, but the well-oiled Brooklyn drag machine was lubricated with vast quantities of liquor, pills, smoke, and powder. That the drugs and the drinks were often free made it even easier to carry into the early morning.

When she was nearly ready to step into the night, it was time to end the livestream. "I have to do stuff that is not good for the young kids that are following me," said Merrie. "I have to be responsible."

In the Facebook comments someone replied, "COKE."

· · · · ·

At Macri Park, two blocks from Merrie's house, she moved, slow and steady, through the crowd. Macri was one of the bars that regularly hosted drag shows in Brooklyn, and as she circulated, dispensing air-kisses and shouting hellos, she noticed a tall, dark-haired boy watching her. When, in the course of working the room, Merrie reached the dark-haired boy with the serious look on his face, she went into automatic hostess mode.

"Hey, babes," Merrie rasped, and introduced herself to the boy and his friend, a pretty girl with curly brown hair. "Thanks for coming out tonight." Greeting people was easy, especially since drag gave Merrie a natural gregariousness and a somewhat proprietary attitude toward any space she happened to occupy. The boy smiled as he took Merrie's outstretched hand and told her his name was Dakota.

Dakota was young and lanky, with black hair and big dark eyes. He'd bleached his eyebrows, and they made his already striking face alluring and somewhat unnerving. Earlier in 2016, he'd graduated from Columbia University, where he'd bonded with another student, a lesbian poet who had come to Macri with him that first night. Together, they binged old episodes of *Drag Race* and went to viewing parties at one of the few uptown gay bars near campus. They whooped and hollered when a queen executed a perfect lip sync and groaned if she sang off-key or came out in an awful look.

Dakota had been playing dress-up pretty much all his life, but he'd mostly kept it a secret. In the liberal DC suburb Silver Spring, Maryland, it could feel like people were always in each other's business. His parents were supportive of his interest in art. He was class president, got amazing grades, and helped out with school dances. He also had a boyfriend in high school and told no one. He just kept imagining what it would be like if his friends' parents knew he was gay, and the whole thing felt awkward and uncomfortable. Dakota loved art and fashion. Designing clothes and making beautiful things became an outlet for self-expression, even as he kept certain parts of himself hidden from his friends and family. At Columbia, soon after he and his friend started watching *Drag Race*, they discovered a scene much stranger and more exciting than what they saw on TV—just across the river.

Dakota's friend had stumbled onto Brooklyn drag a few months earlier, during an open mic at This N That, and once she got interested in something, she went deep. She'd poured over social media, becoming an unofficial encyclopedia of the local scene. At Macri Park with Dakota that night, she was like a scientist doing fieldwork, pointing out local queens, some of whom weren't even in drag.

"These were literally people who'd maybe done drag a handful of times or had done drag years before we were there," Dakota later recalled.

"Dakota wants to do drag, too," his friend told Merrie.

"Well . . . do drag!" Merrie said, not dismissive but also not particularly invested. Lately, it seemed like everyone wanted to be a drag queen. Maybe they were jealous of the attention that queens got in the bars or assumed a few months in heels would land them a spot on *Drag Race* and a chance to make money as an entertainer. However, as a veteran of the Brooklyn drag scene, Merrie felt like she had developed a discerning eye for new talent. Some of the enthusiastic newcomers were genuinely good and legitimately committed. They'd been following drag queens on social media and watching YouTube makeup tutorials since grade school. They understood how to paint their faces to maximize their features, put an outfit together, and hold a crowd's attention during a performance. In that case, Merrie was happy to help. Dakota nodded and smiled shyly at Merrie's lukewarm encouragement.

"OK. Well. I'll think about it."

· · · · ·

Two weeks after that first meeting, Dakota took a bus from his apartment in Union City, New Jersey, to the PATH train that ran between Jersey and Manhattan. From there, he rode the subway to a small studio he rented in Bushwick. There, he got dressed up, and then took the train to Macri Park in Williamsburg. Out in drag for the first time, Dakota had on a massive bow and foundation that was slightly too dark. The baby queen walked over to Merrie, who was hosting the show again that night, and said hello with a nervous wave.

"Yes, Miss Thing!" Merrie shouted.

Dakota looked great—"maybe reconsider the foundation color," Merrie suggested—but this was a genuinely cute baby queen.

"Here's what you're gonna do," Merrie said. "You're going to take a shot and do a number. Not every drag queen performs, but you should see if you like it. Do you have a song in mind?"

Dakota suggested "Girls Just Wanna Have Fun," by eighties pop icon Cyndi Lauper.

Merrie shook her head. "No. Don't do that." It's dumb, overplayed, and doesn't say anything about the queen performing it.

Instead, Dakota performed "Emotions" by Mariah Carey. Her shoes were too small and her hands trembled. As she stood awkwardly on the platform, her knees turned inward. Once the song got going, she stomped back and forth when she remembered to, and moved her arms. When Mariah sang "higher" and hit those ascending whistle tones, Dakota flipped her hair and her wig fell off. She hadn't pinned it on. After she finished, flushed and a little embarrassed, Merrie patted her kindly on the back, and a few of the other queens offered words of encouragement.

Dakota had been nervous about being in drag in public and shy about talking to people he didn't know. This shyness wasn't inhibition or fear exactly: it was a deep and abiding self-consciousness that occasionally gave way to bursts of excitement. He was overflowing with ideas for performances and had even made paper dolls to showcase all the looks he wanted to create. All he'd been missing was a stage. Though it had been rocky, Dakota had survived the first performance and wanted more. Drag was raucous and liberating.

He'd heard that the surefire way to break into the scene was to go out every night and meet as many people as possible. He could see that the other queens spent long nights chatting, sipping drinks, and bumming cigarettes. Unwilling to travel between New Jersey and Brooklyn in drag, he'd get ready at his art studio, stay at the bar until three or four in the morning, go back to his studio, get out of drag, then take the subway to a bus and get back to Union City around six.

Dakota followed other local other drag queens online. Through them he learned about the 2017 Mr(s) BK pageant. Formerly known as the Mr(s) Williamsburg pageant, this was the event where Aja had thrown herself from a balcony railing and launched her career. Though Dakota was new to drag, all the art classes and high school theater had taught him how to carefully plan and execute a performance. He told Merrie he was thinking about competing and, instead of laughing at him, she offered to help him workshop his number. She also booked him for a weeknight gig at Macri Park. While some performers in Merrie's position were threatened by newcomers, Merrie realized that a town as creative and discerning as Brooklyn wasn't going to be satisfied seeing the same five girls perform night after night. While Aja, Thorgy, and Sasha were touring the world as Ru girls, the Brooklyn scene had to keep evolving, innovating, and churning out new talent.

The popularity of *Drag Race* had turned your average gay barfly into a connoisseur of the art form. People who'd never glued down a lace-front wig or painted a cut crease evaluated queens' looks and performances with the discernment of an Olympic judge. But though these fans were sometimes incorrigible fault finders, they were also engaged and showing up. They tipped stalwart Brooklyn queens who hadn't been cast on the show and then followed them on social media. Their reverence for eye makeup and fabric choice and their knowledge of drag references and history further legitimized the art form in Brooklyn as it went from being a collection of close friends to a bigger universe with an established hierarchy, a formidable media presence, and its own modest economy. As one of the most visible Brooklyn queens, Merrie understood that higher standards for performers in the bars meant more good queens out and about in Brooklyn, and that equaled more overall success for her. All boats were rising, and she wanted to be at the helm.

•••••

In January 2017, a few weeks after Dakota first performed at Macri Park, he pressed the bottom buzzer of Merrie's apartment building and waited. He could see that the light was on inside. He shivered, not from the cold as much as nervousness. He pictured his apartment in Union City, New Jersey, where he'd been practicing the number and his art studio in Bushwick, where he'd come up with the look, and he briefly wished he were back there—comfortable, familiar, and alone—before he mustered the courage to buzz again. Merrie Cherry, now very much out of drag, opened the door and welcomed Dakota into the apartment.

"Hello, hello, come on in," Merrie said as he entered a sparsely furnished living room. Merrie took a seat on an antique-looking couch and propped her legs on the coffee table.

Dakota scurried into the bathroom to change. He shed his clothing and riffled through his bags, turning around awkwardly, and emerged wearing what looked like two square pieces of white, almost translucent plastic sheeting sewn together to form a shapeless sack.

What the hell is this girl about to do? Merrie wondered, eyeing the skinny shoulders and chest of scraggly hairs. "OK, babes. Let's do this," Merrie said.

Dakota walked stiffly into place in front of Merrie and kneeled down, the cloudy white tarp spreading around her like a bubble. Her expression was blank, she avoided making eye contact and instead stared at the wall behind Merrie.

Oh Lord, Merrie thought, *this is about to be weird.* She pressed play on the track and a piano began.

A man's voice whispered over the accompaniment, "It was one of those days when it's a minute away from snowing and there's this electricity in the air, you can almost hear it."

Dakota stood up and turned around slowly, continuing to lip-synch along with the monologue. "'And this bag was, like, dancing with me.'"

The outfit, Merrie could see now, was shaped like a giant plastic bag. With the handles at Dakota's shoulders, the almost see-through sack extended to the floor. "'Like a little kid begging me to play with it,'" the monologue, an iconic scene from the Academy Award–winning 1999 film *American Beauty* continued, and Dakota kept spinning, faster and faster, as if blown by the wind. "'And that's the day I realized there was this entire life behind things, and this incredibly benevolent force, that wanted me to know there was no reason to be afraid, ever.'"

Dakota was drifting and floating around the room with the slightest hint of a smile on her face. The painful earnestness of the monologue—"'Sometimes there's so much beauty in the world I feel like I can't take it'"—was the perfect foil for the image of a tall, skinny boy wearing a literal plastic bag. Dakota began to camp it up, scrunching her previously deadpan expression as the monologue reached its corniest and most iconic moment—"'like my heart's going to cave in.'"

The piano ended, and a quiet beat began to pound. Dakota folded in on herself with her back to the audience—in this case, Merrie—and began to fumble with the garment. The thick plastic was unwieldy, and her hands shook as she tied the belt, but she'd practiced for hours over many days to get this transition as smooth as possible.

"Do you ever feel . . . like a plastic bag?" The opening line of Katy Perry's bubblegum-pop hit "Firework" rang out from the tinny computer speakers as Dakota turned around, perfectly in time, to face Merrie. Now belted around her waist, the previously shapeless plastic shrift had been transformed into a perfectly fitted gown. With the simplest of costume adjustments, Dakota's performance had gone from earnestness to pure camp. The back of the bag spread behind Dakota like a cape. It was fashion, style, beauty, mixed with the slightest hint of delusion. It was drag.

The chorus of the original Katy Perry song was "Baby, you're a firework," but Dakota had edited the track to repeat "Baby, you're a plastic bag, plastic bag, plastic bag, plastic bag." As she danced wildly, she could hear that Merrie was laughing. This was good. But *why* was Merrie laughing? The song was fast and it helped that she'd rehearsed, but she still felt like she was falling behind. All her meticulously planned choreography was lost. She threw herself into the manic chorus. Tossing her hair and tumbling to the floor. The movement and music carried on. She had no choice but to keep lip-synching and keep going.

"Plastic bag, plastic bag, plastic bag" her mix droned. She could tell it was funny, but she no longer felt like she was the one in control of the joke. The number ended, and she stood in front of Merrie, out of breath.

The older queen jumped to her feet. "Babes, that was so good. Yaasss. Werk." Merrie was genuinely impressed with the number, though she had some notes. "You've got to look at your audience more. I'm the only person here; you should at least be looking at me a few times." She told Dakota to be careful not to turn her back any more than necessary. "I can see your nervousness, babes," Merrie cautioned.

"Well, I am nervous," Dakota replied somewhat petulantly.

"I don't give a fuck, and neither do the judges. Get yourself out of that."

Dakota pursed her lips and took a deep breath. "Well, that's gonna take time, but I hear you." She could see it would be no good getting defensive. Merrie had enjoyed the number and was trying to help.

"I just don't want to see it on your face," Merrie softened, remembering how nervous she was the first time she performed. "'Cause if I see it on your face, you've lost."

•••••

The first round of the Mr(s) BK pageant took place at Gold Sounds, a gay-friendly bar in Bushwick. Thorgy Thor and Horrorchata were both judging. Thorgy had on a bright orange foam top hat meant to look like cheese over a blue tinsel wig and a matching orange foam bracelet.

"Give it up for Dakota," Thorgy announced. Dakota came onto the stage and crouched down in her plastic bag dress.

"I was very intimidated," Dakota later said. "I wanted everything to be perfect." Her dancer friends helped coordinate the movement and make it even tighter. She had even called several body-waxing studios, figuring that if she was going to win, she'd have to be hairless. Most told her they wouldn't wax a man.

"I didn't say I was a man. You're assuming a lot. There are very hairy women," she'd argued until she finally found a dingy place in Chinatown that agreed to do it for a higher price. The experience took forty-five minutes, hurt like crazy, and was not at all glamorous. But she walked out smooth. She also bought a wig for the first time, a long blond flat front, and she painted full body freckles and a thick gap onto her teeth with black eyeliner, which required her to keep her mouth open for an hour while it dried.

As the music began, intermittent "woo-hoos" and chatter circulated through the antsy crowd.

"Shut up," Merrie yelled from the audience.

They were drowning out the track.

" 'There's this electricity in the air,' " Dakota lip-synched, and then locked eyes with the audience.

" 'You can almost hear it,' " she mouthed. As she turned to make the outfit adjustment, Thorgy glanced over to see what she was doing.

"Yes, queen," she said, and wagged a finger to signify approval. Dakota finished tying the dress's knot just as "Firework" began, and when people clocked the belted bag, which hung perfectly, a tremor of delight passed through the audience. In the next five seconds, the clever reveal sank in and they roared with approval. Dakota's face had changed from soft and contemplative to fierce and seductive. Flipping her hair, twirling, even crawling on her hands and knees, she owned the stage for the next three and a half minutes, through the numerous shifts and changes in the mix, which included various pop culture references to being plastic. The audience loved it. Dakota had done it—she'd managed to be beautiful, fashionable, and well-rehearsed, but most important, she'd been funny and surprising. Merrie was right: the act was a showstopper. Dakota won that round and sailed into the competition's finale.

Dakota had two weeks to prepare a new number. Winning the first round had felt incredible, but she was still a nobody who'd performed only three times. The other competitors were established queens, people with thousands of Instagram followers and years of experience. Miz Jade, a queen who'd gone to SUNY Purchase with Thorgy Thor and performed with backSpace; Hannah Lou, a protégé of Merrie's and a beloved DJ; Momo Shade; and Crimson Kitty, who'd performed with Switch n' Play since before Sasha Velour lived in Brooklyn.

Holy shit, I know all these people, Dakota thought to herself when she saw the finale flier. "I felt like I had a target on my back," she said. "None of these girls knew who I was." If she wanted to win the whole competition, she was going to have to turn out an unforgettable performance. In the "question and answer" portion of the competition's first round, host Alotta McGriddles had asked Dakota what she'd wish for if she were stranded on a desert island. "I'd give America back to the Indians," Dakota replied in a Valley-girl voice with a flip of that blond wig. Dakota's grandmother was Seneca-Cayuga. Her mother had been adopted and didn't have Native American biological heritage, but the culture had been a major part of Dakota's life growing up. This ditzy blond character Dakota had created was well meaning but clueless, and she'd loved pretending to be her onstage. Could she make a bolder statement by leaning in to this character?

Dakota took the drag name West Dakota and created a backstory for the character. She was named after a paradise created when the giant oil snake, the "Dakota Access Pipeline," "slithered its way across native lands carrying four hundred and eight thousand barrels of oil a day from its greasy belly." The persona, a girl with blond hair and eyebrows, had been "one-sixteenth Dakota for seven generations." Once Dakota settled on a character and a theme—a tongue-in-cheek take on white girls appropriating native culture that also incorporated her own history, family, and frustrations with representations of indigenous people—the performance came together quickly.

The night of the finale, West Dakota invited pretty much everyone she knew in New York City. Friends from college took the train across the city to cheer her on. The performance began with West Dakota offstage. A video of the queen in her room played on the screen. "Hey, guys, ummm, it's been a while. I'm gonna do a makeup tutorial, but first I've been getting a lot of requests about where my name comes from—" The video glitched, and West appeared in what she later described as "full native regalia," including a white gown and headdress. When the video of the tongue-in-cheek makeup tutorial resumed, West acted it out onstage.

"This is traditional makeup, not, like, regular makeup," West's bubbly on-screen avatar explained. "I have to start with a base. I'm wearing Estée Lauder double-wear stay-in-place foundation in the color 'Normal.' But you can wear whatever best suits your skin." The jokes were subtle, but the audience was laughing along. "To really emphasize high cheekbones try the Dior color 'Savage.' The markings don't mean anything, so you can just do . . . whatever. That's it. So easy. This is the traditional makeup I wear to one of the largest gatherings of my people. It is a festival where we come together for a week to thank the sun, who is my father; the earth, who is my mother; and the river, who is my third cousin. We call it co-a-chell-a." The crowd hooted with laughter and applause. "Don't forget to subscribe," West's video concluded.

While the judges' scores were added up, the contestants mingled backstage. West Dakota never imagined that drag or nightlife would be the platform for art. She'd always pictured her work in runways or museums, but there was something magical about performing in front of these crowds. It was a way to connect but also be in control. People responded right in front of her, and she was excited in a way she'd never been about a gallery opening. It was art *and* a party. Merrie Cherry was invested in West and believed the gaggiest performance should win. She'd recognized potential and was nurturing it. But should an unknown be able to win the whole competition?

When the contestants reassembled onstage, Dakota shifted awkwardly in her heels. Alotta McGriddles gripped the microphone and ordered the crowd to be quiet. "The winner of this year's Mr(s) BK is West Dakota," she shouted. The audience erupted. Dakota's number had felt fresh and strange. It was artistic, political, and personal. Plus, she had fashion on her side. However, not everyone had been blown away by the number. After the performance, a woman approached and asked if West was native.

"I'm indigenous, and I thought it was offensive," the woman said. West tried to explain that it was a critique of whiteness. But the criticism had her shook. "It was the first time I'd put my art out there and gotten a negative response," she said. "I knew I was playing with a sensitive topic; maybe I was a little bit too new and naive about what I was doing. But it was a genuine message." Later someone posted a video of the performance on Facebook, and West asked them to take it down. "The way things are on the internet, all it takes is for one person to say something for the narrative to spin out of your control." If she ever published a video it would have to be accompanied by an essay explaining her background and the context of the piece. "It was not done carelessly," she insisted.

Plenty of Brooklyn performers did not find anything controversial about West's performance. Merrie was so proud. "She brought something genuine to the table, something that none of us really saw at that time," Merrie later said. "She brought beauty, brought art, but also history. That was the golden ticket, right there. Those things combined in the Brooklyn drag scene, and you're hands down a winner."

Merrie felt more powerful, influential, and important than ever before, but her fame and recognition were always traced back and connected to Brooklyn. Just as RuPaul had thanked Thorgy for bringing BK to *RDR* on season eight of *Drag Race*, club kid James St. James described Merrie Cherry as "the queen of the Bushwick scene." Understanding that her popularity was inextricably linked to her town, Merrie set about mythologizing the local drag scene, its history, and her relationships with other queens in the borough. On social media, she'd post group photos taken at Sugarland back when "brooklyn was just a few girls trying to have fun and get a little coin at the same time" as one caption explained.

She had started to refer to herself as the "Mother of Brooklyn," and while many accepted this without argument, she was often teased and taunted for the "self-proclaimed" grandiose title. "Mother of Brooklyn? Mother of what?" Thorgy would say when Merrie wasn't around and her name came up. "When did she get here?" Thorgy liked Merrie, "but I always looked at her with a skeptical eye. Over years and years of me doing my job, she somehow solidified her own position and declared her own title, which I thought was ballsy, disgusting, and cool. I was like, 'Fuck you!' I never gave myself a title. I just worked my ass off. Merrie could show up to any party; she was the largest, rudest person in the room. She put 'Merrie Cherry Presents' on a party flier and people would fucking show up. Why?" Thorgy screeched. "She would book everyone else and do nothing, show up late, say one stupid thing on the mic that made no sense, and then you would never see her again 'cause she would get in a cab to go to another party that she was probably getting paid for." Thorgy was baffled, but she couldn't fault a queen for having a solid hustle. "I was like, 'Work, bitch!'"

While Thorgy and Aja had become internationally recognized drag queens, without the same exposure, Merrie had no choice but to build her career at home. With young, savvy, talented performers streaming into the scene, she had a choice: compete with them openly or try to envelope them, mentor them even, in the existing scene. Mothers nurtured and guided their young, but mothers were indisputably in charge. Rivals could be unseated; motherhood was for life.

CHAPTER SEVENTEEN
The Rosemont Kids

There was a new queen in town. Many, in fact. In Brooklyn, subway cars full of fresh, untested drag queens, kings, and nonbinary performers seemed to be arriving nightly. They packed into shoddily renovated Bushwick apartments, and they crowded the dozens of bars and restaurants that cropped up along Broadway and Myrtle Avenues. They were more refined than Merrie and her crew had been six years ago and had a worldly, iconoclastic sort of style in which leather jackets and metal chains mixed with lace and satin, Teva sandals and socks paired with rhinestone mesh shift dresses. There was no fear of sparkle or glitter, but there was little love for hippies or normies, or the gays from Hell's Kitchen or Chelsea who wore tank tops that showed off their countless hours at the gym. These young queers were still interpersonally messy—they were young, after all—but came into the scene with a strong sense of self. Many of them had come out in adolescence and had a firm grasp of the rules and expectations of the internet. They loved music and fashion and makeup and, for the ones who'd been watching *Drag Race* since they were preteens, drag was the arena where all these things collided and became unequivocally gay. When Krystal Something-Something, Thorgy Thor, Merrie Cherry, and Horrorchata started drag, it was a scrappy subculture often dismissed by gay crowds as too old-fashioned, too femme, or too messy to be interesting. But thanks to a cultural moment dominated by queer culture—Lady Gaga, *Queer Eye*, the "Transgender Tipping Point," and a growing roster of out gay celebrities—these young, drag-obsessed queers were the epitome of cool. Like West Dakota with her bleached eyebrows, long black hair, and gap-toothed smile, they had the look, the style, the attitude, and the talent. On any given night in Brooklyn there were a startling number of people doing the splits on the dance floor. All they needed was a stage.

Merrie Cherry was happy to provide one. She knew she could not stop the flood of newcomers drawn to the borough and its free-wheeling gay bars, and she didn't want to. A scene that didn't change and grow was doomed. But while the ingenues may steal hearts, the grand dames pull the strings. Merrie set about quite literally putting these youngsters in their place.

"Metro was for the older people," Merrie explained. If you weren't in drag, you had to prove you were twenty-one. "It was not bullshitting with IDs."

There were only so many drink tickets available every night, and once they were gone, it was hard to get a free drink from the bar. "I could do it, of course, but not the average people," Merrie said. "Things needed to change." This change came on Montrose Avenue. The Rosemont opened as a jazz bar in 2016, targeting the upscale, upwardly mobile newcomers in the condos and developments that peppered the eastern border of Williamsburg. From Metro, the Rosemont was nine blocks south, across the street from a park where middle schoolers played baseball games in the warm weather. Despite an airy backyard and round, comfy booths, by the end of the year, it was failing to attract a crowd. No one cared enough about jazz to come out regularly, and there were so many other bars in the neighborhood. In a desperate attempt to drum up some business, the owners dumped the jazz bar concept and lured Troy Carson, who'd previously owned Sugarland

and Metropolitan, back from Arizona where he'd gone to get a break from the grind of nightlife. Troy, knowing he'd been away from the scene for a while, sought out trusted and established local queens to help him book shows and attract the young queers flocking to Bushwick and East Williamsburg.

Believing that the Brooklyn drag scene needed new venues, Merrie got herself hired to do social media, bartend, and book shows at the Rosemont. She dreamed of a trail of gay bars from Metropolitan, the westernmost gay bar in Williamsburg, toward Bushwick. As Merrie saw it, the more spaces there were in Brooklyn, the more of a gay destination it became and the more money everyone made. But a lot of the older, more established queens were uninterested in Rosemont gigs, doubting that the crowds would be big or deep-pocketed enough to sustain their shows. In order to fill the lineup every week, Merrie reached out to green performers she'd seen around or worked with at Macri Park and Metropolitan.

"The only girls that took the jobs were the new girls, 'cause they didn't have anything," Merrie said. "It didn't matter if they filled it up because they were given a stage to perform on that they wouldn't have been given anywhere else."

Soon, she'd filled the lineup with a diverse slew of "daughters," people who she'd mentored over the past year and considered family. Hannah Lou and DJ Ickarus had a party on Fridays called Bitch, Nasty. Dahlia Sin of the Haus of Aja began throwing Skin on Sundays. For Wednesday nights, Merrie hired a queen named Ruby Fox, who'd been pulling outrageous stunts at Brooklyn parties—hanging from rafters, throwing drinks in people's faces, and generally bulldozing anything in her path—and Jacquée Kennedée, a fierce makeup artist who modeled her looks and attitude after early-career RuPaul, to throw a party called Gag. Slang for "fierce" or "yaas," the party quickly came under fire because it shared its name with a long-standing Friday night party at Metropolitan. The group reassessed, made the necessary apologies for accidentally stepping on toes, did some online damage control, and renamed their party Oops.

Once the Rosemont was up and running, there was drag in Brooklyn seven nights a week. Promo for parties started anywhere from two weeks to two days before the event. In addition to being relatively cheap to hire and enthusiastic, Merrie knew that the younger queens would promote their shows widely on Instagram. The expansion of the social media platform from four hundred million users in 2015 to seven hundred million in 2017 coincided with increasingly sophisticated and ubiquitous smartphone cameras. Follower counts along with likes on images became social currency. Performers thrived on the platform where everyone's account was designed to give the impression they were living their best lives both on- and offstage. The endless stream of exhortations—"Party with the gurls tonight"; "Let's get stupid"; "Come to my gig"; "Come to my show"—over fliers and selfies meant anyone who followed more than a few dozen of these local performers would almost certainly know about every gig in the borough. "Shows, shows, shows," was the rallying cry on social media and in the bars. "Giving shows" being the operative term for a lip-synch performance or a moment of spontaneous public mayhem.

Instagram told Brooklyn drag devotees where the parties were, when they started, and who was going to be there. Then, the following day, a ten-minute scroll through Instagram Stories would provide documentation of who'd been there, what they'd done, and how they looked doing it. When Icelandic star Björk ended up at the Rosemont one night, Merrie Cherry used a photo of the singer sitting at the bar to promote her *Drag Race* viewing party. "NOW EVERYONE KNOWS WHERE TO WATCH RPDR!!!! The Rosemont EVERY FRIDAY." As followers of Brooklyn drag were treated to a nonstop stream of fun times at the Rosemont, FOMO—fear of missing out—set in, and curious queers began to flock to the nondescript bar on the other side of Williamsburg. For some, it was closer to their apartments in Bushwick, the crowd was younger, more gender-fluid and more freewheeling. For others, curiosity and the photographic evidence of pretty new faces in the crowd lured them to a bar they might otherwise have ignored.

One of these pretty new faces was a queen who, after experimenting with her name for several years, would come to call herself Chiquitita. Eighteen years old, skinny, shy, bordering on awkward, already world-weary and trauma-tested, she had discovered the Rosemont when Dahlia Sin, Aja's drag daughter, booked her for Skin on a Sunday night in the spring of 2017. After she performed, she watched Magenta, a queen from the Bronx who was also underage, kick so hard her heel flew off her foot and poked a hole in the club's ceiling.

Gaggy, Chiquitita thought. She lived in Jamaica, Queens, with her Salvadoran mother and her older brothers. As a lonely, closeted gay teen with access to really good public transportation, Chiqui (pronounced "cheeky"), as she was known to her friends, took drugs. Streamed porn on her mom's computer. Fought kids from the neighborhood. Made out with her brothers' friends. And, after seeing a drag queen named Willam deliver epic reads on YouTube in a halter top and a honey-blond wig, started dressing up as a girl. First on Halloween, when she wore black thigh-high leggings and a tiny pink tutu and went to a neighborhood party.

"My hood was not the safest place for a crossdresser to be," she'd later say. But that night, mostly everyone was cool; it was Halloween, after all. A straight guy even offered her a pot brownie. She kept dressing up at home, and then one night in 2015 Chiqui went to Pride Lounge, a gay Latinx bar in Queens, and caught a glimpse of her first in-real-life drag queen. Dressed as Marilyn Monroe in a platinum-blond wig and iconic white halter dress, she had luscious, sparkling red lips, and she exited a cab like a movie star at a red-carpet premiere. It was Aja, and Chiqui thought she was the most beautiful person she'd ever seen. "She had that attitude, that allure of 'Oh, hi, how are you? It's *so* good to meet you,' double kiss on the cheek, *mwah mwah*," Chiqui would later say on her podcast *Shows*. Chiqui was seventeen, a student at an especially neglected high school in an especially far-off neighborhood of a generally overlooked borough. No one had ever double-kissed her before, let alone a person who looked this beautiful who was gay and out and booked in drag several nights a week. Chiqui left soon after the introduction, changed forever by the encounter, but trying to make it home before curfew.

After that, Chiqui messaged Aja online and they hung out a few times. It made sense; on paper there were similarities. Both Latinx, both New York City natives. Both understood what it was like to be a sad, gay, attention-starved teenager trapped in a frustrating family. They both loved glamour but touched none of it. They were both scared but also weirdly brave. Being gay got them out of their neighborhoods, but being gay was why they couldn't survive there in the first place.

Aja recognized the similarities, gave some general advice, pro-vided a couple makeup tips on the few times they got ready together, and gave Chiqui some clothes. But this was not a mother-daughter situation. *Drag Race* season nine was about to air, and Aja was overwhelmed with the newfound responsibility and opportunity. She was also in no position to take on any more daughters. Chiqui would have to fend for herself, and she did it the tried-and-true way—by entering Manhattan drag competitions in bars across the city. She never won. She sometimes placed in the top three, but who was she really? A kid who didn't know anyone and who was lying about her age.

Through Aja, Chiqui got her first Brooklyn booking at Don Pedro's, a grungy Mexican restaurant that had shows in the back. She performed the Azealia Banks song "212" and did dip after dip after dip, because she was feeling her shine.

"Why does this girl keep doing dips?" Kandy Muse asked Aja, and Aja just shook her head and smiled. Chiqui liked Brooklyn. It was fun and messy and felt like anything could happen. She started to spend hours in front of her mother's sewing machine, creating velour, Lycra, spandex, and mohair looks. But out in drag at the bars she was terrified to say or do the wrong thing and make a bad impression. She didn't want anyone to know she was underage. Dahlia Sin, from the Haus of Aja, either didn't know or didn't care that Chiqui was a teenager and offered her a spot at Skin. The flier was cute, an anime-style drawing of a brunette with big boobs, and when Chiqui saw Magenta kick that hole in the ceiling, she knew she was somewhere special.

Chiqui kept coming back. One night, in drag, even though she wasn't booked, Chiqui stumbled into the Rosemont during Oops, the bar's Wednesday night party. In a way the party's name said it all. It was a night of low expectations and high tolerance. On Wednesdays, Merrie would sometimes bartend and excuse herself from pouring drinks to give an impromptu show, stranding the other bartender on staff. When Merrie wasn't giving shows, she sat on a stool behind the bar, occasionally opening a beer or making some change for tips. Merrie's stint as a bartender didn't last, but Oops slowly built momentum. The night Chiqui first saw the show, a blond, flat-chested approximation of a reality television Real Housewife was standing on the small stage, giggling into the mic that had become smeared with lipstick and holding a vodka tonic in her other hand.

"Welcome to my sexy party," the queen, whose name was Crystal Mesh, slurred. "Who's ready for shows?" She had on a platinum-blond wig, multiple strands of sparkling fake diamonds, and was balancing on two reed-thin legs in clear, six-inch platform high heels.

Crystal, whose boy name was Jacob, had grown up across the street from a chicken farm in North Carolina. When he was five he told his parents he wanted to be "famous" when he grew up, and in college he auditioned for the *Real World*, got a couple of callbacks but didn't make it onto the cast. He appreciated beautiful things, could tolerate the public, and, though he loved a good time, was trustworthy enough to be alone with a cash register, so after he moved to Brooklyn in 2006 he started working in retail and excelled at his job. As he polished glass and chrome countertops, he watched the chichi customers who frequented the store, making demands and impulse purchases, cups of cold brew coffee gripped in their perfectly manicured hands, and was both disgusted and entranced. It was the same feeling he got when bingeing the *Real Housewives of New York City*. He delighted in the contradictions of the housewives' lives and the way they hustled so hard at nothing, their skill at being themselves—rich, snobby, and talentless. Their egos and their catfights.

When he wasn't working or watching reality TV, Jacob—skinny, blond, freckled, and tall—was at the gay bars. He was a conventionally cute white boy who moved easily in basic gay circles but was drawn to weirdos, including younger people who were obsessed with avant-garde fashion, or who made music alone in their bedrooms, or did drag. Jacob was content being a member of the audience until the summer of 2016, when a twenty-nine-year-old man named Omar Mateen killed forty-nine people and wounded fifty-three others at the beloved Orlando gay club Pulse. Terrified and grieving, Jacob realized, "I could just die, any minute, because I'm a faggot." It was time to make some changes. "If I'm going to keep being a barfly, I should be a barfly with a purpose," he said. Retail paid the bills, he was good at it, but it had no edge and brought no excitement to his life. The

Pulse shooting had made him want to "live [his] life to the ultimate faggotry," he said. For him, that meant doing either porn or drag.

He chose drag and set about creating a persona. Back in 2006, a college friend had jokingly given him the name Crystal Mesh. It was a riff on crystal meth, a drug that was popular in seedier corners of the gay community and associated with multiday orgies, delusional rages, and AIDS. Jacob had little of that darkness, but that didn't mean he wasn't going to have a tongue-in-cheek, controversial name he could laugh about that forced people to take things less seriously. Jacob began experimenting with makeup and showing up at gay bars in Brooklyn dressed in miniskirts and crop tops. Jacob as Crystal would knock on the dressing room door and announce, "I'm here!" to whatever queen was touching up her makeup or doing a bump in front of the mirror. Crystal loved acting delusional, and it helped that she was already over thirty and felt like she had no time to waste.

When the Rosemont became a gay bar at the beginning of 2017, Crystal's tenacious, slightly deranged networking paid off. Her friend Jacquée Kennedée booked her for Oops with the promise of forty bucks and free drinks, and Crystal showed up in a platinum-blond wig, a miniskirt, and a fluffy mohair sweater and referred to the audience as "my babies." The Oops girls booked Crystal for the next week, and then they just kept booking her. The kids, largely in their early twenties, often underage, took to calling thirty-four-year-old Crystal "auntie," and, more comfortable improvising on the mic than lip-synching, she began to host the show, spewing forth a stream of good-natured fantasy that the small but die-hard crowd lapped up with glee.

"I just wanna be sexy and famous, is there something wrong with that?" she'd ask them, and later announce, "I always wanted to be popular and rich, and now I am."

To be a drag queen "you have to be disgustingly optimistic and delusional. 'I'm a star, I'm sexy,' " she'd later explain. It also helps to be self-aware and funny. Jacob as Crystal had started to record songs in the persona of this rich, vapid, sometimes entitled white lady he'd spent so many years watching from behind a shop counter. In "May I Speak to the Manager" Crystal was a woman lodging her complaints about a retail experience. "I'm extremely disappointed / In the quality of service," Crystal sang-yelled into the mic. "I shop here all the time / I'm a very loyal customer." Within a few weeks, Oops regulars knew the words and would shout along when she performed.

One night, Chiquitita, the teenager from Queens, stumbled into the Rosemont and found Crystal, a thirty-something rich-lady wannabe performing one of her songs.

What the hell is this girl doing? Chiqui wondered. She bought a drink from Merrie Cherry, who was working the bar and shouting "yaaaaas" at the performers after each number. As Chiqui lingered in the back, eyeing the cute boys and the general atmosphere of mayhem, she pictured herself up onstage. The crowd was sparse but dedicated, willing to sing along with Crystal's songs and throw dollars into a metal champagne bucket in the middle of the room; the scene felt warm and goofy and Chiqui was immediately comfortable. She took off her jacket and shook her wig, noticing how many pairs of eyes clocked her outfit and her face. She had a gift for makeup, and even on nights when she wasn't booked, which was most nights, she painted to snatch. She watched as two nerdy boys in beanies had a beer-chugging contest and a shirtless boy in stripper heels spun deftly around a pole. After the set, she introduced herself to Jacquée Kennedée and Crystal and name-dropped Aja and Dahlia Sin. Merrie Cherry, who'd been listening in from the other side of the bar, clocked her as cute and up-and-coming.

"Book that girl," Merrie suggested to the Oops crew, and a month later they did.

Like Crystal, once Chiqui was in, she just stayed, coming back week after week in better and better looks—wigs she'd styled with two bright greens buns on either side of her head and a cascade of green curls; a lilac faux fur French-cut bathing suit with matching lilac bunny ears; wide-brimmed hats in embroidered fabrics; three-inch gold hoop earrings; baby curls pasted onto her forehead; fringe; chains; fuzzy hats with horns.

As the Rosemont and Oops gained momentum in the spring of 2017, West Dakota came out of nowhere to win Mr(s) BK and launched herself into the Brooklyn drag scene. She'd met Crystal on New Year's Eve, and, thrilled with their newfound drag personas and the endless possibilities of Brooklyn nightlife, they'd taken a selfie together in the Macri Park bathroom. New Brooklyn queens including Crystal were in awe of West. She'd gone from relative unknown to local star in a matter of weeks and she was smart enough to know not to waste the attention. She began to develop fun, intelligent, fashion-forward looks.

"We want to book you for Oops," the crew cooed one night while they were all smoking outside the Rosemont.

West nodded, of course. She showed up the following week in a floor-length black maxi dress with subtle freckles painted across her face and chest and a modest black turban over her blond wig. She had the kind of style that was a pleasure to look at. Never busy, always thoughtful, and sometimes adorably silly. She loved being able to experiment with her looks. One night, she wore a pair of baggy white shorts cinched at the waist to look like a diaper and carried an oversized blow-up bottle.

"I a widdle babee," she said, shirtless, her blond wig in two pigtails. She kept innovating, and a few months later she tried the look again, this time with a richly embroidered bonnet and a matching pair of high-waisted shorts.

At Oops there was a revolving cast of regular performers, but some people just had chemistry. When West, Chiquitita, and Crystal were together in front of the encouraging audience of regulars and other young drag performers, it felt like a sleepover with no adults. Crystal wrote more music, including a song called "In My Cabana," about being a rich woman lounging in a cabana. She began carrying a tiny white stuffed dog she named Princess Diamanda. Chiqui grew increasingly comfortable in her skin, stopped worrying about whether people knew she was underage, and started taking risks and pulling stunts during her shows. She convinced four guys to carry her on her from the stage out the door; she sat on a stool and ate pickles, chewing into the microphone; she stripped to nothing but a dance belt, often. On one especially wild night, when dressed as a microcephalic character from the TV show *American Horror Story*, she had a desperate need to pee while bantering on stage. As her cohosts cringed, Chiqui availed herself of a nearby cup and then placed it on top of the piano. During her next number, the song reached its climax, and she picked up the glass and drank the urine in one gulp. The audience of devoted regulars shrieked and jumped to their feet, delighted at the lengths Chiqui would go to entertain them. On another occasion, she dressed as a baby and convinced West to change her diaper onstage. As West cringed and protested, Chiqui reached down and ate a piece of smushed brownie she'd crammed into the diaper before her act. Even as a kid singing in the high school acapella group, West had suffered from stage fright. At first, she'd embraced lip-synching as another element of drag, a part of the art form that she had to master in order to be a good entertainer but, as she appeared at Oops week after week, she found that lip-synching helped with the stage fright.

You cannot stop performing because "even if you mess up, the song keeps going," she'd observed.

The wheel was turning, pulling new queens up from the concrete. Kids you'd see one night getting drunk alone were holding someone's props the following week, and a month later were onstage themselves. At first their makeup might be thin and patchy, their clothes ill-fitting or badly tailored. They might have a glow-up, or they might not. There was no recipe for success in drag. A relatable persona helped, but some people got by swimmingly as nothing but a character. Being beautiful never hurt, but it didn't necessarily matter. A quick wit could get attention or a gig, but it didn't always help someone keep getting booked. Pay from the bar was about the same as it had been at Sugarland back when Thorgy, Veruca, and backSpace worked for around fifty dollars a night and as many tips as they could coax out of the measly crowd. But the Rosemont devotees had deeper pockets than the Brooklyn drag fans of the early 2010s and the tips—which were pooled and then evenly distributed among the performers at the end of the night—might add up to another fifty bucks a person. The drag mania that was sweeping the country also meant corporate gigs, fancy soirees, and sponsored events often hired performers to entertain, especially during Pride month, around Halloween, and for winter holiday parties.

Oops was a party thrown by the right people, in the right place, at the right time, and after a few rocky months, it thrived. The crowds got bigger, the queens more popular on Instagram, and some freelance writers in their orbit began publishing stories about their themed parties and gushing over their antics. As the bar found its footing, Merrie's responsibilities dropped off. She stopped bartending and took over as the host of Cakes, the longstanding Wednesday night party at Metropolitan, which featured an ass contest with a fifty-dollar bar tab as the prize. By the end of 2017, though she loved the Rosemont and was proud of what she'd helped build at the bar, she'd get annoyed when someone left a largely empty Metropolitan at two thirty in the morning knowing the party would be raging on Montrose Street. On particularly dead nights, her cohost at Cakes would sometimes sneak over to the Rosemont and carefully avoid having her photo taken so that Merrie wouldn't know she'd been partying at Oops. After the success of Oops, more young queens clamored to host parties at the Rosemont, and then more bars booked drag queens or agreed to let them throw parties. As some drag performers inevitably left town, moved on, or moved up, new ones heard the call, sensed the opportunity, and took their place on-stage. But if Rosemont was the place where cool kids went to watch and give shows, Metropolitan was where working drag queens like Merrie Cherry paid their bills.

CHAPTER EIGHTEEN
Feeling Thorgeous

"I have lots to talk about," Thorgy Thor announced from the stage at Metropolitan. It was January 25, 2018, and she was hosting a packed viewing party for the premiere of *RuPaul's Drag Race All Stars* season three, a special season in which overlooked or promising past contestants returned to compete for a spot in the *Drag Race* Hall of Fame. Viewing parties had become a staple at pretty much every gay bar in New York. Even people who didn't go out to see drag—either because a show that started after midnight was past their bedtime or because they didn't like drag without the glitz and glamour of TV lighting and professional editing—came to viewing parties. It was a win-win for the bars: they could make money off the show's popularity while helping local queens introduce themselves to this broader audience. In a shiny gold top with wide sleeves and red, green, and gold striped pants, Thorgy gripped a microphone and welcomed the hometown crowd.

After *Drag Race* season eight, Thorgy was busy and well paid enough to afford an assistant. Ragamuffin was a droll, former dance major with a talent for abstract expressionist makeup. She and Thorgy were a study in contrast. But ever since Thorgy first booked Raga at This N That, she could tell that the younger queen was "cunty, cool, and smart" and hungry enough to do whatever Thorgy asked.

"What are you doing for the next . . . whatever?"

"Nothing," Raga said.

"I'll pay you to tour the globe with me," Thorgy offered. While on tour, they drank mimosas on layovers, took embarrassing photos of each other sleeping and posted them online, befriended local queens, and went thrifting on their rare days off. They got into drag—night after night, city after city—until their faces were stained with makeup and their feet were blistered.

This was what it meant to be a professional drag queen. It was not a nonstop party, but it was a career, and it afforded Thorgy plenty of opportunities to show off until sunrise. Though her circumstances had improved since being on *Drag Race*, Thorgy Thor was still a sassy, shrieking, good-time girl who haunted thrift stores for women's blazers to wear over sweaty leotards. She still had frizzy wigs hiding two-foot-long dreadlocks underneath. Her legs still looked awesome in tights. She'd stayed close with her pre–*Drag Race* crew and was balancing the demands of a national profile and local responsibilities. Brooklyn was where Thorgy got her start; it wasn't where she was making her money, but she knew that if the world tours and the paid promotions and the TV appearances dried up, Brooklyn would be there for her and, more important, Brooklyn would book her.

That night at Metro, Ragamuffin was hosting alongside Thorgy and sipping her drink of choice: blueberry Stoli vodka and soda. The bar was packed, and the crowd was jovial, eager for a new season of competition, conflict, showmanship, and stunts. Spirits were particularly high because Thorgy was not just hosting the viewing party, she was also a contestant on *All Stars* season three. While they waited for the episode to start; Raga and Thorgy bantered onstage.

"I love doing drag. I love being on the show, but I get a lot of bullshit on the internet," Thorgy said. She typically never reads the comments about her on social media, she told the crowd, but in honor of that night's premiere she'd gone on Instagram and plucked some gems. Looking down at her notes, Thorgy read the first one: "'I know Thorgy gets a lot of hate all the time for everything she does. But I still like her.'"

Raga covered her mouth in alarm and then repeated, "'All the time for everything,'" for emphasis.

Thorgy read another: "'Thorgy is so gross even the producers knew it. Her sisters don't like her. Ew, ew, ew. Thorgy is disgusting. Always looks bad.'"

The crowd booed and Thorgy waited to deliver her punch line.

"'I mean, my dad called me later and apologized, but it still hurt my feelings a little.'"

The episode began, and Raga and Thorgy retreated to opposite sides of the small stage to watch the workroom entrances. The audience at Metro saw Thorgy emerge on screen in the same outfit she was currently wearing—red streamer wig, shiny pants and top. After making her entrance she laughed and did a little tap dance. A few more returning contestants entered and then the camera lingered on the empty workroom doorway. A bike bell rang twice.

"Ayo, sis!" shouted a raspy voice in a Brooklyn accent. Exultant music played as Aja wheeled onto the screen riding a little pink scooter and wearing a pink latex bra, a pair of matching, high-waisted pink panties, and a teal and pink jacket with big spikes of fabric on the shoulder and sleeves. "My name is Aja and I'm here to fuck shit up," she said. A montage reminded viewers of her season nine exploits: the now-infamous backstage complaint about Valentina, her lip syncs, and getting read for her dark makeup by Michelle Visage. In her one-on-one interview, Aja explained that "walking into season nine I was thinking I was the shit. I was gonna win. I was like, *Oh yes, I got this.* And then the challenges and the runways came along and I was like, *I don't look that good. I'm not doing that good. I don't feel that good.*"

Filming for *RuPaul's Drag Race All Stars* season three had taken place only a few weeks after season nine finished airing. Aja, Thorgy, and eight other queens had returned to the workroom for a shot at what some jokingly referred to as their "Ru-demption." The other queens had also upped their game thanks to money from touring and the sobering effect of being picked apart on television. Aja had better clothes, and as she told the rest of the contestants after entering the workroom, a lot of cosmetic assistance. Botox in her forehead. Enhanced lips, cheeks, skin, chin.

"You're a drag queen who got more chin?" Trixie Mattel, the country-singing queen from season seven asked incredulously. Most queens would aim to minimize the size and shape of their chins to appear more feminine.

"Bitch, I didn't have one to begin with," Aja replied.

Privately, neither Thorgy nor Aja expected to win. Aja was determined to have fun and redeem herself after her disastrous meltdowns on season nine, and Thorgy wanted more screen time and a chance to show off her talents as a musician. At Metropolitan, during the first commercial break in the episode, Thorgy lovingly tore into her *All Stars* sisters. "Trixie looks like she's wearing a diaper, right? It's a little diapery," Thorgy said of Trixie's entrance look, a floral bodysuit over heavily padded hips. "I love Trixie. Does everyone love Trixie, or what? She's such a cool chick. So smart. But did anybody notice in her boy interview she has a constant lipstick ring?" Thorgy laughed. "We always give her shit about that. It's just the product she uses. She's like, 'Girl, it doesn't come off, like ever, ever, ever.'"

"That happens to me with my eyebrows," Raga chimed in. She had on a big black beret with mirrors on it, a baggy white mesh shirt, black motorcycle gloves, bracelets, and a red short wig. "It's something about the red that just, like, stays."

"Oh, permanently," Thorgy concurred. "It stays there forever and ever and ever on end." After watching someone insult her outfit during a one-on-one interview Thorgy announced, "Everyone's such a fuckin' bitch. I don't care. The drama is fun. I need to drink something! I want to cheers."

A bartender made his way through the crowd to the stage and handed Thorgy a glass of brown liquor.

"Oh my God, that's a lot of whiskey. All right, cheers," she hollered, and raised the tumbler.

Thorgy gave words of encouragement to the people crammed into the small bar. "I know it's hot in here and this episode is ninety minutes, so thank you, motherfuckers. Free drinks for everybody"— roars of approval—"just kidding."

The commercial break ended, and Thorgy and Raga sat back down on their stools and watched the queens read each other on camera.

Aja changed her look "every five seconds," Thorgy said during the next break. "Nobody had to change, but she was like, 'Hold the cameras, I'm changing my look.'"

"Good for her because in season nine she looked terrible," Raga noted. "So she is feeling the goddamn fantasy, and I love her for it."

The main challenge in this episode was a variety show in which each of the queens had an opportunity to show off a talent. Thorgy played an excerpt from the Introduction and Rondo Capriccioso of a Saint-Saëns violin concerto. Halfway through her number, she did a one-handed cartwheel while clutching the violin, and the music changed to a generic disco mix the producers had suggested. Thorgy accompanied the track—which bore an uncanny resembled to the RuPaul song "Sissy That Walk"—on her violin.

Aja was up next. She strutted onto the runway in a long mint-green jacket. She took off the coat and had on a layer of purple and green fringe underneath. As the song's beat hit, she dropped the fringe layer to reveal a bodysuit with an arrow pointing up from the crotch. She leaped into the air and crash-landed on the stage in a perfect dip, with one leg kicked out in front of her and the other bent underneath. She was performing "Level Ya Pussy Up," an original song she'd written after coming back from filming season nine. "Level one welcome, cunt / I think it's time to pull the stunts," she lip-synched along with the track as she slowly ascended a four-step platform in the middle of the runway.

The show cut to a shot of the other queens who were watching from the side of the stage, "Is she gonna jump from there?" asked a drag queen named Milk, and moments later, Aja did, in fact, jump from there. RuPaul screamed with surprise. Aja landed on her back with her legs splayed underneath her. She rolled languidly onto her stomach and struck a casual pose on the floor. "'Meow to the pussycat, cunt cunt / Meow to the pussycat cat cat, cunt.'"

The crowd at Metro watched, gagged, as Aja lip-synched along with her track before the show took a commercial break.

"Can we just give it up for motherfuckin' Aja?" Thorgy shouted, and the audience obliged with a cheer.

"Also, give it up for Thorgy Thor," Raga continued.

Thorgy waved her finger in the air, brimming with enthusiasm. "I'm sorry, I'm rooting for Aja, bitch. What nobody knows is we actually have to do the number twice for consistency and she did that twice, and both times we were like, 'Aja, you better fuckin' do that, bitch.'"

"It is still so cool to see Aja on TV," Raga remarked between sips of her Stoli blueberry and soda. "I just, like, love her. Like, who was there for, like, fuckin' like Sugarland? Who saw Aja perform before the show?"

There were scattered whoos from the crowd.

"I don't want to give away too much," Thorgy continued, "but when we were there, Aja was the only person in that workroom who was like, 'I'm actually just here to relax.' She was so relaxed, really confident. She was not getting swept away in the drama. She was like, 'I'm gonna paint my face and have a good time today.' I'm like, 'OK, cool, bitch.'"

It was time for the judges' critiques. Michelle Visage complimented Thorgy on her ability to bring classical music to drag. Aja received unanimously positive feedback. She seemed so much better since season nine, the judges remarked. RuPaul asked her what had changed.

"I don't give a fuck what anybody thinks about me. This is me, and if somebody has a problem with it then, that's a you problem not a me problem."

"That's right," Ru countered. "You just jump on they ass."

The guest judge that week had been actress Vanessa Hudgens. "I didn't know who she was," Thorgy told Raga onstage at Metropolitan. When Raga explained that Hudgens had starred in the movie *High School Musical,* Thorgy replied, "Don't care, never saw it. She was the stupidest woman I've ever met or ever seen in my life. She was like, 'I thought you were kind of bashful during your performance,' and I was like, 'You're an idiot.'"

On the tiny stage at Metro in front of a packed room of Brooklynites, Thorgy had come full circle. She had put her fate in the hands of the nightlife gods, and they had blessed her with an incredible career. Was it always easy? Absolutely not. She'd compromised in countless small and large ways—toning down the humor when she went on television or performed for straight audiences, performing with queens she didn't like, worrying over Instagram posts and booking fees. And endured a lot—resentment from locals who questioned her talent, fights with friends who couldn't stomach her success, jokes about the fact that she was white and had dreadlocks, a hairstyle that, she took pains to explain, made it easier to pin her wigs and headpieces into coarse hair. All the while, Thorgy schemed about how to get a gig, make some money, and gain just a smidgen more recognition and status in this world where a growing number of performers were competing for the same small pot of cash and attention. The online scrutiny and meanness were real, the competitive spirit that led her to fight for seventy-five-dollar gigs at the Ritz back in 2011 made it hard to watch other people surpass her in fame and followers. The late nights of partying and the early mornings of travel could be grueling. But Thorgy had fully committed to this life years ago.

"When you sign up to do a living like this, you sign up to do it, and you do it till the sun comes up, and you tire everyone else out and, guess what? They show up to your next show," she said. When she toured the globe doing gigs, she stayed late at the bar and did an extra number, and then she hung out and partied with the local queens.

"You paid me a lot of money to be here, you're also paying for a flight for me and a friend, a great hotel, and all of our meals, and we get tips on top of it," she'd acknowledge if promoters seemed surprised that she was so accommodating. It disappointed her that other *Drag Race* girls could be divas when touring, but she was proud of her work ethic. "I am a drag queen from Brooklyn that loves performing. I shook the hand of every manager and every bar person; I did this in New York for fucking twelve years and that's why I worked so much," she said, reflecting on her career. No matter how far she traveled, she'd always be a Brooklyn queen, the first one on *Drag Race*. People might hate on her, they might not get her jokes or like her looks, but she could always come back to the Metropolitan stage, order a shot on the mic, and it would appear a few minutes later, likely delivered by a bartender she'd known for years. Thorgy knew there were hundreds, maybe thousands, waiting to take her place. That's partly why she seized on every opportunity and squirreled away her money, shopping at thrift stores and living with a roommate in the North Brooklyn apartment she had since before the show.

Thorgy would be eliminated from the season in the following episode. But because reality TV is not real life, Thorgy's career would continue to grow. Later that year, she'd do a forty-date *Drag Race* tour, rejoin the Haters Roast (the comedy show in which *Drag Race* contestants read one another onstage for two hours), and, in July, she'd realize a years-long dream. In a production she'd dubbed the "Thorgy and the Thorchestra," she would lead an orchestra in Halifax, Nova Scotia. A ribald comedy show in a refined setting, Thorgy would tell jokes, pull stunts, and drink copious amounts of alcohol as she performed orchestral standards by Aaron Copland and Tchaikovsky on the violin, viola, and cello in full drag. It would be the clearest indication yet of how far she'd come from the queen in a tutu and dirty tights riffing on *Swan Lake* on a Tuesday night.

Watching herself on TV while tossing off insults with Ragamuffin and making jokes in front of a crowd at her hometown bar, Thorgy was deep in her element. After the judges gave their critiques, she called for another Maker's Mark and sat back on her stool. During the next commercial break, she told the crowd, "I got offered to do a lot of viewing parties and I said, 'Absolutely not!'" She had hosted viewing parties of *Drag Race* season eight, *All Stars* season two, *Drag Race* season nine, and now *All Stars* season three, all at Metropolitan.

"I always come right back here because I love you guys, and I hope you come back every fuckin' week."

CHAPTER NINETEEN
"Your Makeup Is Terrible."

Thanks to nonstop touring and four-figure booking fees since the season nine cast was announced, Aja was no longer broke. She'd been able to buy herself a wardrobe she was proud of, and she had approached this return to reality television for *All Stars* season three with a newfound sense of calm and enthusiasm.

"I'm giving you silhouettes; I'm giving you fashion; I'm giving you Aja's perspective, my full look," she told *Out*. "I'm giving you just me. On season nine, I feel like I had the opportunity to show me, and I let it slip out of fear." Going forward, the point was to be fearless. She'd moved out of her mother's house and away from Momo, and the relief she'd felt from the validation that came from being one of the chosen few queens to be cast on the show was real.

"People talk about the glow-up and I'm just like, There really isn't a glow-up, I'm just not suffering from an immense amount of anxiety and depression. I'm just actually able to breathe," she said to journalist Evan Ross Katz during an on-camera interview for Mic.com.

Not everyone appreciated the new and improved Aja, however. Her makeup, in particular, had become a point of ridicule and derision among online fans. It started as soon as season nine aired. "I don't think I've ever hated anything more than Aja's makeup," tweeted one viewer with 240 followers.

"Hi drag race stans! why does aja's makeup look like shit?" asked another.

"For those of you saying the makeup is bad, it's not her makeup, it's her skin underneath that's bad," someone wrote on Facebook. "She has severe acne scars."

"She ugly."

"Aja was boring and talentless."

"Fuck off bitch."

What? Aja would think to herself. *I don't even have acne, I have burn scars.* The comments were relentless and cruel. Aja tried to focus on the positive: on the people who gushed over her looks and who embraced her, on the money and the clothes, and on all the concrete ways her life had improved since she'd gone on the show. But as the season went on, it got harder and harder to tune out the hate.

At one point, when things got particularly heated online, Kandy Muse texted to check in. "Hey, sis, you OK?"

"I just don't even know anymore," Aja replied. "People are literally just dragging me left and right; it's like I should be happy, but I don't even feel human anymore."

Some *Drag Race* aficionados felt a loyalty to their favorite queens that led them to defend their honor at every opportunity. Sometimes viciously. Demure and at times delusional, Aja's fellow season nine contestant Valentina was a fan favorite, especially among the younger viewers, to whom she represented flawless beauty, innocence, and a kind of treacly star power that was rare in actual drag clubs. After the episode in which Aja complained about the judges' preference for Valentina's runway looks, Valentina's fan base attacked.

"Aja, Valentina could give you her skin, makeup and wigs and you STILL wouldn't get it," tweeted one fan.

To Aja, the rant had been mostly compliments and hardly even qualified as a feud. It was a careless outburst born of stress, exhaustion, and a backstage cocktail. But now that the show was on VH1, drag and drag queens had been introduced to an audience that couldn't always see the difference between television and real life, who had no experience with drag queen banter and run-of-the-mill shadiness.

At meet and greets before or after drag shows, fans would ask Aja if she and Valentina were "cool."

"Yes, love," she'd reply, trying to remove all sharp edges from her voice. "It was a thirty-second interaction that happened months ago." Among queens who saw themselves as performers first and reality TV personalities second, meet and greets, where fans paid extra and stood in line in order to take a photo with the queens, could be frustrating. They required performers to get ready earlier. The exchanges were intentionally brief, and yet some fans found time to offer deeply personal information about their own family rejection, struggles with addiction, or debilitating illness, which could be draining. Other fans smelled bad or were too clingy or repeated catchphrases from the show ad nauseum. The normal rules of decorum governing first encounters between strangers seemed to not apply. Kim Chi, a season eight queen who admitted on camera to being a virgin continued to be asked about it years after her season aired. If a queen was abrasive or came off badly on television, some people at the meet and greet would make a point to tell them: "I hated you on the show."

For those people who'd grown up following YouTube influencers and reality TV stars online, the distinctions between regular people and celebrities could get murky. Fans watched drag queens talk about their struggles—for love, family, identity, security—and some started to feel as though they knew these queens. That deeper sense of connection drove an economy of conventions, tours, merchandise, and sponsorships. It also fueled a litany of online abuse. When a favorite queen lost a lip sync and had to sashay away, the person who sent her home could expect a fire hose of rage online. If the offending queen was Black or Latinx, some of that abuse would inevitably be racist. Fans routinely tweeted slurs and bigotry at non-white queens. Someone even threatened to burn season ten contestant Asia O'Hara alive. Hackers took over the Instagram account of Shea Couleé, the Black Chicago queen who lip-synched against Sasha Velour in the finale, and posted pictures of slaves in chains along with the caption, "Sheas family back in the days."

In addition to mean-spirited comments online, a few fans had lashed out at Aja in person. At one club event in Denver, someone spit on her. At another, a Valentina fan bought a ticket to her meet and greet in order to confront her and threatened to hit her in the face. Even though Aja and Valentina had given each other shit on the show, they loved each other. They texted encouragement and liked each other's pictures on social media. Aja admired the coherent and polished look that Valentina pulled off after less than a year in drag.

Why are these people so invested in our friendship? she'd wonder after one of these awkward fan encounters. Sure, it was a meme-worthy moment, but didn't people realize this was a TV show? It was real, but also, like, not.

•••••

Despite her glow-up, Aja did not win *All Stars* season three. In the season's fifth episode, the challenge was "Soup Can Realness" and the queens had to design a soup can and wear it down the runway. Aja was eliminated after the judges found her "Sugar Tits" brand soup to be lacking. *Drag Race* girls often released original songs the week of their elimination or after they'd won the season. The music was usually a dance track with some playful rapping in which they joked about their time on the show. Season eight winner Bob the Drag Queen made a catchy song called "Purse First" inspired by her habit of entering the workroom every morning holding a handmade purse out in front of her theatrically. Monique Heart released a single called "Brown Cow Stunning" riffing on a giraffe print that she'd mistakenly identified as "brown cow" on the runway during season ten. The joke didn't have to be major, it just had to be salient and give them something to promote when *Out* magazine, *Entertainment Weekly*, or *New York* magazine interviewed them about their departure from the show. To get the most out of these fifteen minutes of fame, it was good to have some bit of content or a product to plug. As season nine was airing, Aja had put out "Level Ya Pussy Up" as a single, and on March 1, 2018, a week after she was eliminated from *All Stars* season three, she released the song—"Finish Her!"—and spent thousands of dollars to produce an accompanying Mortal Kombat–inspired music video where various Aja avatars in campy pastel looks fought each other with fists and swords.

Aja found that making music—in particular rap music—was more than just a way to cash in on her brand. She'd been writing lyrics and rapping in her bedroom since she was young, and now that she had an audience, she loved the power that came from performing her own songs onstage. During an interview with *Out* after her elimination, she revealed that she'd been working on a rap album, "which I feel is not touched territory for *Drag Race* girls," she said.

Aja felt like a *Drag Race* girl had a shot at mainstream crossover and real success beyond the drag world. "Imagine a *Drag Race* girl nominated for an Oscar, or a Grammy," she said. "Wouldn't that be insane?"

Increasingly, getting dressed up, putting on a full face of makeup, and lip-synching to someone else's hit song didn't feel like getting her life; it felt like work. The schedule was brutal, and while the fans could sometimes be kind and uplifting, Aja felt hemmed in by their expectations. She was a full person, not a TV character. She wanted creative freedom, something she thought couldn't exist at the drag shows and the pride festivals that were paying her bills. After a year spent being relentlessly picked apart online by fans of a TV show, music seemed like a way to regain control over her image and an outlet for artistic expression. In an interview with the queer online publication *them*, Aja further distanced herself from the art form, explaining that she wasn't just a drag queen. "I think my art is not . . . solely drag," she said. "Just because I've done drag does not mean my music is written from a drag standpoint."

Promoting her music was one thing, but this caught the attention of journalists and *Drag Race* devotees alike. In May 2018, during that on-camera Mic.com interview, Aja said, "I don't want to do music as a drag queen. I don't look at myself as a drag queen who does music. I look at myself as a musical artist who just happens to do drag." She had appeared out of drag in the music videos for her songs, and she explained that Aja, the drag persona, was "just a channel of expression."

Many of Aja's die-hard fans celebrated the music. But a vocal contingent of *Drag Race* devotees online were unimpressed. "Your music is too draggy and it lacks professionalism," one person tweeted. "Youre an amazing drag queen but i dont know if music is the way for you. BTW you were excellent on all stars."

"What is draggy about my music . . . . . . ? Also drag? I don't even consider myself a 'drag queen' anymore - I'm a queer artist," Aja replied. The unsolicited feedback and the condescending tone of familiarity in the original post left her feeling misunderstood. She hated that feeling and, just as she'd clapped back in the bars when someone criticized or disrespected her, she lashed out. "This EP was my heart and soul," her post continued. "It had nothing to do with drag. This EP was me as a person."

And what was drag, even? Increasingly, Aja felt like *Drag Race* was a weird fetishization of one type of drag: cisgender men dressed as hyperfeminine women. "People be like, 'Oh you're so good at drag,' and I'd be like, 'I'm good at putting on clothes?'" she said, confused. Aja loved drag, but she didn't understand how something that was supposed to be a radical act of artistic self-expression could be judged to be good or bad. The show was not a contest to find the best drag queen in the country, it was reality television, heavily produced in favor of drama and emotion. Aja, though brimming with both, was desperate to be taken seriously beyond her ability to stir conflict.

Aja had been raised deep in Brooklyn—"the hood," as she called it. She was accustomed to gunshots, racism, and brawling on the street. As the producers of *Drag Race* and the many haters online had learned, conflict was Aja's canvas and one of her strategies for survival. She'd battled her way to the top of the Brooklyn drag scene while older queens accused her of stealing and called her ratchet and ghetto. She'd worked hard to prove to local queens that she was trustworthy, that she could draw crowds and hold their attention, that her looks were polished and her performances energetic. "Then, I went on TV and I was like, Girl, I gotta freshen up even more," she said. She'd spent money on clothes, improved her makeup, tried to hold her tongue when people said rude or offensive things during shows or meet and greets. She'd been desperate to please the judges, the fans, and the other queens, and yet she ended up miserable.

"I whitewashed myself for television," she said later. "I wish I didn't. It showed me that there was parts of me that I was ashamed of."

She'd wanted to help her mother pay off her house; she'd wanted to build a life as an artist. Instead, she was floundering. Despite the crowds, the money, the outfits, and the opportunities, she felt alone, yet again.

CHAPTER TWENTY
A Professional Party Girl

On a Tuesday night in the middle of June 2018, Merrie walked two blocks from Metropolitan to Macri Park to meet her girls for a night out. Merrie's style when out of drag: an allover-print T-shirt designed by a local Brooklyn artist underneath a ripped jean jacket, or a wide-brimmed hat, a pair of track pants, and her trusty flip-flops. For Merrie, it was a point of pride to be out as often as possible. She knew she was one of the rare few who'd made Brooklyn nightlife a full-time gig. Also, it wasn't just a job, it was her life. How could she expect other performers to support her parties if she wasn't showing up for theirs?

In the new drag economy, maintaining a successful career required constant networking. As she watched the shows at Macri, she tipped the queens, handing over dollars with a kiss or a matter-of-fact nod, presiding like a foreman on the shop floor. If something was outrageous, a drag performer in a pair of lacy panties dropping cereal and milk down her back and onto the floor or a skinny queen doing a jerky, annoying dance practically in Merrie's lap, she'd shake her head, eyes wide with mock rage. Merrie couldn't help but pull focus. Her face often conveyed more fear, joy, or hostility than the drag performers on the stage. Even in a T-shirt and jeans, Merrie was giving shows. Not everyone loved her for it—there would always be people who got annoyed when Merrie popped off, or who found her too loud, too Black, or too confrontational. But when Merrie reacted, everyone noticed.

New York City's Pride weekend was a few weeks away and Merrie's gigs were piling up. She was booked to perform with the rapper Lil' Kim at a nightclub in Manhattan. She was emceeing a Bushwig Pride event headlined by Willam, the sassy blond drag queen-slash-actress with a million YouTube subscribers. She'd been invited to Vancouver Pride in August, and the club owners were paying for her flight. She and her drag sisters were literally getting paid to dress up and party. They had thousands of followers, racks of clothing, and bags of makeup. People took them seriously, greeted them with kisses and compliments, and listened when they talked. It was hard to complain, and yet, there were plenty of hassles. The hours—midnight to four or five in the morning several times a week—were brutal and meant that your friends also worked in nightlife or were young enough to withstand the late nights. Drag was uncomfortable. It took pounds of spandex, Lycra, underwire, foundation, and plastic hair to make Merrie Cherry into a bombshell. After a night pacing the concrete floor of Metro, her feet were numb, her legs ached, and her chest sagged.

Merrie understood that, as a big, flamboyant person who turned looks for a living, her life seemed exciting to someone with a boring job who came to the bar for an escape and a sense of fantasy. And it was, a lot of the time, but between the genuine moments of emotional release, cheering, and infectious abandon, there were long stretches of Britney Spears or Ariana Grande for the twentieth time that week, of no one on the dance floor or near the stage, of cranky bar managers and bitchy cohosts, and of drunk fools yelling in your ear about their problems. When someone was telling Merrie their life story at the bar, it could feel like they were suckling at her tit and slurping up her energy. "I have learned the art of having a conversation and not talking to someone," Merrie said of the nightlife demands. Sometimes after walking away from a conversation in which she'd been laughing and reacting, she'd think, *I have no idea what we just talked about.*

The things that made these stretches of time tolerable, that shrunk them to manageable, forgettable chunks of the otherwise decent night, were shots and cocaine. A lot of the time, Merrie didn't even have to ask. The drinks and coke were offered by generous bartenders, kindly drug dealers, or friendly fans. The buzz gave the night a sparkle, made people funnier, boys cuter, music sweeter, and talking on the mic more enjoyable. On particularly great nights out, when everyone dances and no one fights or gets weird, it could feel like a secret spreading through the whole bar.

"Do you have coke?" someone might ask a stranger, and even taking the drugs was a giddy diversion, conspiratorial and ritualistic, snorting off a key or a fingernail in the bathroom as people pounded on the door.

"Do your drugs in the open, we've got to pee," someone might finally shout, frustrated by the slow line.

Then, it was back to the bar for a shot and another shot. Suddenly, alcohol didn't make you sloppy, it made you sharp. Instead of having an awkward conversation with someone she barely knew, Merrie could offer a bump or a shot and, afterward, they'd comfortably go their separate ways. For some, a bump made it possible to carry for hours and turned a tedious night into one of promise. For others, a bump wasn't going to cut it. Especially if the coke was gritty or pasty or cut with laxatives and caffeine. By 2018, Merrie was hosting several nights a week at Metro and performing paid shows around the world. She was, undeniably, somebody. Drugs helped keep the gears turning and the party going.

That night in June, Merrie had three little bags of cocaine, and she did some in the bathroom. All was well. The drugs made whatever shame, confusion, or insecurities that had hounded her during the daytime disappear. She was fierce and fabulous. She was mother-fucking Merrie Cherry. The chalky trickle ran down the back of her throat, she sniffed, and her mind cleared. She washed her hands and returned to the bar, carefully lowering herself onto the stool near the stage before taking a generous sip from her pint of beer. The pints flowed, punctuated by tequila and wrapped in a cloud of cackling. All the girls were out because it was a Tuesday night and most queens weren't booked. Though Merrie loved performing for packed rooms of sexy guys, nights like these were almost as special. If late-night cuddles and spirited debates were going to evolve into close friend-ship outside the club, you had to put the time in, send the texts, and make the brunch plans, and be ready to spend six hours in the bar out of drag on your night off and then, when the bars closed, head to a nearby apartment for "afters" until the sun came up.

The evening wore on. Untitled Queen, her best friend Lucy Balls, Horrorchata, and Merrie Cherry all made their way to the Rosemont for a queen named Patti Spliff's monthly show, Sad Songs, where, as advertised, a diverse group of performers did their most maudlin numbers in front of an intimate crowd. Patti Spliff had been in the Brooklyn scene almost as long as Merrie. She often wore a beret or hat over her trademark braids, which framed her doe-eyed face. At the Rosemont, there were more drugs, more jokes, more sarcastic eye rolls. Merrie made the rounds, chatting up everyone she knew and a bunch of people she didn't and, by the end of the second set, at around 1:30 a.m., she had taken ten shots of tequila and was most of the way through her third bag of coke. Not unheard of, but the night was a wild one.

"I'm going to Metropolitan," she announced to Horrorchata. When barhopping across "the holy trinity" of Brooklyn gay clubs, she preferred to finish close to home. At Metro, she passed on a shot and ordered a beer. The room was spinning. She thought about going across the street for a bottle of water, but had no cash, so she opted for sleep instead.

"I'm fucked up, I'm going home," she told the people she'd been chatting with and mumbled a few goodbyes. Outside the loud, sweaty bar, she climbed the stairs slowly, her breath heavy. Inside her apartment, she collapsed on the bed and fell into a deep sleep.

The next day, when Merrie opened her eyes around noon, her mouth felt dry and her head throbbed, but there was something else. She rolled over and her arm hung like a dead weight at her side. She couldn't feel her hand. She got up and stumbled to the kitchen, disoriented, and drank some water with her left hand. She instructed her phone to google "drunk numb hand." The results were inconclusive. She thought she might have Saturday night palsy, when someone falls asleep so deeply they compress a nerve in their arm and it goes numb. It wasn't permanent, but according to the internet it could last for a week or longer.

Gradually, the hangover fog cleared and, to her great relief, she was able to move everything but two fingers. She had a gig DJing that night. Walking around at the bar, she could tell her hand was not OK. The next day, she went to the hospital and they confirmed what she'd already suspected—it was Saturday night palsy. Merrie went home, canceled that night's gig, and ordered delivery—filet mignon. She considered calling Horrorchata because she was bored, but then remembered that Horrorchata had a gig.

She spent the next few days mostly in bed, scrolling Instagram and dozing. Then, about four days after she'd first lost feeling in her right hand, she tried to pick up her phone, and the hand wouldn't move. *Weird*, she thought. She got up to go to the bathroom and found that her right leg was dragging. The right side of her face was tingling, too. Had it always been tingling? Something was not right. The internet said that even if her arm stayed paralyzed, the feeling should have fully returned by this point. The arm was numb. Merrie called out to her roommate across the apartment.

"I'm feeling really weird," she explained. "I still can't move my hand."

Her roommate looked concerned. "Go to the hospital."

Merrie's heart was pounding as she picked up her phone. By the time she got to the emergency room at Mount Sinai Hospital in Manhattan, she could barely walk. An unsmiling nurse took her vitals and asked her to describe her symptoms and then disappeared. She waited. After four hours a nurse came into the room and announced, "We're admitting you now." "Why?" Merrie asked. "No one told you? You had a stroke," the nurse replied. The hospital staff unlocked Merrie's bed and rolled her down the hallway, onto the elevator, and into a room full of beeping machines. That's when the crying started. Merrie had never spent more than a few hours in the hospital for anything worse than a sprained ankle. The idea of sleeping there alone, with machines all around her beeping and dinging, was terrifying.

The stroke, Merrie would learn, had likely been caused by a combination of high blood pressure, sleep apnea, heavy drinking, a family history of strokes—her mother had suffered four, the last one fatal—and far too much cocaine. As the night wore on, Merrie kept crying. A nurse rushed in to warn her that panicking would raise her blood pressure, increasing the risk of another stroke. Merrie picked up the phone with her left hand and slowly scrolled to her grandmother's number. "Grannie, I'm in the hospital." Merrie paused to stop herself from choking up again, and she explained what had happened.

On the other end, her grandmother sounded calm. It wasn't clear what she was feeling, but her voice was resolute: "You need to be strong."

"I don't want to be strong." Merrie liked to joke that her grandmother, stoic and inspirational, was always acting like Maya Angelou. "I want to cry and be hysterical right now," she sobbed.

"Don't cry, don't cry, you're going to be strong and get through this," the ninety-four-year-old said. Merrie's grandmother warned her not to get overly excited.

"Do what the doctors say," she encouraged.

Merrie took a deep breath, said goodbye, and took her grandmother's advice.

Lying in the hospital bed covered in sensors and tubes, Merrie tried to tune out the machines and relax. She'd been doing cocaine pretty much every day for the past year. For a long time, it was only three or four times a week. Maybe on Tuesdays and Saturdays. But somehow, she didn't know why exactly, things had gotten crazy, and she and her friends had become a bunch of cokeheads. As it was happening, she hadn't given it much thought. They'd always done drugs. Before coke it had been ecstasy, or Molly, but Molly had always made it hard to get onstage and be coherent. Cocaine was different—it made her feel sharp and, most of the time, it cut the effects of alcohol, too, so then you could even drink more. Though it had landed her in the hospital, it had also helped her career, Merrie was sure of that.

Her mind cast around for happier thoughts. If she was going to recover and live, she would need to make changes.

The first step was coming clean to her friends and followers about what had happened. Word of Merrie's stroke had already started to spread through the borough, and people had been sending worried texts all day. ("Are you OK?" "I heard you're in the hospital, I'm so sorry." "Merrie, what happened? Where are you?") From her hospital bed, she posted on Facebook.

Hello friends and family! Right now I'm sure it's starting to get around that I'm currently in the hospital. Three days ago what I thought was a simple drunken moment turned out to actually be a minor stroke. Trust me I'm just as shocked as you are. But this is my reality at the moment. I was lucky enough to catch it early and my doctors feel as if I will have 100 percent recovery. . . . Thank you for all the messages I've received. I will be taking a month off to rest and get myself in a better State of Mind. My unhealthy lifestyle has officially caught up with me. And in a weird way I see it as a blessing because I know I cannot continue going on the way I have been. I have some great people taking care of me and I have no doubt with their help and knowledge I will have full recovery. I will not be able to celebrate Pride properly with you all, but I hope you celebrate for me. Please be safe and happy Pride.

Always remember, cherries belong on top!

PART FOUR

CHAPTER TWENTY-ONE

We Love You, Merrie Cherry

In the hospital, time crawled. For the first few days, Merrie dozed and cried and picked at the sad meals left at her bedside. She was alone aside from the physical therapist and the rotating cast of nurses and aides who came to check on her. On Merrie's third day in the hospital, Horrorchata and Untitled showed up, lightening the mood by cooing and fussing over her in her hospital gown, adjusting the blankets. The next day, two men appeared at the door to her room while Merrie was giving a urine sample. One gripped flowers in his fist. Merrie, who had just finished peeing into a cup, recognized neither of them.

"Hi, Merrie," they chirped.

"Uh, hey, what's up?" she asked, confused and a little nervous. They looked vaguely familiar. Maybe people from the bars. Or were they actual friends and the stroke had damaged her memory, too?

"How did you find me?" she asked. She had tagged her location— Mount Sinai Beth Israel hospital—on a video she'd posted to Facebook. Since then, she'd been receiving a steady stream of flowers and stuffed animals from well-wishers who'd seen the post. The guys, who were indeed regulars from Metro, had called the hospital to find out what room she was in, the one with flowers explained.

"So weird" was how she'd later describe the event. But just like she did at work, she chatted with them briefly and then made an excuse— she was tired, which actually wasn't a lie—and moved them along.

During her second physical therapy session, the therapist asked Merrie to show her what she does when she performs.

"Oh, you want a demonstration?" Merrie asked, teasing. She stood up in her light blue hospital gown and paper-thin robe. Bon Jovi's "Living on a Prayer," was on the radio, and Merrie turned on the shows. Kicking up her leg, raising and lowering her arms, and shaking her chest. The therapist pulled out her phone to record, and Merrie focused on the camera, giving sexy eyes and a characteristic pout before fatigue and self-consciousness stole her thunder.

"OK," she said, laughing, then flashed a peace sign and waved at the therapist that she was finished.

Once word got out that Merrie had survived, friends sprung into action. The warm wishes and concern cheered her. Horrorchata and her Bushwig cofounder, Baabes Trust, launched a GoFundMe to help raise money for Merrie's recovery. The fundraising message included a plea from Merrie. "For me drag is not just about nightlife, its a way to reach out, to bring people together regardless of who they are—drag is about finding out who WE are, together . . . If I ever made you smile, gag, dance, and laugh or if you think I might do in the future then girl, NOW is the time to show me some love.

"And by love I mean paper . . . of course."

The five days in the hospital were some of the loneliest ever, but Merrie also realized that, unlike when she'd first arrived in New York City, she was no longer alone. The social magic she'd been making across Brooklyn meant nightlife friends and barflies posted her GoFundMe far and wide. This was a test of their ability to help a sister—the question of whether the community could come together. It was an opportunity to prove that the scrappy scene, in the cheaper borough, could show up with real funds and support when someone was in need. No one forgot Merrie Cherry; instead, they'd rushed to her aid.

The hosts of Bushwig's Pride event, where Merrie had been a

headliner, coordinated a video greeting and got the entire crowd to shout, "We love you, Merrie Cherry," in unison. Messages poured out on social media.

"How many crazy adventures I can't even count!!!," Isis Vermouth, a bearded queen with a trademark deadpan sarcasm who'd recently moved back home to upstate New York, posted on Facebook. "Merrie Cherry has been the most amazing partner in crime and she even came to my wedding! I'm reaching out to everyone to chip in."

Untitled Queen posted a photo of her and Merrie spooning on a white tile floor after a photo shoot. "Remembering we met during Pride Month when I started doing drag, and she saw me out at a Hot Rabbit party when it was at Nowhere Bar, and came up to me and asked if I wanted to do a little competition she was throwing in Brooklyn called DragNet. I said yes! and when I won I got to host the next three months with her. I never was on a mic (never thought I could), let alone on a stage for very long and she taught me so much. How to engage people and how to just GO FOR IT, because there was no time to second guess yourself. I cherish a lot of those Jefferson St memories at her (two different apts on the same street) where we would just get Popeye's and get in makeup together and go nuts! I am also posting a link for her Go Fund Me. Please help if you can while she is recuperating she cannot work."

The Brooklyn crew hosted a fundraiser at Metropolitan. Performers included Horrorchata, K.James from Switch n' Play, Magenta the underage queen from Oops, and Untitled Queen—and everyone donated their tips to Merrie Cherry. The cash was flowing in. As polarizing as she could sometimes be, Merrie was the type of person who you wanted to help. The source of enough free shots and moments of fantasy and gay joy to encourage people to open their wallets. Even in her illness, she was legendary. In the end, they raised more than six thousand dollars.

The day Merrie came home from the hospital, she announced to friends that, from now on, she was vegan and would only have two drinks a night. She was grateful that she'd quit smoking a few months earlier and made it clear that she would absolutely, under no circumstances be doing cocaine.

On the mic out at the bars in the weeks after the stroke, however, some Brooklyn mainstays were skeptical. "Doctors can be such alarmists," announced one queen during an early evening show. "Mine told me that if you do cocaine, your heart could just—stop."

"Do you know what city you live in? Eating Popeyes and doing cocaine—that's all we do," her cohost replied. "Well, you do it till you have a stroke—and then you change your life." The jokes hinted at a darker truth. It wasn't just Merrie who was living this way and it could have just as easily been a number of other people in her place.

About a month after leaving the hospital, Merrie Cherry was back in drag. Her beat was light, and she'd grown her eyebrows back—her right hand still couldn't grip a pencil, let alone a makeup brush. But the point was to return to normal—a new normal, one without drugs or drunkenness—and normal meant work. Merrie wanted to put the stroke behind her, but it wasn't easy. Those first few weeks back, she fielded a steady stream of well-wishers and gawkers. Every night, friends and strangers paused to pay their respects as they passed. It even happened when she wasn't in drag.

"Oh my God," a girl had gasped one afternoon when passing her on Lorimer Street. "You're alive!"

What the fuck? Merrie thought.

The second time someone commented that she wasn't dead, Merrie laughed. She was outside Metropolitan, on her way home from the movies.

"Are you fucking joking?" she'd responded. "Do you think that's what I want to hear right now?"

The third time it happened, she didn't even reply. Most people wanted to know if she was OK. "How are yooooou?" they'd ask, soft, vague concern in their voices and worry in their eyes.

"I'm good. I'm good." Merrie would usually say. But occasionally she'd pop off. "I'm good! Are you good? How are you?" she'd snap.

She didn't know how long she could keep having these conversations. Just recovering was hard enough. She regularly posted healthy, smiling photos online, commenting that she was feeling great. She did feel better. Her hand wasn't 100 percent yet, but she knew she was healing. She went to Vancouver for Pride and did her gig in light makeup and flats, but she went nonetheless.

Two months after her stroke, at Metropolitan bar on August 16, Merrie Cherry and a drag queen named Lady Havokk hosted a night of all Madonna songs to celebrate the diva's sixtieth birthday. The dance floor was lively, boys in short shorts grinding on one another, bouncing on the sofa and sipping tequila sodas out of tall glasses. It was the steamy, wilting end of summer, so hot in New York City that kids waited until dark to play on the playground and everyone had on the smallest amount of clothing possible. When it was time to start the shows, Merrie cautiously climbed the step onto the stage and took her place next to a twerking boy in a shirt so ripped it was nearly falling off. She side-eyed the dancing boys, picked up the microphone, and bellowed, "When there's a drag queen on the mic, get the fuck off the stage." The boys scattered.

"Give it up for Merrie Cherry," Lady Havokk said into the mic. "She's sticking to her plan being healthy."

The crowd cheered, "Yeah, Merrie!"

"For one day, we're not going to talk about that," Merrie cut her off. "We're just going to have fun, but after this I'm going to put my slides on. Trust and believe—I don't want to always be the bitch who just got out of the hospital."

The DJ cued her first number. During the emotional introduction to the song "Like a Virgin" Merrie reached up and adjusted the track lights on the ceiling so that their light framed her and reflected off her blond wig. Under her makeshift spotlight she executed her trademark step up, high knee, step back, and her face was warm with feeling. Merrie gave the crowd what they wanted, a joyous release at the song's climax.

"You should wear more blond wigs, Merrie," Havokk exclaimed on the mic between songs.

"No, you white devil, I'm not going to oppress myself more by wearing a blond wig," Merrie snapped playfully at her cohost. During her second number, Merrie motioned for a girl with a nose ring to come onstage. The girl refused and backed away from the stage. Merrie gave her the middle finger, and the performance went dark. She twirled and snarled, flipping her hair when the synths came in.

When the song was over, Lady Havokk took the mic and addressed the crowd. "I just want to say, Merrie Cherry is the reason Brooklyn drag and nightlife is actually a thing right now. She's the most amazing human being I've ever come into contact with."

Merrie stared at her, open-mouthed and unblinking. After the set was over, Merrie moved to the back of the bar and stood, sipping her pint of beer with a straw so she wouldn't smudge her lipstick.

People came by to pay their respects, murmuring, "How are you?" "Love you." "You OK?" arms outstretched, shaking their heads, their lips pursed in sympathy. Merrie accepted their gentle arm squeezes and shoulder pats and thanked them and explained that, yes, she was doing well, she was getting better, she was feeling great, thank you.

By this point her recovery consisted mostly of "sitting on the couch, not doing shit." Being out and working was an improvement, but a sense of balance eluded her. For the past six years she'd gone out almost every night, submitting herself to nightlife without a plan for the future or a sense of whether it was a good idea to be in a bar most of her waking hours. Nightlife was what she knew and what she loved and, as she told people when she described her work, it was her sense of survival. It was the thing that got her out of a sad, lonely life and into a spotlight, even if it was just the overhead track lighting at Metro.

Nightlife was also, if she was being honest—and surviving a life-threatening illness felt like a good moment for honesty—a complete and total psychic drain on her. "I got into this industry because I discovered I'm a person who can change people's energy. I gave so much energy to people for so long and now I'm like, what do I have left?" she said of her circumstances since getting out of the hospital. That feeling, of people slurping on her emotional tit as a distraction from their own lives, was exhausting in a way it hadn't been before. All the concern and coddling from friends and strangers didn't help. Merrie understood that Lady Havokk was trying to be kind when she praised her on the mic, but she kind of hated that she'd done it. She didn't want to be the sick person anymore. She needed a regular life, or at least a healthy one. She felt this most acutely on nights like that one, when the heat was strangling and everyone seemed a little unhinged. Before the night was over, two drunk people threw a potted plant at the woman working the door, and Merrie left the bar to find a bush lying on the sidewalk surrounded by a hill of dirt. When Merrie had been in the hospital, Santiago Felipe, a jovial, bearded, bearish photographer who'd been taking pictures of the scene since Thorgy Thor's early years at the Ritz, texted, "It's your stroke of good luck!" Merrie had laughed at the time, but maybe it was true. She had been auditioning for *Drag Race* for several years, and while she knew the producers watched her last audition tape more than ten times, she hadn't yet been cast. "Get some footage of you in that hospital gown for the audition tape," Santi had advised her, not joking. *Drag Race* loved a story of survival and triumph over hardship: Ongina breaking down on the runway during season one and revealing that she was HIV positive; Roxxxy Andrews telling the season five judges her mother had abandoned her at a bus stop. Was this Merrie's ticket?

What she really needed was for her career to flourish, or else none of this—the drugs, the stroke, the paralyzed hand, the fighting, and the swollen ankles—would be worth it. In those sweltering, frustrating first weeks of recovery, the path seemed clear: Merrie was going to overcome adversity and then reveal all on reality TV. Drag was the thing that paid her bills and that she was good at. It was drag or nothing.

CHAPTER TWENTY-TWO
Hello, Bushwig!

Merrie Cherry pulled open the door to the Knockdown Center, a twenty-thousand-square-foot concert venue on an industrial block at the border of Brooklyn and Queens, and a blast of dance music rushed to greet her. A square, pleather handbag swung from her elbow as she crossed the floor. She had woken up that morning with stabbing pain in one of her molars and though she normally scanned for every glimmer of attention, she was distracted by the toothache. Instead of her usually open, searching expression, she seemed focused on something in the distance.

"Merrie!" Someone in a red bathing suit with matching stones glued to his face caught her eye. Merrie's faraway look transformed into a warm smile.

"Hi, babes," she rasped, and offered air-kisses and a gentle pat on the arm.

"Merrie Cherry, hey girl," someone else said, and in response she waved like a beauty queen on a small-town parade float.

It was a sunny afternoon in early September 2018, at the seventh-annual Bushwig. Over the course of two twelve-hour days, more than one hundred and fifty performers would put on shows for an audience of around three thousand people. Bushwig had grown up with the Brooklyn scene, and while it was still edgy—people never stopped doing lines in the bathroom and huffing poppers in the

273

crowd, and at least one performer usually peed, got fisted, or douched onstage—there was now an army of volunteers, a glossy promotional photo shoot weeks before the event, security guards, food trucks, and insurance. The crowd that started trickling in at 2:00 p.m. didn't come just to watch the shows. Attendees in hoop skirts, headdresses, tulle capes, corsets, and jockstraps resembled haunted dolls, antebellum brides, cowboys, butterflies, beauty queens, gargoyles, valley girls, geishas, MILFs, and men in wigs. Girls in devil horns and thigh-high boots and boys in fishnet bodysuits rushed back and forth between the main stage and backyard, mingled in groups, and stood gaping, eyes wide, cell phones aimed at the runway, ready to capture every gag-worthy moment. Though wearing heels on the concrete floors and the gravel yard meant they'd be sore to the shoulders on Monday, anyone worth looking at was hobbling.

Merrie's "walk-around look" for the first day—what she wore when not hosting or performing—was a full-length bodysuit covered in ornately curled strands of white plastic. Hundreds of crimson zip ties attached to the suit stuck out like a layer of spikes, topped off with a headdress covered in longer zip ties. Anyone who leaned in for an air-kiss or a hug was in danger of getting poked in the eye. When the ties caught the light in this bright, airy venue, her head looked like an angry Koosh ball. After a few laps around the space, Merrie's tooth was throbbing, so she made her way to the VIP dressing room, where she'd spend most of the afternoon high on edibles, joking with the other headlining performers. That Bushwig now had a VIP dressing room was also evidence of how far the festival had come since its 2012 debut in a rocky backyard with a stage full of loose nails. Once there, she changed into a red spandex off-the-shoulder, leopard-print gown. She was elated that August was finally over. The heat made layers of fabric and makeup even more uncomfortable. By late summer, everyone who didn't leave town for the beach or the woods was cranky and antisocial. But now, the weather was bright and mild, perfect for drag. Bushwig was a jubilant howl celebrating the end of the sweltering madness.

Merrie knew that that day, people would be whispering yet again about the stroke. Bushwig was the weekend when her community—the one she'd helped build over years of late nights, cardboard props, and tequila shots—put on its best pair of heels and showed itself to the wider world. It was Merrie's time to prove she wasn't just fine—she was better. She had survived, and she would thrive onstage. But first, she would eat a little more of the pot cookie in her purse.

As the sun crawled westward in the sky, the five-minute sets went by in a blur of confetti, sequins, and thumping bass. At around seven o'clock, the evening light reflected off the venue's windows, and the specs of dust and glitter in the air gave the space a deep-sea aura. It was the golden hour, the final minutes of daylight before the festival became a party. People were arriving in bigger groups, streaming in through the front doors on the east side of the venue. The music was louder, the bass heavier. The growing crowd was twisting and nodding along with the music.

"Hellllloooo, Bushwig!" Merrie yelled into the mic.

The audience yelled back, and the light reflecting off the screens of their cell phones twinkled. Prominent Brooklyn drag performers didn't just give shows at Bushwig, they also took turns emceeing—joking with the crowd and introducing the other performers. By the time it was Merrie's turn to bring up the night's headliners, the sun had set and the people who'd been kiki-ing outside—smoking weed, sipping frozen drinks, and posing for photos in the hazy light of the early evening—wandered to the main stage, drawn by the increasingly loud cheers.

"This next bitch"—Merrie paused, and the cheers quieted—"this next bitch, she is a Brooklyn girl. One of my favorite local queens.

You might know her from a little show she was on . . ." Merrie was taking her time. "It was called *RuPaul's Drag Race.*" She paused again so the crowd could holler. Even in the most avant-garde corners of Brooklyn, people bowed to the obvious indicators of success—in this case a spot on a season of reality television. "This girl is fierce, she is fabulous, she is my sister, give it up for . . . . Aaaaajaaaaa." Merrie's voice disappeared into the roar of the crowd.

Aja walked onstage looking demure in black gloves and a black ruffled robe that resembled Victorian mourning clothes.

"Come on, mama!" someone in an evening gown and high-tops shouted from the floor. The song, "In My Head" by AlunaGeorge, came on, slow, with a round bass line and simple drumbeat. The whispering, ethereal vocals, intimate and sexy, praised a steady, supportive lover.

Aja had on a wide headdress that looked like two flat white horns. Her body movements were contained, and her hands punctuated the trills in the song. A performance that begins with neck-to-ankle coverage can mean only one thing: costume reveals. The black dressing gown came off mid-twirl to reveal a bejeweled ombré sack dress. After a series of seductive turns up and down the runway, the sack was cast off. As the song's second verse started, the dress underneath the sack—a rainbow flapper tunic—immediately began shedding beads. Aja ignored the wardrobe malfunction and peeled off her black gloves with an economy of movement that was daring in a room this big. Determined to show her layers, she lost the flapper dress and then the matching corset underneath the flapper dress, until all that remained were two tasseled pasties and a pair of high-waisted panties.

Aja had hoped that her appearance on *All Stars* season three would redeem her in the eyes of the fans. She had been more relaxed on the show and in the workroom. She was more comfortable in her skin, and it didn't hurt that her skin had been lasered smooth by a doctor. She had toured relentlessly, and she had faithfully hugged her fans before and after every show. Aja's profile had exploded since being on TV, but she continued to grapple with challenges to her authenticity, respectability, and worthiness.

"I've been working on my burlesque and my live music; I don't really have the drive to dance and flip flop and be doing dips," she told an interviewer for the queer online publication *them*. "It's something that is part of me, but it's not something that I'm carrying into the future."

The plan was to transcend the label of "drag queen," and while some fans cheered her self-expression and streamed her music avidly, others responded with mockery and disdain. Sarcastically dubbing her a "burlesque rapper," *Drag Race* fans on Reddit and Twitter latched onto this moniker and harangued her with it online. "Disrespectful for [Aja] to still be attending DragCon when she doesn't identify as a drag queen, tobeperfectlyhonest," someone posted. "She should go to BurlesqueRapperCon instead."

On stage at Bushwig, AlunaGeorge's sweet voice rang out of a catchy synth line and a house beat. " 'When my head's surrendered to the darkest hour, I can hear you calling / Drowning out the people that be fronting me,'" Aja lip-synched. The song built to its climax. Aja stepped left lightly, and pivoted right. Staring down the runway, she leaned back, sat down, lifted her right leg, and licked it.

"OK, bitch, OK." The music ended, and Merrie was back, shouting into the mic. Aja waved and walked offstage. "Give it up for Aja. We getting crunk tonight, girl? Aja, are you gonna party with me tonight?" Merrie asked to no reply.

Merrie walked casually down the runway and spotted a tip someone left on the floor during Aja's number. "Aja, you left some money out here, girl." Merrie held up the bill. "It's a twenty," she said into the mic, and gave the crowd a devilish look. Aja would always be from Brooklyn, but the farther she traveled from home the less connected she felt to the drag community where she'd gotten her start six years earlier. Aside from the occasional night of drunken debauchery with her drag daughters, she'd never been a big drinker—she didn't even like to stay up late unless she was working—so now that she was touring, giving several shows a week around the world, her presence in the bars of the borough was scarce. Most of the performers that weekend were unpaid, but the Bushwig organizers did spend money on headliners, typically *Drag Race* girls or touring musicians. This was Aja's first year as a headliner, and she knew that a spot on *Drag Race* and this elevated status had earned her a lifetime of taunts and passive-aggressive digs from Brooklyn queens struggling to get ten thousand followers on Instagram. Aja did not reappear to claim the cash. As the audience howled and hooted, Merrie stuffed the money into her bra.

When Aja came back onto the stage for her second number, she had on a black, white, and red outfit that looked like a deconstructed motorcycle jacket and chaps. "Make some noise," she implored the crowd. "Make some motherfuckin' noise." Though Aja was cashing in on her fame as a drag queen, she was also working hard to write and record music, hoping this would be the next phase of her career. For her second Bushwig number, she'd perform her music live in Brooklyn for the first time. "I grew up on these streets, bitch," she told the crowd. "I sucked dick on these streets. I ran these streets, shit." It was nerve-racking, bringing her rap music to a drag festival in the city where she started out, among people like Merrie, Thorgy, and Horrorchata, who had booked and berated her for years. But she picked up the mic and released a stream of frustration, excitement, and raw emotion into the venue.

"And no, I'm not fakin' / Smudge me with that sage shit / Los Santos, Orichá, qué bonita," she was performing "Brujeria," the second song off *In My Feelings*, which she'd released that spring. She had recently rediscovered the Lucumí religion, an often-maligned Afro-Caribbean spiritual practice sometimes known as Santeria. She had struggled to embrace it during that difficult and uncertain first year as a teenage performer in Brooklyn, but now, as she grappled with challenges to her authenticity, respectability, and worthiness, these traditions brought self-esteem and a sense of purpose. She crouched down and twerked.

"Y cada día hago brujería" (I do witchcraft every day), Aja rapped, referencing her power as an artist and her dedication to brujería.

The crowd nodded along—some were confused, but all were willing to support Aja because she was from Brooklyn and because she was, as always, her charming and baffling self. Aja looked out at their faces and stomped up and down the runway, three feet of blond wavy hair swinging behind her. Onstage, at one of the world's biggest and most exciting drag festivals, it was starting to feel like drag Aja had to die for the real Aja to thrive.

·····

"Merry Christmas, faggots!" shouted Charlene on the second day of the seventh-annual Bushwig drag festival. Since competing against Aja for the Mr(s) Williamsburg title four years earlier, she had come out as a trans woman and come into her own as a magnetic truth teller. For many in Brooklyn, Charlene was the first word on politics, pop culture, and the significance of Cher to the queer community. The previous week, she had been a headliner at Wigstock 2.0, a revival of the beloved East Village drag festival founded and hosted by Lady Bunny that had gotten a serious upgrade thanks to financial backing by actor Neil Patrick Harris. Gone were the days of port-o-potties on the Hudson Piers; Wigstock 2.0 was held on the rooftop stage at Pier 17, a stunning open-air venue overlooking the East River. Charlene's Wigstock 2.0 performance was going to be featured in a forthcoming HBO documentary on the festival. Soon the whole world, or at least those with access to HBO, would have the opportunity to watch Charlene, a vision in rhinestones and red fringe, toss aside her cowboy hat, bra, and thong during an exultant performance of the Cher song "Just Like Jesse James."

That night at Bushwig, Charlene was emceeing in a pair of purple lace underwear over a jockstrap. "Y'all ready for a lesbian on this stage?" she yelled. The crowd, which was growing denser and sweatier by the minute, cheered back. Charlene threw up her arms, and Miss Malice of Switch n' Play, the femmecee and women's college graduate, wiggled up the steps and onto the stage in a floor-length mermaid dress. The gown oozed 1960s glamour with a plunging V-neck and a psychedelic pattern of black and white circles down the front. Her wig was six inches tall, black, and after being teased to within an inch of its life, it swooped out around her shoulders. Malice was plucked and primped for the gods. Her black acrylic nails filed to a sharp point and her lips painted bloodred and stacked with glitter. She was flanked by her partner K.James and Vigor Mortis, a drag king and Switch n' Play member who'd discovered the group after taking a local drag king workshop in Brooklyn. The boys wore understated black blazers and fedoras.

"This is my femme-spiration," said Charlene, who, like Malice, loved faux fur, feathers, and perfectly mussed hair and had a devotion to acrylic nails that bordered on religious.

Dusty Springfield's version of "Spooky" began and the group swayed slowly in unison. The stage filled with artificial smoke, and Malice smirked. The piece de resistance of her outfit was a colony of plastic bats that were attached to her wig and appeared to be swarming around her head.

"In the cool of the evening, when everything is gettin' kind of groovy," Dusty Springfield purred. Malice lip-synched to the song, a knowing look in her eyes, as she and her dancers' shimmied. This was her first time performing at Bushwig, and Malice had taken the time to make an act, commission a gown, and practice until she felt confident she could hold the crowd's attention. During the song's saxophone solo, Malice blew a kiss with both hands and scooted down the runway, stopping at the end to lift her arm, stroke her long, dark armpit hair, and pantomime licking her hand. It was her signature move. In the song's outro, Dusty Springfield repeated the word "spooky," and Malice lip-synched her way offstage, K.James and Vigor on either side of her. She'd been asked to perform last year—"We need your energy here, we'll load any song you want, just do an impromptu lip sync," Merrie had implored. But Malice didn't feel ready. Back in 2017, she had mostly thought of herself as a member of the Switch n' Play collective, and she didn't know the Bushwig queens and many other people in the drag scene well enough to feel comfortable on the stage. Since then, she had performed with Untitled Queen as part of Sasha Velour's post–*Drag Race* NightGowns tour. She hosted the Brooklyn Nightlife Awards with Merrie Cherry, and she performed at Horrorchata's Be Cute party, where Charlene had referred to her as a "dyke" in her introduction, a term she liked even more than "lesbian" because it had a more aggressive edge. These warm welcomes made her proud to have shared her "big dyke energy" with the wider Brooklyn drag community.

Merrie wasn't out among the crowd much that weekend; her aching tooth had put her in a bad mood and the pot she'd eaten to help with the pain had made her antisocial. But she knew what she was there to do: give a memorable show. Merrie had started planning her number back in July. While lying in her bed, doing her physical therapy exercises or scrolling Instagram, she dreamed of a number that would demonstrate to the whole community, and maybe the world even, that she was back, better than ever, and ready to slay.

The song "Proud Mary" is a classic rock paean to those who abandon the stability of their everyday lives to seek meaning, fortune, and adventure. It's about finding community—the people on the river who are "happy to give"—and bucking the constraints of the working world. The Ike and Tina Turner version of the song begins with a pulsing, understated acoustic guitar line and a beat that's mostly hi-hat cymbal. During the introduction, Tina tells you what to expect. ("We're gonna take the beginning of this song and do it easy, and then we're gonna do the finish rough.") Tina's raspy voice echoed over the sound system at the Knockdown Center and the crowd was quiet for once. As much as "Proud Mary" is a song about escape, it's also a story of persistence, the way that life keeps turning and burning, rolling on the river. Merrie could relate.

The past two months had been a much-needed respite and a panicky free fall for Merrie Cherry. A mixture of elation that she'd survived and dejection over her slow recovery and weak and largely immobile hand. The song was iconic but would hopefully be surprising to the young, pop-obsessed crowd. With a cloud of fog obscuring the view, Merrie stepped into a wheelchair at the side of the stage, and a local DJ slowly pushed her toward the runway. The audience gasped. Merrie was wearing a hospital gown and a shoulder length auburn wig. Her cherry-red platform heels stood out against the chair's chrome footrests. The first section of "Proud Mary" goes on for nearly two minutes, the verses conclude, and Tina and the backup vocalists harmonize the phrase "rolling on the river." It sounded like the song was over. But then the drummer hit the snare with both sticks. The organ began to wail and Merrie Cherry leaped out of her wheelchair, tore off the hospital gown, and tugged down a red skirt with white polka dots that she'd been concealing inside her tights.

While in the hospital, Merrie had promised herself that she wouldn't cry once she left. She'd mostly kept the promise. She broke down only once, in front of her roommate, because people kept asking if she was OK—she was, but also she wasn't. Every time someone said, "How are you?" she was reminded of the stroke. The stress and the fear sometimes got so intense she struggled to breathe, but she had to keep going.

The horns blared, Tina roared, and Merrie kicked her feet out in front of her and raised her hands above her head. The outfit shined under the spotlight, and Merrie stomped and shuffled, pointing into the rapt audience. From four feet above them, there was no sign of illness, no hesitation or grief, just Tina Turner's guttural trills and hollers and Merrie Cherry sweating and shining through the smoke.

CHAPTER TWENTY-THREE
Take It to the Runway

A few weeks after Bushwig, Merrie Cherry woke up in the previous night's makeup, touched up her eyeshadow and lipstick, threw on a blue stretchy bodysuit and a fluffy pastel pink boa, and called a Lyft to the Jacob Javits Convention Center on Manhattan's West Side Highway. It was the third day of RuPaul's DragCon, and she was going to be on a 1:00 p.m. panel called "Secrets of a Drag Queen for Everyday People" with several former *Drag Race* contestants and a drag legend named Sherry Vine, who'd been part of the 1990s drag boom in New York City. Simon Doonan, a writer, beloved reality TV guest judge, and the creative ambassador-at-large for the department store Barneys would be moderating.

Merrie was running late. "Everyone's running late—for this event and always," she reminded herself, and was reassured by her ability to touch up her face in thirty minutes. As she recovered from the stroke, she'd developed a new way of holding her makeup brush, and her lines were much steadier now.

"I'm still mourning the fact that my hand's not gonna be normal for a while. Trying to remember I'm lucky. The way my hand looked before, I really thought I'd never be able to hold the brush," she said. As she adjusted her dress in the back seat of the car, she caught the driver leering at her in the rearview mirror.

"Would you stop looking at me," she commanded forcefully. "You need to drive and mind your business."

The car dropped her at the entrance of the block-long glass building, and an assistant whisked her down a stairwell and through a loading area with a concrete floor. At the front of a vast conference room full of folding chairs and lined with heavy red curtains, Simon Doonan told a story about a roommate he'd had in London in the 1970s who would wait "for the cover of night," to go out in drag in order to avoid skinheads and threats of violence. "Merrie, do you want to talk about how the fuck you get to the gig?" he asked sweetly.

"I'm blessed," Merrie chuckled. "I live six blocks from most of my gigs."

Sherry Vine told a story about walking from Avenue C to the Pyramid Club in the East Village.

"Did you wear heels, girl?" one of the queens asked.

"No. Tennis shoes."

Even the queens who hadn't been on *Drag Race* described the ways the show had changed their lives. "I've traveled the world," Merrie said, "and now I'm making 'Merrie Cherry's Cherry Chocolate Chip Oatmeal Cookies.'" It was true—Merrie had been making vegan cookies and bringing them to the bar for the past few weeks in a half-hearted attempt to launch a branded baking venture.

"Did you bring any?" asked fellow panelist and season six *Drag Race* contestant Darienne Lake.

"No." Merrie replied, and Darienne threw an empty water bottle in her direction.

Merrie Cherry and Horrorchata, who had both sat on DragCon panels about being local queens and the Brooklyn drag scene over the years, lent street cred and grit to this much more accessible and kid-friendly event; in exchange they got a chance to meet *Drag Race* producers and other business types who hired queens for corpo-late gigs and sponsorships. "DragCon amazes me. People say, 'Oh, DragCon is so stressful,' but I fucking love it. You see that World of Wonder and RuPaul, they created an entire industry that everyone that I work with, from drag queens to clothing designers to jewelry designers to wig stylists, can live off of," Merrie said of the event.

As time went on, the show by, about, and for gays, seemed to increasingly cater to audiences who didn't identify as queer and who wouldn't necessarily see or do drag on their own. Some criticism was unavoidable. Ru's objective seemed to be mainstream celebrity. Ideological purity or allegiance to a scene or subculture did not appear to be part of the plan. While many celebrated the fact that Ru was the first openly gay spokesperson for M·A·C cosmetics, they side-eyed him for gleefully endorsing everything from Squatty Potties to essential oils and for selling RuPaul-brand dolls, shoes, and chocolate bars. They knew all the lyrics to his more popular songs but groaned at his shameless plugs for his albums every episode. The show's laser focus on one type of drag—gay men dressed as women—continued to rankle local queens. When RuPaul questioned the validity of women and trans people in drag, Charlene, one of the highest-profile Brooklyn-based trans performers, wrote in an article for the queer website *them* that "trans queens more than meet RuPaul's requirements for the show, of being 'men who reject masculinity.' It's a full-time rejection! RuPaul is just being a transphobe because, by his own logic, trans women are the real heroes. I know some girls who have put off transitioning because they wanted to compete on the show. There are plenty of trans girls who are really primed for this show, who really could be on *Drag Race* . . . but they can't."

Merrie Cherry saw things differently. To her, RuPaul was a legend who had earned his spot at the top of the drag pyramid. "I'm sorry [RuPaul] may not think the way you do or do things the way you think he should do them. But guess what? You can't control what other people say or do. That man has done so much for our community and is the reason why so many of my sisters and I are free from the corporate 9 to 5 machine . . . Leave Ru alone," she wrote to her community in a Facebook post. "He has done more for the QUEER community then [*sic*] we can ever hope in our lives. Lets watch and learn instead of bringing down."

As a kid, the only Black male role models Merrie saw on TV were Michael Jordan, Bill Cosby, and LeVar Burton. That is, until RuPaul Charles stormed the stage on MTV. Watching the Wigstock documentary and the movie *To Wong Foo*, in which RuPaul plays a queen named Rachel Tensions and wears a Confederate flag–inspired evening gown, the little boy who would grow up to be Merrie Cherry came to understand he was gay and so was Ru.

Merrie's admiration of RuPaul influenced her own aspirations. "I don't want to be fifty-five and doing drag unless I'm RuPaul," she told her friends after her stroke. RuPaul had gone from a scruffy, avant-garde performer to a glamorous diva. Merrie wanted to make that move, and so she took notes. She built a wardrobe of custom looks—a sexy, Barbara Eden–inspired genie costume, a rocker chick with a Mohawk and artfully bleached dress, a fairy princess in pink tulle—she answered every press email. She put herself out there, over and over again. She met people in the bars and she friended them on Facebook or followed them on Instagram, and she liked all their posts. You never knew who might be putting together a feature for the *New York Times* or organizing a panel on the future of drag.

It was this strident networking that got her invited to DragCon year after year. After the panel, Merrie took a break from browsing the Sugarpill makeup counter to open her gift bag. Inside was a fan with the word "Shade" written on it and a pile of facial masks and gels. "This is so cute, I'm glad I took two bags," she said as she changed into her flip-flops and headed down the pink carpet. If Merrie hoped to do more than just sit on panels and collect gift bags, she'd have to ascend. She needed a booth of her own, a VIP line of people waiting to pay her for photos, and the imprimatur of the most famous drag queen in the world. She needed to be cast on *RuPaul's Drag Race*.

• • • • •

A few months later, Merrie Cherry's apartment had been transformed into a makeshift runway, the furniture in the living room shoved against the wall. It was early January 2019, and the casting call for *RuPaul's Drag Race* season twelve had gone out a week earlier. Prospective contestants had about a month to make their tapes. By season twelve, the audition rules and requirements were clear, firm, and extensive. Queens needed to show thirteen original looks. Those who, like Merrie, knew long in advance that they were planning to audition, stockpiled custom outfits and made sure to keep the best ones off Instagram or social media. They rummaged through friends' closets and ran up obscene credit card bills hopefully to be paid off with the exponentially greater booking fees they'd demand after appearing on the show.

Videographers were enlisted, some of whom charged thousands of dollars and promised music-video-quality production. Most were friends or people in the community who had access to a decent camera and some video-editing software. By the time *Drag Race* entered the mainstream, Santiago Felipe had been photographing drag queens for a decade. A rare Brooklyn nightlife staple who got along with pretty much everyone, Santi had a warm chuckle, and a uniform of black baseball hat, black T-shirt, and long black coat. He could, and did, talk shit with the best of them, but he showed up when you needed him. He'd made Thorgy Thor's and Aja's successful audition tapes and gained a reputation as someone who knew how to get a queen on the show. He'd also been hired as the tour photographer for the

Icelandic experimental pop icon Björk and the personal photographer for actor Billy Porter, who made waves when he walked red carpets in gowns, dripping with jewels.

Despite his success, Santi, as he was known, was a Brooklyn local, holed up in a cramped Bushwick apartment with his growing pile of external hard drives and photo equipment, shooting parties until 4:00 a.m. for fifty or one hundred dollars and a few drink tickets. He and Merrie were particularly close. Their friendship was equal parts bickering, mockery, and collaboration. He'd already made three of her seven or so *Drag Race* audition tapes, and getting her cast had become a test of his skill and savvy.

Once the casting call had gone live, chatter in the bars inevitably turned to the show. Who was auditioning, who wasn't, who'd gotten calls from the producers last year and thought they had a chance this year. Queens auditioning for *Drag Race* can see how often their tape has been viewed by producers, and Merrie's last video had been watched thirteen times. This year, as Merrie was recovering from her stroke and trying to level up her drag, Santi yet again put himself in charge of the tape. He'd arrived at Merrie's house around 2:00 p.m., stepping around a pile of upturned end tables, suitcases, and massive men's running shoes, and began to set up his ring light, camera, and tripod. He was brimming with ideas. Though Merrie wanted Santi's help, she did not want to be told what to do, and the arguing began as soon as he walked in the door.

As part of the audition tape, wannabe contestants have to show two different celebrities for the Snatch Game. For the tape, Santi wanted Merrie Cherry to impersonate 1980s iconic TV dad and convicted sex offender Bill Cosby. Jokes about quaaludes and pudding pops were already dancing through his head, but Merrie was resistant.

"I just think it'll be funny," Santi said. This was full of pitfalls for obvious and not so obvious reasons. A despicable sex criminal who'd allegedly harmed dozens of women, Cosby was also a man. Historically, on the show, dressing up as a man for the Snatch Game was high risk, high reward.

"I don't want to trigger women who might have been sexually assaulted." Merrie pouted.

"You're not doing it for women, you're doing it for Ru. It's for Ru to watch," Santi said.

Merrie considered the point, weighing the risks. Ru enjoyed irreverence. He was adamant that even disturbing subjects can and should be fodder for drag queen humor. No one would expect a queen to do Bill Cosby. She'd have surprise on her side, and it wouldn't be the first time Merrie had flirted with tastelessness and controversy (in 2015, she dressed as a skyscraper while Hannah Lou impersonated an airplane and flew across the stage to knock her down in a tribute to September 11). Merrie, recognizing that Santi was right and that Cosby was someone she could impersonate without too much difficulty, gave in.

"I'll do it," she capitulated, and Santi cackled, picturing her dressed up as the predatory sitcom star.

A stylist Santi had called to freshen some of Merrie's hair emerged from the kitchen and placed a feathered, dirty-blond wig on the table. "Doesn't she look so much better?" the stylist asked, referring to the hair he was fluffing.

"Yes! We're in this together," Santi yelled to Merrie, carrying the wig into her bedroom. "You need to listen to me; I'm going to lead you to success."

"I think we should have footage of me making my audition tape because after I get on *Drag Race* I'm going to want to do a Netflix documentary about my life," Merrie told Santi, who shot her an irritated look.

"Cleveland, I hope you can shoot video while lacing a corset," he muttered to Merrie's assistant. Merrie and Cleveland met earlier that year. Cleveland had moved to Brooklyn from the Midwest and was managing an Airbnb in exchange for a place to stay. Merrie needed someone to help her get dressed and run errands. Quiet and handsome, with glasses, a stuffy nose, and a weakness for gossip, Cleveland had proven to be a fast learner and an eager baby drag queen.

Merrie was feeling her fantasy. "This is the beginning of the rest of my life," she sang the line to one of RuPaul's many inspirational dance tracks while rubbing lotion across her arms and shoulders. "Well, I mean, my life is pretty fabulous, but it's the beginning of the rich part. I'm tired of being broke. I mean, I'm not broke; well, I'm hood rich— Aaaayyyy." She shook her chest in the now-tight corset.

Merrie clomped out of the room, and they discussed whether to leave the plush baby blue couch as a prop in the runway shots. Merrie suggested seating some stuffed animals on it.

"Oh yeah, an audience!" Santi exclaimed, loving the absurdity that Merrie always brought out in him.

Merrie was sweating and giving directions to move the couch and open the door, but Santi ignored her. Frustrated, she took off her orange wig and executed three swift martial arts kicks in his direction. Santi responded by giving her the finger.

The minutes ticked by. "Let's go!" Santi called out as Merrie waited for Cleveland to put the backs on her earrings. Her hands still weren't strong enough to do it herself.

"I am rushing, I don't know why you think I'm not," she yelled at Santi. They emerged after fifteen minutes. Merrie, in a Mohawk wig and an artfully bleached and patched T-shirt dress, asked Cleveland to put on the seventies metal band AC/DC so she could get into the mood.

An hour after Santi arrived, they were ready to film. Merrie's wig grazed the top of the doorframe when she walked from her bedroom into the living room. She got into position, and Santi checked the camera and signaled that he was recording.

As Merrie stomped down the makeshift runway, she kicked her legs and pumped her fists. This year, Santi had turned down numerous requests from other local queens who'd heard of his success in making audition tapes. He'd agreed to work only with people he thought had a shot of getting cast or old friends who'd bugged him until he relented. As he watched Merrie smile, turn, bevel with her foot in front of her and her hands on her hips and push her chest forward with a finger to her lips pantomiming "shh," he marveled at her charisma. He wanted to land another girl on the show this year, to get his work in front of the *Drag Race* casting agents and justify his reputation. Like Aja and Thorgy, Merrie had a talent for being herself. Santi was betting that her status as the Mother of Brooklyn could get her a spot in the cast. He knew that Merrie could tell her story and make it resonate with people who had boring lives, or wished to dress as a beautiful woman but didn't have the courage. People who needed to know there was a big, loud, Black gay man out there living his fantasy.

Merrie put on a red sparkly cheetah-print, one-shoulder gown, with a red boa and that big blond hair she had just had styled.

"You look so good," Cleveland murmured.

In front of the camera, she posed, her eyes big and flirtatious. She glanced sideways and tilted her head back in mock laughter. Santi looked at Cleveland in the corner, scrolling through his phone, and grumbled, "I wish I had Cleveland's job and I could take breaks whenever I want. It's OK, Cleveland, take a break—you've been putting up with Merrie Cherry."

"For seven hours!" Cleveland shouted, exasperated.

Santi was unsympathetic. "Try eight years," he barked, and turned back to the camera's viewfinder.

CHAPTER TWENTY-FOUR
Proud Merrie

Audition tapes for season twelve were due on March 1, 2019. Merrie Cherry, Dahlia Sin, Momo Shade, Kandy Muse, Crystal Mesh, Horrorchata, and dozens of other Brooklyn queens had made one. Their tapes, along with thousands of others, were uploaded to a website for *Drag Race* producers and casting agents to watch during March and April. Most received a cursory review, but tapes by the favored candidates might get ten or more views. The previous year, the producers had watched Merrie's season eleven audition tape thirteen times and even asked her to submit a video with more Snatch Game impersonations. After they reached out, she called Santiago to give him the news. Should she call some local designers and have them get started on her custom looks? she wondered. Drag queens don't officially hear about the casting decision until a few weeks before they leave, sparking a mad scramble for outfits and wigs.

"Merrie! Do not do anything," Santi cautioned. If she started contacting designers to order a slew of special garments with a wink and a nudge, people would start to talk. It would be embarrassing to have everyone assume she'd been cast only to learn later that she hadn't.

The interest in Merrie's season eleven tape and the addition of a gripping and personal anecdote about surviving a stroke made season twelve feel like a sure thing. She'd assiduously upgraded her wardrobe, carefully crafted her responses to questions about her drag persona and career, and triumphed over a life-threatening medical event. Before she uploaded her video, Merrie showed her audition tape to some friends who gave her some notes and feedback. When she told Santiago, he was furious and he refused to make any changes.

"I told you, if I was going to do this, it was going to happen my way," said Santiago, frustrated that his opinion wasn't being respected. Merrie didn't understand why he couldn't let her be in charge of her own audition tape, and in a flurry of heated text messages the drag queen and the photographer had it out.

Merrie couldn't relax, and she couldn't ignore any critiques, even those from people who had little experience with drag or the show. Instead of trusting Santi's judgment—and her own—she made the edits herself, sent in the tape, and waited. Out at the bars the following month, she overheard queens discussing their audition videos, mentioning the number of views they'd gotten. While producers had watched some of the tapes five, six, or even nine times, her video had received only three views in as many weeks. When she'd hear that a queen had gotten more views than her, a little voice in her head would say, *They're going to pick that person this year. It's not going to be you.* Later, at home, she'd look at other queens' Instagram pages and wonder, *Are they better than me?*

March became April, and then it was May. At the bars, she heard whispers that some queens had gotten calls from the show. Casting on *Drag Race* was supposed to be a secret. But in such a tight-knit scene, secrecy was impossible. Of course their roommates, lovers, and best friends were going to find out, and of course those people were going to tell their roommates, lovers, and best friends, and so on. Insider knowledge about casting was currency, even in Brooklyn, where it was still cool to ignore *Drag Race*. Being the first to know who was cast was a flex few could resist, especially if the queen cast was part of your inner circle.

June was Pride month, when every business and corporation with even a mild tolerance for LGBT employees or customers hung rainbow flags from the rafters and held Pride-related events and promotions. For drag queens, it was the busiest and most profitable time of the year. A beloved local queen with a solid online following could make upward of ten thousand dollars working corporate events for companies like BuzzFeed, Target, and Levi's—even the NASDAQ stock exchange hired a drag queen for a Pride event. This year was special, the fiftieth anniversary of the Stonewall riots, in which a motley group of bar goers who were fed up with police raids and harassment staged a three-day revolt. The riots were celebrated the following year with the Christopher Street Liberation Day parade honoring the quest for "Gay Liberation" and the "militant" and "revolutionary" spirit of the 1969 riots. In 2019, to commemorate the anniversary, Lady Gaga performed on a stage built outside the Stonewall Inn in an event with corporate sponsorships that included United Airlines, T-Mobile, and Diet Coke.

Eager for the cash flow and the distraction from her *Drag Race* angst, Merrie threw herself into the festivities. She performed Whitney Houston's "I Will Always Love You" on a boat for the Pride event in Hudson, New York. She and Horrorchata were interviewed for LogoTV, the network where *Drag Race* originally aired. In the interview, they basked in their status and visibility talking about bringing drag to museums and Bushwig becoming an international event. At last year's Bushwig Berlin festival, Merrie Cherry's Grindr account "was just like, bloop bloop bloop," Horrorchata said, making an exaggerated swiping motion.

"They wanted the chocolate goodies," Merrie shouted, and shook her chest back and forth joyfully.

"Darling, they wanted chocolate, girl," Horrorchata cackled.

Merrie was featured in a Google Pride campaign. She flew to

Toronto for the city's Pride celebration and then to Vancouver. A photo of her in a wide-brimmed red hat with white polka dots alongside a quote, "As a queen and queer person I try to fight for my community and carry the herstory forward," appeared on an Airbnb ad plastered across the city. Brooklyn Boulders, a local rock climbing gym, hired her to appear in drag for their Pride month party. In white patent leather go-go boots and a teased red wig she gripped the climbing holds and foisted herself an inch off the floor. "I climbed," she proclaimed, and after the joke's novelty wore off, she returned to lip-synching and chatting with the events' attendees.

Just after Pride, the season twelve cast left to film *Drag Race*. The gigs and the gossip died down. The party was over, the lights went up, and reality set in. There was no longer any question about who'd been chosen. Queers in Brooklyn noted who was "away on vacation" and who had canceled their gigs. Santiago's texts to a Manhattan queen whose tape he had also filmed went unanswered. Merrie had known for months that she hadn't made it, but in July, after Pride month, she and all the other queens who auditioned but never heard back were forced to confront the fact that yet another season of *Drag Race* was filming and they weren't on it. Merrie's disappointment was especially acute. For the most part, once the filming was underway, she refused to discuss the show and her rejection. She'd already spent thousands of dollars on looks, and she'd organized her life around the expectation that she'd eventually be cast. It took up so much space in her brain, she'd sometimes hesitate before posting something snarky on social media or complaining about a particular *Drag Race* girl on the mic, worried that any moment of negativity or shade might get back to the producers. It was like the audition never ended.

When it came time to make a tape for season thirteen, she and Santiago were still not speaking. Merrie thought they'd be friends again someday, but he was going to have to apologize. Santiago was too stubborn to reach out, so even though he missed his frenemy, he consoled himself by looking at old photos of her in bad makeup and busted looks.

Despite what Ru and some contestants claim, the show was not "the Olympics of drag." Plenty of accomplished and polished queens were passed over for people more likely to deliver the drama and help make good reality TV. Merrie knew this. Merrie also knew that despite her many years at the center of the Brooklyn scene, she was a work in progress when it came to performing and turning looks. That some queens had been able to secure a spot on the show because of their charisma only made Merrie even more insecure about her star qualities. What did it take to get on *RuPaul's Drag Race*? She had put years of real work into her drag. She had hustled to build not just her own career, but a whole universe in Brooklyn. Didn't this mean she was entitled to as much fame and success as everyone else? She'd helped to elevate other performers and some of them had surpassed her. Not everyone in a scene can break out and wanting something badly wasn't enough to make it happen. The show's producers, her peers, even her own body were saying in one way or another that she wasn't going to be cast on *Drag Race*. Everyone knew her name, many people appreciated and respected her, but when it came to accessing the largest drag platform in the world it didn't seem to matter that she was the Mother of Brooklyn, and it didn't help that she'd given herself this title. Even though Sasha Velour had spent little more than a year performing in Brooklyn, post–*Drag Race* she was seen by many as the ambassador of Brooklyn creativity. Aja was the emissary of Brooklyn attitude, and Thorgy was the exemplar of its hustle. Merrie had tried to be the scene's North Star, but as she worked to hone and polish her drag to be more palatable for a TV show, she'd lost her way.

For all of her delusion, even Merrie recognized that her ambitions had begun to control her life. It was time to find something else to be passionate about. On February 1, 2020, Merrie posted a diptych on Instagram. It was a photograph of Harriet Tubman, stoic in a head scarf and a black shawl in the mid-nineteenth century on the left, and a picture of Merrie, in her own head scarf and shawl in 2020, on the right. Along with the photo, Merrie included a short biography. "Harriet Tubman, born March 1822 was an American abolitionist and political activist. Born into slavery, Tubman escaped and became a warrior in the freeing of slaves." On February 2, she posted another diptych, this time Michelle Obama was on the left with a photo of Merrie dressed as Michelle Obama on the right. Every day in February, Black History Month, Merrie posted one of these tributes to a Black woman of historical importance. Entertainer and expat Josephine Baker, model Naomi Campbell, trans activist Marsha P. Johnson, Black Panther Kathleen Cleaver, singer Mahalia Jackson, Oprah. She dubbed it her "Black Women Empowerment Project." To some, especially at first, it seemed random and grandiose. Some of Merrie's ideas over the years had been misguided, but in Brooklyn, she was often celebrated for the camp quality of her iconic missteps. Earnest projects like this weren't what people expected from Merrie. But as the images kept coming each day—Diahann Carroll, Lorraine Hansberry, Zora Neale Hurston, Dominique Dawes—these women who were beautiful, brilliant, and strong, who'd triumphed over adversity and made indelible marks on history, crowded into Merrie's timeline and demanded consideration. The project's strength was simplicity.

As praise and attention flooded in, Merrie made another seemingly pivotal decision about her future. On March 11, 2020, she sat on the love seat in her living room and posted her most recent *Drag Race* audition video to Facebook. At first dressing up had been about connecting with people. Then drag had been about getting fucked up with her friends. When it turned into a job, trying to find security and success had become a burden. She loved *Drag Race* and believed her life was better because of the show. She had auditioned for years and now she had come to accept that "I was not what they were looking for," she wrote in the video's caption. She had heard that queens who posted their unsuccessful audition tapes online would be disqualified from future seasons. "I know by posting this I am officially saying goodbye to that dream but I am so excited for the future . . . I want to be a big star, but it's going to be on my own terms and under no one else's hand," she wrote.

She stepped off the stage and into the abyss. She had some dreams and some plans—write a one-woman show, take singing lessons, have an exhibit of her photographs—but no idea that just a few days after posting this video, New York City, and then the world, would face a global pandemic. Two weeks of lockdown would become two months and then six and then an entire year lost to an illness that would kill nearly four hundred thousand people in 2020. That most drag shows would be on hiatus for the rest of 2020 and many would never return. That the killing of an unarmed Black man named George Floyd in Minneapolis would lead to daily protests across the country and find drag queens out on the streets, inspired by this demand for justice and excited for a chance to put on a wig and hype up a crowd. Merrie herself would lead Black Lives Matter marches, parades, and rallies in full drag with an Afro wig and a megaphone. But she wouldn't do another indoor drag show that year. She wouldn't see her grandmother until December, when the anxiety and worry became too much to bear and she would fly to California, quarantine for two weeks in Sacramento, and return to her Berkeley home to find her granny alone and twenty pounds underweight. Merrie would stay in California to care for Grandma Ruth until May 2021, when after a series of strokes, her grandmother passed away in the hospital just before her ninety-eighth birthday.

But on the eve of the pandemic, as Merrie sat on her love seat, her mind was on *Drag Race*. After she posted the audition video, she scanned the Facebook comments—"You're my favorite NYC queen to ever exist." "I feel like you already ARE a big star!" Merrie decided to be positive about the future. "I don't want to be a fifty-five-year-old queen fighting twenty-two-year-olds for gigs or keeping a gig because I'm a 'legend' that's respected by the community. That's just not what I want my life to be like in eighteen years," she said.

She'd posted the video in order to chart a new path for herself in drag. But the uncertainty of a year spent locked down during a pandemic, with no gigs, press, costumes, or crowds, can make a person yearn for even the most disappointing relics of the pre-Covid era. The isolation would also help her put aside what she'd realize were petty grievances. Soon after lockdown in 2020, she and photographer Santiago Felipe reconciled. There was no big resolution or apology, no one took responsibility for the fight; Merrie just started messaging him occasionally, and after leaving her messages "on read" for a few weeks, he replied. They were like siblings, they fought and sulked, but they were always going to be friends. When the call for *RuPaul's Drag Race* season fourteen audition tapes went out, Santi convinced her to try out yet again, even though she assumed that posting the season thirteen audition tape disqualified her.

"You never know," Santi argued. "You have nothing to lose; just try. It's easy, I'll help you."

After a little prodding, Merrie figured, *Why not?* The truth was that Merrie longed to be a star, and when she was making her audition tapes with her friend, stomping up and down her living room floor like it was a Paris runway, she felt like one.

CHAPTER TWENTY-FIVE

Bitch, I Won

At around 7:30 p.m. on March 7, 2020, Aja and her boyfriend, Mark, spun through the revolving doors and up the escalators of New York University's Kimmel Center for University Life. Delta Lambda Phi, the school's fraternity for gay, bisexual, transgender, and progressive men, was hosting its eleventh-annual HOTT *Drag Race* competition, and Aja was the celebrity judge. The crowd was mixed. College students in sweatpants, some of whom were under twenty-one, slouched in folding chairs next to young women with heavily contoured faces and designer car coats. Some of that night's ten competitors had friends in the audience to cheer them on and at least one queen had invited their parents. Aja was wearing a pastel sweatsuit made by a local Brooklyn designer and a chin-length teal wig. Mark had on all black and a single dangling earring of stars and moons. During the cab ride over, Aja had been streaming live on Instagram. As she rode through the night, examining her makeup, which was light, little more than foundation and a smoky eye, and tossing her hair for emphasis, she once again explained why she no longer identified as a drag queen.

Aja had known since she was a kid that she was not the gender she was assigned at birth. "I feel like I'm a woman in a biological man's body," she once said. Around the same time Aja released her EP, *In My Feelings*, she began to publicly identify as trans feminine and it became increasingly difficult to reconcile her life as a drag performer with her gender identity. For many performers, drag is an art form of transformation, but Aja had begun to feel like "there was not much transformation happening on the inside. I did not want to be performing my gender, I wanted to live it. I didn't want to feel like, Oh, I'm a different person 'cause I put on a wig."

Aja didn't want to do dramatic makeup, wear synthetic wigs, or glue down her eyebrows. "I want my real eyebrows, I want to do makeup on my own face, I want to wear human-hair wigs. I need people to think this is my real hair." If she was being honest, even as a teenager drag had been a way to express her gender. She knew that plenty of trans and nonbinary people did hyperfeminine drag and understood that, for them, it wasn't at odds with their gender identity. But, for Aja, drag heightened her sense that her body and her gender identity weren't aligned. She loved drag, she told her fans watching her on Instagram live, but she was a transfeminine artist, not a drag artist.

Aja released her first full length album, *Box Office*, in February 2019. The day it came out, one hundred thousand people streamed it on Spotify. The music was hip-hop with punk influences and a confrontational vibe. Aja felt inspired by the response, and she liked the music she had made, but her status with some fans continued to be contentious. During a European tour in early 2019, Aja was sick, her nose so congested she could barely breathe, running a fever and unable to sleep. She showed up to some gigs in pants and a jacket without a wig on. On Twitter, when she asked whether she should dress in drag for a London concert dozens of people tweeted supportive comments filled with heart emojis and professions of love, but a few balked.

"People do PAY and they want you in drag," one fan chided.

Trying to strike out on her own while distancing herself from the

Drag Race brand was not only emotionally and physically exhausting, it was bad for business. In March 2019, she traveled to Australia to do five shows in five different cities. Aja did her best to entertain the crowd, performing songs from *Box Office* to the hundred or so people in the audience. She'd had to give away most of the tickets to the meet and greet, because they hadn't sold enough. Despite the lackluster attendance, she jumped off the stage to dance among the fans in the crowd and gave a rousing speech about doing what she loved and following her dreams. After the tour, she tweeted that she wasn't ashamed to admit that the ticket sales were disappointing.

Though she tried to keep her head up, she was falling apart. While she knew at some level that she should ignore her haters, she kept railing at the Redditors and critics on Twitter. *Drag Race* wasn't real life. She was a person, not a persona. It was unfair to expect her not to change and grow. She didn't want to just dip and split and say thank you at the end of the night. Frustrated and exhausted, she broke down on Instagram live. "I don't think I'm better than any-body. I don't think I'm better than drag. I love doing drag . . . I think I've suffered this year with being very confused and not knowing where my identity fit into my art form and I apologize if I've hurt anyone else in the process, cause I definitely have hurt myself. I can't be perfect. I'm not perfect. I never have been and I never will be. All I can do is move forward authentically and be myself.

"Yes, I did become known through *Drag Race* as a great lip-syncher and performer and whatever," but lip-synching was "not what's in my heart" she continued. "What's in my heart is to make music, and, I get it, a lot of people don't like my music and don't give a fuck. I get it. But that's just where my passion is and I cannot change that." It was so confusing. People cared, they paid attention, but they didn't seem to listen or understand. "To a lot of people and promoters I am honestly just a dollar sign. A person who competed on *Drag Race*. And you know what? People are right. I do need to accept that, but that doesn't mean I should not have goals or dreams . . . I am very insecure, but I do believe in myself. I'm not saying I'm the best shit that ever happened. I don't think that. I never thought that. I'm my biggest critic." She shrugged and looked down. Her face was drawn, her eyes looked sad and tired. "I've been really just suffering from a lot of depression. I've been on the road for a long time and I need some 'me time,' and I really just need to stop seeking validation especially from people online who are never gonna like me. I need to stop getting upset over dumb shit and I just need to stop having social media vomit."

After *All Stars* season three aired, Aja had around a million followers on Instagram, but as she continued to distance herself from drag, argue with fans, and vent online, her follower counts dropped. She worried that her career would be cut short and that her relationships would suffer. She took her anger out on the people around her, sulking and yelling when things got overwhelming. If Aja could have picked a lane—caring and capitulating to the fans, or cutting the cord and striking out on her own—she may have avoided some of the criticism. She likely would have been less frustrated when it came her way. But she couldn't stop trying to assert her creative identity *and* expecting to be appreciated on her own terms. She couldn't stop feeling disappointed when people either misunderstood or didn't accept these willful acts of self-determination, and so throughout 2019 she continued to swing wildly between defiance and contrition.

"I don't consider myself a Ru girl anymore," she said in September on Instagram. "Nobody owns me. I don't pay a check to RuPaul. People say, 'Don't bite the hand that feeds you. She made you.' She did not make me. I sent in a tape and got picked by a casting firm. I made myself, every single person on that show made themselves."

In October, when she tweeted "I am no longer a drag queen or a drag artist. I used to be. I was on a TV show about drag twice, I know. Sorry if this offends you or confuses you." The responses were scorching.

"The fans weren't there for rapping. Just say you don't wanna do drag anymore and go," wrote one commenter on Reddit.

Aja felt like her approachability, the fact that her fame was confined to a passionate subculture, made her an easy target for haters. She understood that being a public figure opened her up to criticism. She knew she had to endure some scrutiny, but she didn't know how to deal with it except by lashing out and fanning the flames.

"I'm someone who spirals very easily," she acknowledged. "I fell into such a depression." She started to think about killing herself. One especially lonely night after staying up for several days straight, she called a suicide prevention hotline. "I disassociated. It was dark shit."

As she distanced herself from drag, the Haus of Aja was also coming apart. In a way, this was inevitable. Kandy Muse, Dahlia Sin, Momo Shade, and the newest member, Janelle No. 5 (rhymes with CHANEL N°5), wanted to continue their careers as drag queens. They'd started taking more gigs in Manhattan, where bar goers waved fives and tens instead of singles and a popular queen could make a few hundred dollars in tips on a busy weekend night. They wanted to be on *Drag Race* and to step out of Aja's shadow and experience fame. However, since the very beginning, they'd had to fight to transcend their reputation as sidekicks—Aja was the house's namesake and mother, after all. They were frustrated and argued constantly among themselves. Mostly, the fights were between Momo and the others over gigs, shady comments, and old resentments. Momo was barely in drag during 2019. She had moved with her boyfriend, Michael, to a cozy middle-class neighborhood in Queens that wasn't even accessible by subway. He made her outfits, drove her to her gigs, brushed her wigs outside the gigs, and collected and counted her tips. He was a proper drag boyfriend, and when she wasn't doing shows, she liked to hang out with his family and break her low-carb diet to eat homemade Italian food. Sometimes his cousins came to her gigs. They were a gaggle of young, attractive, mostly heterosexual, Italian-Americans dressed in all black, with dark hair and nasally laughs. There was security in having a boyfriend to dote on. In the bubble of Michael's world, Momo had found another family. She loved being included.

One night, in the summer of 2019, Momo had it out with Kandy and Janelle. Downstairs at Pieces Bar in the West Village after their weekly show, Kandy and Janelle told Momo her drag was inadequate and that it felt like she'd stopped trying, Momo later recalled. "Fuck you, bitches. I'm done with this shit," Momo shouted. It seemed clear to Momo that the other girls had decided to fire her from the gig. "I was so depressed, I felt so deflated," Momo said. "I wanted to do drag, but I had so much sadness, it turned me bitter." Soon after, Momo told Aja that she wanted out of the drag house altogether.

Aja could relate. The Haus of Aja had depended on their mother for gigs and visibility, but now that Aja was making music more seriously she was less inclined to do shows with her drag daughters and less interested in getting in the middle of their arguments. For Aja, being associated with the house meant being associated with drag. The other girls tried to be understanding and supportive of Aja's career shift, but it seemed like Aja was walking away from the very thing they wanted most in the world. She had been turning down drag queen roles in film and TV and she refused interviews that weren't about music. To people desperate for a bigger platform in drag, this was absurd.

"I was being told left and right by people in my own life that I was stupid for giving up drag, that I was delusional and crazy to think I could leave this," Aja later said. However, she was adamant. She wasn't going to be seen as some anonymous "man in a dress" who danced and did splits on command.

After months of group texts, arguments, and side conversations, Kandy Muse posted a photo with Janelle and Dahlia on Twitter. The trio posed in black latex bodysuits. In a series of tweets, Kandy explained that Aja was going to be focusing on her music career and "Momo is no longer in the picture." Henceforth, Kandy, Dahlia, and Janelle would be known as Doll Haus.

•••••

Aja had become a queer celebrity overnight. But she was still a local performer who could be hired to judge your college drag show. It made for a strange kind of fame. "People know you, but they forget that you don't know them," Aja said. "It's a weird level of approachability. You can't just go down a block from your house and see your local Ben Stiller, but you can go down the block from your house and see your local drag queen." She appreciated a lot of her fans and had even become friends with some of them. They texted regularly and a few had stayed at her house when they came to New York. They'd show up in Aja's Instagram videos of cab rides through New York City or meals at Brooklyn restaurants. "Girl, you're friends with your fans?" other *Drag Race* queens would ask incredulously. "When I started having fans I didn't look at them as fans, I looked at them as supporters," Aja explained. "If the vibe was right, we'd chat and maybe do something nice—it was very that." Nevertheless, most of the attention she got felt impersonal, like it had been borrowed from the broader *Drag Race* fandom. Once, while Aja was on a date that was going poorly, a fan interrupted an argument to ask for a photo. Another time, while she was eating at a restaurant, someone sat down next to her, snapped a picture, said, "I love you," and left. Was she supposed to feel grateful for this attention?

"There's a sense of entitlement; people think that if they can't approach you in the way they want, you're an asshole, you're a bitch, you're terrible," Aja explained when retelling this story. "It's like the persona is famous but the person behind it is nothing."

Aja had always been uncomfortable with the sense of ownership people felt over her. She'd started out as a brash, clumsy child stumbling around in heels lying about her age. In drag she served a fantasy, but now the reality—that she was trans femme and Black and creative and from Brooklyn—was all she cared about. Though drag once felt like her ticket out of Brooklyn, it had become a burden. Music was an art form in which she felt she could be her authentic self, but music was not what paid the bills.

"OK, I guess I'm doing drag," she said and announced some upcoming gigs. She took heat for that online as well.

"Ain't making that much coins anymore with the rapping gig, going back to drag," someone speculated on Reddit after Aja posted a flier for a gig.

At the door of the NYU auditorium, she stopped to greet the frat's president, Andrew Schlager, a junior who was clean-cut and in boy clothes but for a pair of black patent leather stiletto ankle boots.

"I'm not supposed to see the girls before the show," Aja joked as some of the queens competing that night gathered shyly in the corridor.

"You look beautiful," Aja encouraged. "Don't get pregnant—or do—I don't know your life." She retreated to a small room to wait for the show to begin. After warming up the crowd, the host introduced the judges: Andrew, the fraternity president in the short stiletto boots who was originally from Lancaster, Pennsylvania, "the Mennonite who keeps it tight"; a member of the Kappa Kappa Gamma sorority; and "our celebrity guest for this evening. You might know her from a little underground show known as *RuPaul's Drag Race*. From season nine and *All Stars* three, representing Brooklyn and brujería, give it up for Aja!"

Aja emerged from the back of the room and leaped onto the stage as the RuPaul song "Call Me Mother" played. She took a seat next to Andrew the Mennonite. All the competitors that night were NYU students. While they weren't all active drag performers, many aspired to give shows beyond the fraternity's social network, and some had already entered open drag competitions in Manhattan and Brooklyn. It was college drag—creative and expressive, if not always palatable. The performers dressed in sequins, tulle, and lots of spandex. They dipped, they split, they climbed off and then back on the stage. Someone jumped rope, someone else twirled a baton, and a cow-print-clad queen named Mooriah did a burlesque number that involved grinding on judge Andrew. Several of the queens packed seven-minute megamixes with songs and pop culture references, under the assumption that more is more. A pretty queen in a pink sequin bodysuit and a long black wig included a clip of Aja's now viral season nine tirade about Valentina in her mix of songs and moments from popular TikTok videos.

After the queen was finished and stood panting on the stage, the judges weighed in. "The energy was amazing," said Andrew.

Next it was Aja's turn to give feedback from the table. "I was like this bitch is banjee, you have such a bad attitude and I love it . . . I just wanted you to be a little less nervous 'cause you were having so much fun. Every time you hit the stage, take a deep breath, remember even if it's a competition, there's no competition 'cause you have to walk in saying, 'Bitch, I won.'"

"One question. 'Did you stone that body suit?'" one of the hosts asked, making yet another reference to Aja's rant from season nine.

As a judge, Aja was playful and encouraging, recognizing that baby queens want their performances to be clearly understood and that these performances are often extensions of themselves. "You have a really good control of your energy," she told a queen who'd pulled off a long blue wig to reveal a bald cap decorated with a single eye. "I love that there was a buildup. It was so dramatic."

When she did offer a critique, it was gentle. "I don't think the number needed the jump rope, honestly. It was a cute addition, but I think we could do better without it," she told a queen named Lolita Coppola who was dressed as one of the pagan worshippers from the movie *Midsommar*.

The final number of the evening was a nearly ten-minute "ode to Black female talent in the past twenty years," by a queen named Chiffon With a Period. To a megamix including Beyoncé, Rihanna, and several other Black female vocalists, Chiffon dipped, flipped, and lip-synced her heart out as the audience lost its collective mind cheering and hollering for her performance. Afterward, Aja weighed in. "When you first came out I was like, she needs to go to charm school 'cause this bitch is bad. Your melanin is so beautiful. You came out here and you were the only Black girl in the cast, and I'm gonna say this 'cause this is important: Black drag queens—Black artists period—have to work ten times, a hundred times harder than anybody else to get an equal amount of representation to get an equal amount of feedback, and bitch, you ate that." Aja tossed her hair and the gold hoops in her ears shook back and forth as if in agreement. "Even in the harsh lighting, you were so soft. For me it was tens across the board."

As the scores were being tallied, Aja stepped onto the stage and began chatting up the room. "Give it up for everybody who came here tonight—your hostesses have been lovely as fuck. The girls are fuckin' killin' it. Y'all are enjoying it. I'm enjoying it. My boyfriend made a full judge sheet in his notepad and sent it to me. I was like, 'Oh you're helping me, that's cute.'"

Aja had stipulated that she would not lip-synch that night, but instead was performing her own music live. "I'm doing my rap shit for y'all. Period. Let's hit that shit, baby," she instructed the DJ. "Put it as loud as you can and put my mic as loud as you can 'cause we got this." The music began and Aja performed "Brujería," hyping up the crowd by twerking and spinning.

After the judges crowned Chiffon With a Period the winner of the competition, the queens and audience members migrated to Aja and lined up for photos. They circled around her, peppering her with questions about how to audition for *Drag Race* and whether she was touring internationally.

"Was the drama real?" a girl asked of Aja's time on *All Stars*.

Aja nodded. "I talked so much shit, they could have given me a really bad edit," she told them.

Watching from next to the stage, Mark, Aja's boyfriend, was hungry and ready to leave. "These people are going to be accountants," he said later. "They don't need your advice." They might not have needed it, but they wanted to know Aja's thoughts—on the show, on voguing and ballroom culture, on their drag performances and their friends' outfits. It was her job as a queer celebrity and a reality TV star to be approachable and outgoing, to maintain her composure when answering the same question for the fourth time that night and to be indelibly herself. Aja had a flight to Los Angeles the following morning and would continue on to Australia the next day. She hated traveling to Australia—it was far and the time change screwed up her sleep schedule. Usually, by the time she acclimated, she was on the plane back to the United States. Aja was also worried about the coronavirus that was spreading from Asia to Europe. Italy was in quarantine; she was asthmatic and a self-described hypochondriac in normal times. Being afraid of getting sick was almost as bad as being sick.

As the world stood on the precipice of the Covid-19 pandemic that would change everyone's lives forever, Aja finished talking to the crowd of fans and made her way to the nondescript room where she'd stashed her things. As she packed up, people ducked their heads in to say hello and utter words of praise.

"I saw you at Bushwig, you were amazing," said one queen.

"I love you, you were my favorite," echoed a skinny boy in eye makeup.

"You're honestly one of the frat's biggest inspirations, and we love you so much," said Andrew, the frat president. "What you do, not only as a queer performing artist of color and bringing recognition to trans women and people of color—that is just beautiful."

They exchanged air-kisses and a brief hug. Aja rode the escalator to the Kimmel Center's ground floor, walked through the revolving doors, and into the night.

By the time Aja's Australian tour was over, the United States would be in full lockdown. Aja and Mark would spend weeks in Los Angeles quarantining in a friend's apartment. Drag tours would be canceled. Bars and clubs closed. But for Aja, the pandemic brought a moment of reprieve and unexpected opportunity. She finished writing an album called *Crown* that described her spiritual journey deeper into the Lucumí religion. She and Mark began obsessively beading instruments, appliques, and outfits. She gained weight and started an OnlyFans account in which she posted tasteful, not-suitable-for-work photos of herself out of drag. The money from the OnlyFans subscriptions helped fund the rest of the album and allowed her to help her mother stay afloat during the worst months of the plague.

The world would never be the same and drag, which had enjoyed yet another heyday over the previous ten years, would undoubtedly change with it. That was part of its power. No matter how mainstream, how recognizable and popular drag got, some freaky, loud upstarts would come along to challenge people's assumptions about gender, performance, nightlife and queerness, and make the art form their own. If drag performers were good at anything it was hustling and entertaining under duress—especially when money, opportunity, and respect were scarce. As the lockdown set in, some performers began to do digital drag shows and post videos shot in the backyards and living rooms, soliciting Venmo and Cash App donations. Venues would shutter permanently, budgets would be slashed, people would move away and some would get sick and not make it.

But drag performers would find new stages, new audiences, new gigs, and new forms of expression. Chiquitita, the Rosemont girl and Oops performer who'd helped usher in a new generation of Brooklyn drag, created a ten-foot-tall, Valentino-inspired, zebra-print gown for a national drag competition that was held digitally because of the pandemic. West Dakota helped to organize a fifteen-thousand person rally for trans rights. She also campaigned against cash bail, and appeared in ads for Michael Kors and Ketel One. Crystal Mesh retired from drag and started doing porn under the name Jake Lawrence. Momo Shade became a business manager for the Bobbi Brown makeup line, broke up with Michael, and got her own apartment for the first time. The other former members of the Haus of Aja continued to cement their legacy on *Drag Race*. Dahlia Sin appeared on season twelve and was eliminated after wearing a broccoli costume in the very first episode. Kandy Muse, the lovable Bronx bombshell and shit stirrer, landed herself a spot on season thirteen and made it all the way to the finale. Aja found herself back in drag and forced to accept the label of "drag queen" once again. "If somebody wants to book me for a drag performance for a couple thousand dollars, why am I gonna say 'no' to that?" she said. "I'm not making that much money off my music and I felt like by punishing people, I was punishing myself."

Drag Race itself evolved and adapted in the years after Thorgy, Aja, and Sasha graced the stage, casting a trans male drag performer on season thirteen, several out trans women on season fourteen, and a self-described AFAB (assigned-female-at-birth) performer on the third season of the United Kingdom's *Drag Race*, one of several international spinoffs. The show remained a contest for explicitly high-femme drag performance, but this progress did not go unnoticed by fans and gender nonconforming hopefuls. Though Santiago's efforts to get Merrie Cherry cast on season fourteen of *Drag Race* were unsuccessful, in 2021 she appeared in the fourth season of *Dragula*, a televised horror-themed drag competition hosted by the Boulet Brothers, two stalwart Los Angeles–based queens known for their matching gothic glamour. Merrie did not win, but she did introduce a whole new audience to her raucous personality and get to bathe in the attention and battle the criticism. As the pandemic raged, sputtered, and limped along, drag would continue to be a balm for brutal, uncertain times. A fun, adventurous outlet for people who refused to disappear just because they were locked down. Not even a global pandemic could stop these talented, charismatic attention seekers from making art and mayhem in Brooklyn.

ACKNOWLEDGMENTS

First and most, I'm grateful to the many performers and nightlife devotees who spoke with me about drag and queer art at the bar, over meals, in their homes, on the way to the gig, and on the telephone: Aja, Alotta McGriddles, Amy Campbell aka Whiskey Dixie, Angelica Sundae, Charmin Ultra aka Charmy, Chelsea Rodriguez, Chiquitita, Chris of Hur, Cleveland Miller, Courtney Conquers, Crystal Mesh aka Jake Lawrence, Daphne Always, Darlinda Just Darlinda, Dèvo Monique, Emi Grate, Emma Mendelson, Esai Andino aka Momo Shade, Hannah Lou, Holden Bucy, Horrorchata, Ickarus, Ja'mie Queen West, James Coppola, Jessica Bennett aka DiBa, K.James, Krystal Something-Something, Lady Quesa, Linda Simpson, Madame Vivien V, Marqui Jordan, Martyr, Mary Jo Cameltoe, MaryKirk Pollard, Merrie Cherry, Mini Horrorwitz, Miss Malice, Ms. Ter, Miz Jade, Mor Erlich, Nancy The Girl, Nicky Ottav, Queen Robert, Paradise, Paul Irvine, Jesse fka Ragamuffin, Shane O'Neill, Shaquanda aka Andre Springer, Shiny Penny, Simon Doonan, Thorgy Thor, Untitled Queen, Vena Cava, Veruca la'Piranha, Vigor Mortis, West Dakota, and Zoe Ziegfeld. Thank you for your generosity, insights, stories, and company over the past three years.

There's nothing I love more than going out with my friends. Brian Ferree, Daniel Griffin, Ben Hudson, Michael Federico, Zach Nutman, Hugh Ryan, and Eric Schmalenberger, knowing you would one day get to read this kept me writing during lockdown. No way could I have done it without you all. I am so proud to call you family.

Enormous gratitude to my agent, PJ Mark, for his unwavering support for this very gay book. Megan Hogan at Simon & Schuster brought sharp edits, grace, and kindness. Zack Knoll provided endless enthusiasm, expertise, good ideas, and friendship. Seriously, I am so lucky.

This book has benefited immensely from the deep well of talent at Simon & Schuster. Erica Ferguson and Sherry Wasserman, your style guide was a work of art. Thank you, Hope Herr-Cardillo, Rex Bonomelli, and Jackie Seow for your vision and creativity. I am grateful to Carolyn Levin for her thoughtful counsel. Thanks also to Beth Maglione, Amanda Mulholland, Jessie McNiel, Maxwell Smith, Kassandra Rhoads, and Elizabeth Venere. I am thrilled to have worked with you all.

Amelia Schonbek and Matt Wolfe were loving, whip-smart, and imaginative readers and advisors even in the messiest of times. Along with Will Hunt, Heather Rogers, and Cody Upton, they have been a generous and brilliant writing community for nearly a decade. I'm indebted to Wiley (aka YP aka Aaron Cohen) and Michael Glennon for their humor, friendship, and deep knowledge of drag in Brooklyn. Katia Bachko and Liz Flock brought stellar and much-needed editorial insights. Rosecrans Baldwin and Andrew Womack of *The Morning News*, we don't deserve you. A piece I wrote about Aja and another about the history of lip-synching for *Slate* were expertly stewarded into the world by Bryan Lowder. From the day we met, Santiago Felipe has been an integral part of this project.

This book is the story of a community and my own has been an inspiration and delight as I've worked on this project. Nandini Ramachandran, Jesse McElwain, Ki Wi, Manny Castro, Helena Ribeiro, James Martin, Katie Miles, Isa Knafo, Dominic Mondavi,

James Cavera, Jennie Shanker, Jess Perlitz, Emily Squires, Alan Chelak, Pablo Trujillo, Ali Herrmann, Liz Hodgson, Kahn Miller, Mike and Scott, Tyler Baldor, Shayan Lotfi, Barbara Maier Gustern, Sarah Heck, Baker Overstreet, the crew at Dean Street especially Emily Msall and Annie McEwen, Jenna Loyd, Mark Vareschi, Kate and Sam, Summer Minerva, Seth Fowler, Andrew Leland, Courtney Bowles, Mark Strandquist, Leah Guadagnoli, Dane Terry, Patrick Robbins, Jeff and Abby, Zach J. Couch aka Debby, Shelton Pritchard Lindsay aka Cupcake: thank you for the late nights, conversations, long walks, text messages, dinners, shots, and sleepovers.

There is surprisingly little historical documentation and scholarship on drag in the twentieth century, but what does exist is priceless. I am indebted to the work of Esther Newton, George Chauncey, Joe E. Jeffreys, Nelson Sullivan, James St. James, and RuPaul.

Thank you to the staff at *The Journal*, *Every Little Thing*, *Crime*, and *Vice News Reports* for inspiring me every day with your journalistic integrity, creativity, and storytelling chops. In particular, I'm grateful to Ashley Cleek, Adizah Eghan, Annette Heist, and Annie-Rose Strasser for accommodating my many deadlines.

I wrote some of this book while a resident at Millay Arts and during a virtual residency at the Watermill Center in 2020. I also had funding from the Mid Atlantic Arts Foundation. Heartfelt appreciation to those institutions for their support of countless creative projects, including this one.

Wendy, Paul, Adam, Carla, and Dorene, I love you very much. Paul Jackson, for our house, our dogs, our jokes, and our life, thank you.

ABOUT THE AUTHOR

Nicole Pasulka writes about gender, activism, and criminal justice for publications such as *New York, Harper's, Mother Jones, Vice,* and *The Believer.* She has received numerous prestigious fellowships and had her writing anthologized in the Best American series and featured on NPR's *All Things Considered. How You Get Famous* is her first book.